Freekeh, Wild Wheat & Ancient Grains

In memory of my father, who lunched on a fresh
wheat loaf of bread every day...

Freekeh, Wild Wheat & Ancient Grains

recipes for healthy eating

Ruth Nieman

Foreword by Judi Rose

PROSPECT BOOKS

2021

First published in Great Britain and the United States in 2021 by Prospect Books, 26 Parke Road, London, SW13 9NG.

British Library Cataloguing in Publication Data:
A catalogue entry for this book is available from the British Library.

ISBN 978-1-909248-68-7

Set in Goudy Old Style by Catheryn Kilgarriff and Brendan King.

Printed and bound by the Short Run Press Ltd., UK.

FSC
www.fsc.org
MIX
Paper from
responsible sources
FSC® C014540

Table of contents

Foreword

Einkorn, emmer, Ezekiel bread – the very words seem to conjure up ancient worlds and exotic, half-imagined flavours. Since biblical times, the fields and hillsides of the Levant and Northern Israel have yielded scores of wild grains and seed-bearing grasses. For millennia, they have been foraged, gleaned, milled, tamed and turned into pottages, breads and more. I picture Sarah, wife of Abraham and matriarch of the Jewish people, whipping up a batch of "hearth cakes" at the behest of her husband with "three *seahs* of fine flour", in much the way my mother, legendary Jewish food writer, Evelyn Rose and I would make scones and griddle cakes five millennia later.

Throughout history, recipes, techniques and traditions have been passed down, evolving and adapting to new circumstances and even technology. My mother loved to regale us with memories of her Latvian born grandmother taking her to the local golf course in South Manchester to forage for "the wild herb" for *schav* – sorrel borscht. As the years passed and times changed, sorrel was replaced with farmed watercress and the old family *hackmesser*, or hand-chopper, with a food processor. Yet the threads of heritage and family history bind the two soups together. Curious to experience the tastes of my late mother's childhood, I recently grew some sorrel in my London garden. After a good deal of what Mum used to call "experimental" – our family jargon for rigorous recipe development – I succeeded in recreating a delicious *schav*. I like to think great-grandma would have approved.

Ruth Nieman is a woman after my own heart. Through meticulous academic and hands-on research she revives the rich history of ancient grains and explores the role of these historical staples and lost crops in our culinary heritage to reveal how they influence the way we eat today. And while the ingredients and their stories hail from long ago, the author has also used her version of "experimental" to create innovative recipes that introduce them to Western tables, weaving past and present into something fresh and new.

Of the many "new" grains we meet in these pages, from khorasan and kali to carmel and teff, it is the eponymous freekeh that perhaps most captures Ruth's imagination. The archaic agricultural process of harvesting young, unripe wheat, then briefly roasting it over a smoky fire, is still practiced across the Levant. In Northern Israel she learned how to cook the freshly smoked grain from a group of Arab Israeli women, savouring their heritage, sharing these healthy staples fresh from the fields, connecting the land to the plate. And it was also in an Arab village just outside Jerusalem, that Navin, an accomplished cook, introduced me to the smoky, nutty, comforting pleasures of this deliciously versatile grain by way of *shorabet freekeh* – Palestinian freekeh soup. On complimenting my hostess on its exquisite flavour, and asking about the recipe, she duly presented me with an enormous bag of her home-smoked freekeh to take home to London.

Thanks to recent nutritional research, we now know that whole grains are vital for a healthy diet and can reduce the risk of heart disease, lower "bad" cholesterol, and promote gut health. Ancient supergrains, in particular, are especially rich in plant protein, dietary fibre, not to mention a host of minerals and vitamins such as zinc and iron that are important for building immunity. Yet this is not news. A thousand years ago, the medieval physician and philosopher, Rabbi Moses Maimonides extolled the health credentials of "coarse" (wholemeal) flour in preference to its "fine" counterpart (what we'd now class as a less healthy "white carb"). Once again, the old has become the new.

As you read and perhaps cook from these pages, I hope you too can picture the generations of growers, gatherers, bakers, and home cooks who "brought forth bread from the earth" – and much more besides. This is their story. As my mother liked to say, may you enjoy it in good health.

Judi Rose
London, 2021

Introduction

"Like liquid gold the wheat field lies,
a marvel of yellow and russet and green..."
Hamlin Garland

Freekeh, wild wheats and ancient grains have re-emerged into our culinary landscape as we connect again with the importance of our agricultural heritage.

In this book I will lead you into the discovery and cultivation of wild wheats and ancient grains over the passage of time, and methods of early farming. Over the course of 10,000 years, our knowledge of these ancient grains and cereals, the history of bread, loaves and artisan bakers, together with biblical citations of freekeh, wheat and barley, will be explored, and we will look at the domestication of wild wheats from within the 'cradle of civilisation'. The dawn of agriculture saw the farming of wild wheat, barley and millet, and marked the transition from hunter-gathering to crop husbandry. This all took place in the region that was known as the Fertile Crescent, spanning the countries from the mouth of the river Nile to the northern tip of the Persian Gulf. This includes Israel, Palestine, Syria, Jordan, Lebanon, Iraq and Egypt and covers centuries of agricultural, anthropological and culinary history.

It is from the Book of Ruth and the fields of Bethlehem, that "a parched grain" was referenced and distinguished as smoky green kernels of freekeh, the long-established staple of the region's diet. The annual harvesting of the unripe green wheat is an agricultural tradition that is still practised in the lush Galilean terrain by Arabic farmers. When roasted on open fires in the wheat fields, this unripe green wheat leaves a chaffed kernel, rich in essential nutrients that has remained a core carbohydrate of the Arabic diet.

Wild wheat stalks of emmer were rediscovered in 1906 at the foothills of Mount Hermon, together with barley. Historical discoveries of the first known beer brewery in Palestine, and archaeobotanical findings of charred emmer and wild barley, unravel the eating habits and lifestyles of forgotten civilisations. In a recently coined phrase, "the old is the new", wholesome wild wheats and ancient grains, rich in protein, iron and minerals, are revered by the health-conscious and environmentally-minded.

Gluten, the group of storage proteins found in wheats, barley, cereal grasses and hybrid species from the Triticale genera, has unique properties of elasticity and viscosity that allows for doughs to rise and form a soft, open crumb structure. Wild wheats and ancient grains all contain gluten proteins, but to a lesser degree than modern bread wheats, so although they are unsuitable for sufferers of coeliac disease, they are a healthier option to prevent stomach distension and inflammation. Sorghum and teff are classified as flowering plants from the grass family, gluten-free and nutritious substitutes for wheats and grains.

Through a clear historical knowledge and botanical background of each supergrain, *Freekeh, Wild Wheat & Ancient Grains* will undoubtedly interest a new decade of healthy eaters who want to know and understand the historical roots of what we consume, the role of ancient grains in our food ancestry, and their sustainability in a world of modern food production. This culinary treasure trove of traditional and contemporary recipes features a health bread from the writings of philosopher Maimonides, biblical stews heralded by the prophet Ezekiel, original fermented sourdoughs from ancient Egypt, and authentic freekeh dishes from local Galilean Arabic women. Paired with contemporary flavours and modern techniques for cooking and baking with freekeh, emmer, einkorn, spelt, khorasan, barely, rye, sorghum and teff, each recipe will excite Western palates with Eastern flavours.

Chapter one

Grains and pseudocereals

Freekeh, wild wheats and ancient cereals formed the staple food of past eras, and these grains, many of which have been lost or fogotten with the passage of time, are now beginning to reappear again on our plates, reenergising our palates and replacing the missing nutrients from our diets.

During the First Temple period of 1000 BCE, the wheat and barley harvests of the ancient Israelites were put under sustained threat by the authoritarian rule of a rising kingdom, which ordered farmers to surrender their crops to the realm. By virtue of the obligatory weekly sacrifices in Solomon's Temple, grain crops were protected, and it was permitted to bake unleavened goods for religious offering. These were offered to and consumed by the high priests as nourishment for their righteousness. It was in the Neo-Babylonian Empire of 586 BCE that the First Temple and its "threshing floor" was pillaged, destroyed and conquered by King Nebuchadnezzar.

However, following the building of the Second Temple in 515 BCE, biblical writings led to the realisation that the Land of Israel lay within a flourishing belt of wheat, barley and cereals, and a belief that grain, flour and bread would become the universal staple from their prolific yields and versatility, as prophesied in Ezekiel 4.9: "Further, take wheat, barley, beans, lentils, millet, and emmer [spelt]. Put them into one vessel and bake them into bread." Without grain, life could not have been sustained through the ages of mankind, and become the central component in global cuisine, through sharing food and "breaking bread".

It is in Genesis, the opening book of the Old Testament, that the wheat harvest is first mentioned, when Reuben the eldest son of the biblical patriarch Jacob, ventures into the fields and finds mandrakes, small purple flowers that grew in among the wheat sheaths and which were widely believed to enhance fertility. From this first reference in the scriptures, wheat is listed as the most important agricultural crop of the land of Israel and the core ingredient of bread, which gained recognition as "the staff of life". It was inscribed in Deuteronomy 8.8-9 that the Israelites would be bestowed "a land of wheat and barley, of vines and fig trees and pomegranates, a land of olive trees and honey, a land in which you will eat bread without scarcity, in which you will lack nothing".

Dr Tova Dickstein is the Biblical Food Expert at Neot Kedumim, Israel's natural landscape reserve that nestles within the Judean hills. She states that young wheat with a slight green tinge to each grain was known in biblical times as 'carmel'. Due to the agronomic stage of the growing cycle of the wheat, the carmel was picked before it was fully ripe in the early spring months. It was harvested before the arrival of the hot winds and the swarms of insects that the heat brought with them, preventing destruction of the annual crop. Once threshed in the fields, the young unripe grains were set alight on open fires and winnowed vigorously to remove the chaff, before being eaten whole, or ground into coarse meal

Young, green ears of wheat

between two milling stones, for bread or gruel. This is the first recollection of the process of producing freekeh, the immature green wheat that was understood by culinary historians to have been first grain offering in the temples of Jerusalem.

Dickstein adds that the carmel was seen as a form of a miracle, after the meagre harvests that resulted from a prolonged drought. The explanation during this period of famine was recounted by a disciple of the prophet Elijah who unexpectedly brought "twenty loaves of barley and fresh ears of grain" which he was instructed to give "to the people that may eat". Bewildered the servant replied, "How can I set this before a hundred men?" to which Elisha retorted "Give it to the people to eat. For this is what the LORD says: 'They will eat and have some left over.' Then he set it before them, and they ate and had some left over, according to the word of the LORD" (2 Kings 4:42-44). The miracle of the twenty loaves of bread stretching to feed over one hundred mouths and the leftovers fed to the starving flock, is a story repeated a number of times in the Bible, and started with the first fruits of the land, namely wheat and barley. It remains customary within Jewish law to offer the gift of food as charity to the poor and needy, and in celebration of religious festivals. This comes from the time when the gleanings from the harvested fields were not considered worthy of the sanctification of offerings, and therefore the loaves of bread were considered a true blessing from the Lord in sustaining life.

In another early biblical tale, an indication of how nature affects wheat crops is clearly told in the story of Joseph, where he interprets Pharaoh's dreams to reveal "seven years of great abundance are coming throughout the land of Egypt, but seven years of famine will follow them" (Genesis 41:17-32). During the abundant years, the grain was stored for the years of scarcity, which again illustrates the early practises of farmers who sought to protect their yields by harvesting the young, green grains of freekeh.

In the Book of Ruth, one of the writings of the Old Testament, the story is believed to have taken place at the start of the wheat and barley harvest in the ancient city of Bethlehem. Pronounced "Beyit Lehem" in Hebrew which directly translates as "The House of Bread", Bethlehem has remained an agricultural market town, enveloped by the wheat and barley fields, that nourished and sustained Ruth and Naomi, and saw the birth of Jesus.

The biblical story of Ruth in the Old Testament shows the arduous toil she endured reaping, gathering, threshing and winnowing wheat and barley in the fields of the landlord Boaz, and the love and respect she gained from him through her sheer determination and work ethic in the long, hot harvests. In an article entitled 'The Book of Ruth: Reaping Redemption' by the late Batya Uval, a culinary writer and tour guide at Neot Kedumim, Uval recalls that Boaz insisted Ruth ate her share of the bread to maintain her strength. She mentions "kali", the freshly picked, roasted wheat grains which we understand to be yet another reference to the early husbandry of freekeh. Kali was considered to be the fast food of the biblical era, as the field workers often did not have enough time to make bread, so gathered the remnants of grain left on the ground and quickly roasted them near to where they found them, on open fires, as a means of nourishment and energy.

This is Uval's recipe for Kali: Roasted Grain from the Book of Ruth, which she based on the ancient biblical practice. I have assumed from her recipe that the kernels should be cooked on either a modern gas fire, barbeque or even a hob, as she concludes by writing "that the grains will cook faster over a good campfire".

Kali: Roasted Grain

Ingredients:
1 cup / 200 g whole wheat kernels
2 tablespoons / 30 ml olive oil
1 teaspoon of salt, to taste

Method:

❖ *place wheat kernels in dry frying pan over high heat*
❖ *cook, stirring frequently until the kernels start to brown, then add olive oil and salt*

❖ *continue cooking for about 10 to 15 minutes, until the kernels are dark*
    brown, slightly charred & soft enough to eat

I have used whole wheat berries for this recipe, but you can use any other
whole grain of your choice. Place the kernels in a double-handed frying
pan, with a dash of extra virgin olive oil smeared over the base for flavour.
Do keep your eye on the grains and keep them on the move as they will
suddenly turn very dark in colour and burn if you don't. Once they are a
rich golden colour, remove the pan from the fire and drizzle some more olive
oil over the toasted wheat and plenty of coarse sea salt. Eat as a nutritious
snack or sprinkled over salads for some extra crunch.

Roasted Kali

Archaeological evidence from excavations in the Near East, show that the origins of wild wheat go back to early Neolithic times, more than 10,000 years ago. The prehistoric communities of the Fertile Crescent started the transition from hunter-gathering for food to agricultural farming of cereal crops, which marked the initial cultivation of wild emmer wheat. The remnants of the harvested grain date back to 9600 BCE, and were found to be from the Damascus basin, near Mount Hermon, situated in what is now Northern Israel.

It was around 7800 BCE in Çayönü Tepesi, southeast Turkey, that einkorn was discovered and subsequently domesticated. The spreading of cultivated ancient wheats beyond this region soon spread to Greece and as far as India by 6500 BCE. By 3000 BCE, wheat was found to be cultivated in England and in parts of Scandinavia, and in China over 1000 years later, making wheat the most successful global cash crop, due to its high yield and ability to grow in temperate climes. In these flourishing agricultural belts known for their rich and well irrigated soils, wheat, barley, millet and rye became the founder cereal crops domesticated for human use and would become the most widely grown and consumed grain throughout the world.

These early grain farmers also became the first millers of ancient wheats and grain, releasing the small, oval shaped seeds from the glumes of the spikelet, before parching, roasting and grinding the kernels into flour. This formed the basis of their nutritional sustenance, be it flour for bread, or as a thickening agent to add in gruel, soup or stews. Ancient grains continued to evolve through agricultural developments, and the cultural practice of the early harvesting of wheat has survived through the millennia, producing annual yields of freekeh, which remains a culinary staple in the Middle East.

DNA studies of einkorn conducted by archeobotanists in modern day Turkey, have shown that it was the first cereal to be gathered and threshed for cultivation in the pre-pottery Neolithic Age, before selective breeding of wheat was commenced prior to the Middle Ages. By the seventeenth century, emmer and einkorn were both cultivated in their natural habitat and cross-bred to create "landrace" cultivars, in other words those that are locally adapted to suit temperate climates and natural environmental forces.

The Dagon Grain Museum, situated in the Dago Silo of Haifa Port in Northern Israel, was the creation of Dr Reuben Hecht in 1955. Here, an archaeological collection of farming tools and grain storage pieces from Palestine and the surrounding region of the Levant are exhibited, dating back to the Stone Age of 6000 BCE. Hecht's idea was to document the historical links between the basic human need to sustain life, and grain. The Dagon collection exhibits archaeological artifacts from the era of hunter-gatherers to the birth of agriculture and the domestication of wheat

Storage jars from the Dagon Archeological Grain Museum, Israel.

and barley, intertwined with the biblical and mythical symbolism of grain and bread as the staple food of mankind.

Basic field tools used by hunter-gatherers to collect wild grain are displayed alongside the first agricultural implements used by the early farmers to thresh and harvest the wheat. Ploughs were developed in the late Neolithic era, and were harnessed to oxen to plough the land. Once the wheat had ripened, the painstaking task of harvesting the grain by hand took place, using a sickle that was made of animal bone, either the cheek, rib or jaw bone of an ass or a donkey. Serrated blades, either flint or the extracted teeth of a wild boar, which were long and sharp, were inserted into the round shape of the implement to ease the reaping of the grain.

The quern was the earliest known grinding implement. It was made of stone and shaped in the form of a shallow bowl with a flat underside and convex on top. The grain was placed inside the quern and, using a large round stone, the grain was ground by hand, with forward and backward movements. The quern was considered an essential tool to process the flour for bread making. Grinding the grain into fine powder was laborious and tedious, and tasked to the women. Using these basic stone tools, approximately 800 grams of flour was produced from an hour of solid grinding, which was just enough to bake a loaf of bread for the hungry men. The museum exhibits many stone querns, as it was over thousands of years later before grinding tools were improved and milling became more efficient. Storing the grain from the annual harvest was considered to be of the utmost importance to protect the community's economy. Dagon's collection of storage pits of the Palaeolithic era (12,000–6000 BCE), together with Canaanite pit shaped jars (2100–1900 BCE), communal storage structures and intricately decorated stone jars, adorn the museum.

Hippocrates of Kos was an ancient Greek philosopher and physician who became widely known as the "Father of Medicine" by transforming the way medicine was practised during the Hellenistic era (323–33 BCE). He advocated harmony between health and nature and the importance of understanding the role of dietetics on the human body. Hippocrates heavily influenced the theories and principles of Galen of Pergamon, who became renowned for his medical and surgical skills as a physician during the Roman Empire.

Galen researched and wrote extensively on the effects of food and diet, and developed the theory of the "humors" that had to be blanced to maintain human health. He viewed the line between food and medicine as blurred, often prescribing food as medicine, particularly for ailments of the digestive tract. Galen wrote prolifically in his thesis entitled *On the Power of Foods*, where he avidly discussed the influence that grains, fruits and vegetables have as sustainable ingredients and their effects on the health of the Roman Empire, dedicating a whole chapter to the medicinal benefits of barley. His chapter, 'On Barley Soup', argues that "everything that is good is assembled in barley soup", and that the cleansing, thirst quenching and hydrating ingredients in his recipe have the ability to rid the body of harmful disease, while also boosting the body's natural strength as a highly calorific grain.

Galen's original recipe was called "Ptisana". It featured in Oribasius' *Medical Compilations*, which collated manuscripts and essays from medical writers throughout ancient Rome and Greece. Galen's Barley Soup was highly calorific and was considered to be full of natural goodness, as well as having a cooling effect on the body's temperature, so it could serve as a medicine for fighting infection. Barley was easily accessible and affordable to all, therefore a soup of this kind would have been a staple dish of many of the poorer households in the Empire.

In Galen's recipe for Barley Soup, written in Latin, the barley is softened in water, which is helped by the addition of vinegar. A touch of salt is added but "not too much" and the addition of olive oil will not "harm the cooking". He goes on to state that nothing else needs to be added apart from "a little leek and dill weed" which I can only deduce will add some aroma to the otherwise thick, rather bland soup.

This is my take on Galen's Barley Soup, a refreshing broth with aniseed flavour from fennel and dill, accompanying the protein rich, soft pearls of barley. As with the original recipe, I have kept the sweet sauteed leeks as the basis of the soup, and added black kale for extra fibre and antioxidants. Barley soup was typically thick in consistency similar to a porridge, nourishing and full of calories but often tasteless; this is appetising, fragrant and undoubtedly full of flavour, enhanced by the addition of salty feta cheese, crumbled over the top.

Pearl Barley Soup with Fennel, Dill & Feta

Ingredients (serves 6-8):
3 tablespoons / 45 ml olive oil
3 leeks
2 large fennel bulbs
¾ cup / 150 g pearl barley
1 teaspoon fennel seeds
6 cups / 1 ½ litres vegetable stock
3 tablespoons / 30 g dill
juice of 1 lemon
4 cups / 120 g black kale
salt & pepper
¼ cup / 50 g feta, crumbled
dill or fennel fronds, to garnish

Method

❖ *wash the leeks well, as they collect mud and grit in between the layers, remove the fennel fronds & outer layer of the fennel bulb & slice both vegetables finely*

❖ *place the olive oil in a large saucepan, I like to use extra virgin olive oil as it adds flavour from the outset, then add the leeks & fennel & fry over a medium heat for 5 minutes until beginning to soften, meanwhile toast the fennel seeds in a dry pan until the flavour starts to release, then grind to a powder & set aside*

❖ *once the leeks & fennel are soft, add the pearl barley & ground fennel seeds & stir to coat, add the vegetable stock, for which I use a good quality stock pot, but you can use whatever you have in your cupboard, bring to a simmer & cover, leave on a low heat to cook for 40 to 45 minutes, until the barley is just tender but still has a slight bite to each kernel and the vegetables are soft*

❖ *finely chop the dill, add to the soup with the lemon juice & season with salt & pepper, add the kale & cook on a low heat for a further 10 minutes, check the seasoning, adding more salt & pepper if needed, but remember there is salty cheese to follow; serve in bowls with crumbled feta & extra dill or fennel fronds*

In Classical Greek literature, the poet Homer, the historian Herodotus, and the naturalist Pliny, all made reference to an early grain variety known as zea, which was considered a symbol of fertility.

Herodotus wrote in his histories that this ancient grain was far superior to wheat or barley due to its high nutrient and fibre content. It was said that zea was given to noble warriors, including Alexander the Great, to give him strength and energy during his battles, whereas the inferior wheat or barley grain was merely used as fodder for animals. Herodotus wrote passionately and emphatically that "Other nations live on wheat and barley, but among the Egyptians it is the greatest disgrace to a man to make his diet on these grains."

Pearl Barley Soup
h Fennel, Dill & Feta

Zea was believed to be the wild cultivar of emmer wheat. It was the grain of choice for the making of bread, as well as the basis for thick and nutritious drinks, by coarsely grinding together zea and wheatberries and making it palatable with the addition of milk or water. Together with wheat, barley and other species of grain and cereals, zea became a focus of interest in the writings of Dioscorides, the Greek physician, pharmacologist and botanist, who understood the cereal's impact on health and healing. Dioscorides recommended the use of soft wheat bread as a compress for inflammation around the eyes. He also recommended wheat flour mixed with sweet wine or vinegar to be applied to the forehead to combat ocular streaming.

Wild emmer wheat became the prominent crop in the classical era, with dishes emerging such as *tragos*, a wheat-based gruel or porridge. It was deemed to be "most useful food" by the physicians and botanists of ancient Greece, who believed it provided a healthy sustenance for all. A preparation of ground wheat, mixed with a nutritious liquid, formed the basis of this widely consumed food. Galen, Pliny and Dioscorides gave this blend a variety of names which included pudding, cereal or drink, however the recipe remained one and the same. "Cracked emmer was boiled with milk and dried in the form of lumps. These could be conveniently stored and carried, and, when wanted, boiled again to make a porridge." (*Food in the Ancient World from A to Z*, Andrew Dalby.)

For centuries to follow, *tragos* became the staple to sustain life among the poor, sick and vulnerable in the insipid, bland form of gruel, with bran replacing the protein rich wild emmer, and water used instead of milk.

In the tenth-century agricultural anthology *Geoponika*, a recipe for Byzantium porridge resembles that of modern breakfast food made from barley, spelt or oat flakes. The particular strain of wheat used for this cereal was called *olyra* similarly considered superior yet documented as a "rice-wheat" hybrid, rather than the refined emmer. Some culinary historians and archeobotanists claim the ancestry of zea and *olyra* to be one and the same: wild emmer wheat. "One must take the wheat called Alexandrios and one must soak, separate (sc.in nodules) and dry it in the heat of the sun; and in doing that, discard the husks, shells and fibrous parts of the wheat. One must dry and store the *tragos* (made) from *olyra* wheat of superior strain."

The Middle Ages saw global agricultural practices transformed. This was primarily due to the improved irrigation from the watermills built by the Romans, but also owing to the introduction of crop rotation by the farmers, a practice found to improve yields and soil fertility. They began the method of three-field crop rotation, which delivered cereal harvests in both spring and autumn in two of their three fields, allowing for one field to remain fallow every third year, and simultaneously enhancing the nutrient content of the soil.

Wheat and rye were commonly planted in the autumn months, and barley and oats followed in early spring, allowing for profitable harvests that would provide a cash income for the farmers, when sold for bread or beer. However, the timing of each harvest became of vital importance during this new agricultural era, ensuring the maximum yield of each cereal crop. In a blistering heat the wheat would dry out and the grains drop to the ground, but in cold, wet weather the cereals would rot in the damp soil, so a temperate climate was preferable to produce the optimum harvest. Common wheat, *Triticum aestivum*, was highly valued during this era in Medieval England, as the gluten content in this species was esteemed for the making of bread, that sustained and nourished the lords of the manor. Climatic conditions could so adversely affect the growth of the wheat, that during this revolutionary farming period, the immature green grains were reaped for the annual food source, which led to the ancient cultural practice of harvesting unripe wheat. To ensure that the grains were palatable, the young wheat stalks were gathered in large bunches and thrown onto open fires in the fields, where they were roasted until charred. The grains were then sifted from their blackened husks and sold to the lords, or stored for leaner times, and known as freekeh.

Freekeh was first documented in the form of a recipe by Muhammad bin al-Karim al-Baghdadi, an Islamic caliph who compiled the earliest known Arabic cookbook during the thirteenth century. In *The Book of Dishes*, Al-Baghdadi writes of *farikiyya* which he describes as a "porridge of new wheat, cooked with milk and meat", and gives the following recipe: "Stew fat meat, which has been cut up small, in melted fat, then cover it with water and throw a little salt and a stick of cinnamon on it. When the meat is done, throw a bit of ground dry coriander on it, then add a little more water. Take the necessary amount of new wheat, rub it from its ears, clean it, add it to the pot and leave it until it thickens – thicker than *hintiyya* [wheat]. When it grows quiet on the fire, take it down and ladle it out. Put finely pounded cumin and cinnamon and a little melted fresh tail fat on its surface, and eat it." (A *Baghdad Cookery Book*, translated by Charles Perry.)

Ancient freekeh grain has been at the heart of Levantine cuisine for centuries, and is traditionally paired with meats, vegetables and spices. Freekeh stuffed pigeon or squab, was an ancient Egyptian delicacy, gently poached in a spiced broth and rumoured to have been served to young couples on their wedding night. The cooking of freekeh is about the liquor that it softens in, which is a meaty stock, made from pieces of meat that are then shredded on top of the grain and delicately spiced with cinnamon bark, black peppercorns and bayleaves. Maintaining its authenticity and traditional spicing, this is an easy meatless recipe for freekeh, that is still cooked in the kitchens of Levant and then served with meat, fish or vegetables, instead of rice, pasta or potatoes. You can make it with chicken stock and add chunks of succulent chicken on top, however the flavour of the nutty grain is delicious on its own.

Freekeh with Pinenuts & Almonds

Ingredients (serves 4):
1 cup / 180 g freekeh
1 medium onion
3 tablespoons / 45 ml extra virgin olive oil
1 teaspoon baharat
1 teaspoon cinnamon
1 ½ cups / 350 ml vegetable stock
⅓ cup / 50 g pinenuts & slivered almonds
salt & pepper

Method
❖ *soak the freekeh in a bowl of cold water for 5 minutes, drain & rinse well under cold running water for a couple of minutes to remove any grit or chaff from the grains*
❖ *finely chop the onion and place in a saucepan with the olive oil & cook on*

*a low heat for 5 minutes, stirring occasionally until the onions are soft &
beginning to turn colour; when cooking in the Galilee with local cooks I was
given the tip of cooking with cold olive oil, which gives extra flavour to the
vegetables from the outset*

❖ *add the freekeh & the spices to the onions & stir well to coat the grains with
the spicy oil; I like the warming fragrance of baharat, a blend of nutmeg,
cloves, cinnamon, cardamom, marjoram and black peppercorns that is
ground together and used in savoury Arabic cooking; add the vegetable stock
& bring to the boil, reduce the heat & leave to simmer gently without a lid
for 20 to 25 minutes, until all the liquid has been absorbed but there is still
a slight bite to the grain, turn off the heat, place a tight-fitting lid on top of
the saucepan & leave the freekeh to stand for 10 minutes, to allow the steam
to continue to soften the grains, similar to cooking rice*

❖ *toast the nuts in a pan with a dash of olive oil until brown, set aside,
before placing the freekeh in a serving dish, add the nuts & serve at room
temperature*

Freekeh with Pinenuts
& Slivered Almonds

The agricultural revolution of the Middle Ages saw the introduction of more sophisticated farming technologies that would enrich the land and improve the drainage for new cereal crops. It came in the form of the heavy-duty mouldboard plough, that could turn over the heavy clay earth, loosening the top soil and providing the essential nutrients for the crops to thrive. During the same period, the Arab Islamic rulers from the Iberian Peninsula that bordered North Africa were restoring the Roman built aqueducts to improve the irrigation of the fertile land and ultimately the grain harvests. The propagation of these new crops included durum wheat (*Triticum durum*), spelt (*Triticum spelta*) and the pseudocereal buckwheat (*Fagopyrum esculentum*), all of which flourish in the harsher conditions of the Northern European landscape.

Durum comes from the Latin, meaning "hard"; a tough wheat species with high levels of gluten and a rich source of protein and fibre. It had a strong resistance to milling and so was turned into coarse middlings rather than pure flour, which made durum the ideal wheat for pasta and couscous. There remains a controversy as to the origins of pasta, with some culinary historians believing Marco Polo first encountered "long noodles" made from hard wheat flour on his journeys through the Far East, and that it was he who brought the staple to Italy during the Middle Ages. Others believe it was the Muslim geographer by the name of Abu Abdullah Mohammed al Edrisi, who travelled extensively throughout the Mediterranean and completed a thorough geographical survey of Sicily for King Roger II, shortly before his death in 1154. noted "long strands" made from a hard wheat and found in the markets of Trabia, which may be the first citing of spaghetti.

Spelt is also known by the German name dinkel wheat. The cultivation of spelt is referenced as far back as biblical times and the exodus of the Israelites from Egypt. Spelt was first thought to be the grain used for the unleavened matzah that they managed to hurriedly take with them on their journey through the wilderness, although culinary biblical historians have since realised that it was more likely to have been emmer. Cultivated predominantly in Germany and other parts of Northern Europe, spelt became a chief trading crop in the Middle Ages, due to its adaptability to a colder climate. As a hulled wheat, the removal of the outer husks allowed the grain to thrive in this agricultural environment for many years.

Buckwheat, also a relict crop from this era, was believed to have been domesticated in Southeast Asia around 6000 BCE, before finding its way across to the Middle East and Europe by the Middle Ages. Classified as a pseudocereal, it was mentioned in the eighth-century historical Japanese chronicle *Shoku Nihongi*, which urged farmers to plant this cereal in case of a poor rice harvest. Around 1400 BCE, buckwheat was given the name of "Saracen" which Europeans gave to many things that originated from the East. Favouring a cooler and wetter climate it found its way to America two hundred years later, where this non-grass cereal established its status as a low maintenance, economical crop.

It was in the mid-eighteenth century that an eminent Swedish botanist, Carl Linnaeus, became famous for the scientific classification of plants and cereals. He is considered to be the "father of modern taxonomy". Up until Linnaeus's time wheat had been classified into two categories: free threshing and hulled, whereas Linnaeus recognised five distinct species of domesticated wheats. Nevertheless, wild wheat was not properly classified until the nineteenth century, mainly due to the lack of botanical evidence of any wild cereal grasses in the Near East.

In 1906, wild emmer wheat was discovered to be growing in Palestine by the Romanian agronomist and botanist, Aaron Aaronsohn (1876–1919). Aaronsohn studied agriculture in France, before moving to Palestine where he and his family became pioneers of the first agricultural settlements in the first wave of Zionist immigration. The wild emmer wheat that Aaronsohn found was deemed by him, and subsequently proclaimed by many other botanists, to be the "Mother of Wheat", a title that has always remained with this species. Already the leading expert in the plants and cereals of the fertile land of Palestine and its surrounding areas, Aaronsohn found the wild wheat whilst trekking through Upper Galilee, at the foothills of Mount Hermon and the area of Southern Lebanon. Some historians documented his discovery nearer to the Lebanese town of Rachaiya, and others towards the Palestinian countryside of Amiad, close to the old town of Rosh Pina. Wherever the point of actual sighting, this became the single most important botanical find in the history of the Middle East, and made Aaronsohn a leading name in the world of agronomy. He strongly believed

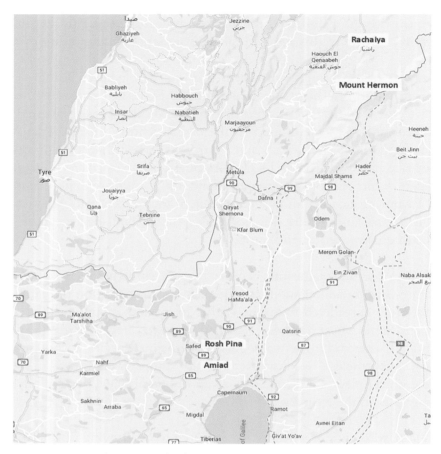

A Map of Aaronsohn's discovery of wild Emmer wheat

that wild emmer was the original ancestor of all domesticated wheat and was able to survive in extreme weather conditions, which would therefore lead to the evolution of this cereal's cultivation and agricultural usage.

Wild emmer wheat is categorised as hulled, a type of awned wheat that can self-cultivate from its long wheat spikelets. It is a brittle, tetraploid plant that contains four full sets of chromosomes in the two genomes of its genetic composition. The wild spikelets have tough glumes or husks, and can hold no more than three grains per spikelet, which shatters spontaneously in the hot, dry winds of the Middle East. In comparison, the glumes of most domesticated wheats, being soft and fragile, were easily threshed. It was during the early 1900s that agriculturists identified the DNA composition of wild emmer with other artificially selected wheat strains, and established the cereal crops to cultivate. This produced prolific yields, which fostered the development of domesticated wheat and hybrid cereal crops for global consumption and economies of scale.

The first documented hybrids of domesticated emmer produced the bread wheats *Triticum aestivum*, Polish wheat *Triticum polonicum* and durum wheat, *Triticum durum*. They were all discovered to be high yielding common variants of wheat and highly adaptive to climatic changes. Spelt is also an heirloom wheat, and wild spelt was found to be growing alongside wild emmer in Northern Israel. Spelt is genetically similar to bread wheat, but with a divergent, water soluble gluten composition, making the grain easier to digest and therefore reducing bloating of the stomach. The process of wheat domestication from the wild genus of emmer and einkorn was characterised by the assisted selection and manual sowing of seeds, rather than natural dispersion. Upon maturity, threshing, ploughing and winnowing of these hulled grains were required for harvesting, but with each glume only holding three kernels, the yields were insufficient for the global market. This led to the domestication of wheat being conducted in earnest.

The domesticated grains inevitably fell into a global agricultural recession in the late 1800s, due to disease, flood and war. This left the fertile land barren and a lack of farmers, who joined up to fight for their countries, creating hunger and poverty worldwide. The early 1900s saw the modernisation of

**Wild emmer wheat
spikelets & glumes**

the ancient stone flour mills to industrial grain mills, which together with the major advances in genetics, led to the development of the semi-dwarf stemmed, high yielding, disease resistant wheat varieties that would boost the production of bread for the future. This work was promoted by the American agronomist Norman Borlaug, during the 1950s and 1960s. Borlaug became known as the "Father of the Green Revolution" and was awarded a Nobel Peace Prize in 1970 for his work on sustainable crops. Global production of the ancient cereal subsequently tripled to become the second highest generating global crop, with only rice beating it to pole position.

Professor Assaf Distelfeld is a Molecular Biologist and Plant Geneticist at Haifa University, Israel, whose research interests lie with the wild emmer wheat that can still be found growing throughout the Zavitan Nature Reserve, in the lush terrain of the Golan Heights in the Northern tip of Israel. He categorically states that the wild genus contains more proteins and minerals than its domesticated counterpart, and has a positive impact on gluten intolerance. Wild emmer, einkorn, freekeh, spelt and many other relict cereal crops are still considered to be the natural and more nutritious choice of staple in our diet, due to a higher content of proteins, fibre and minerals. As sustainable and functional requirements of our diets, they are making a timely return to the global food market, connecting the modern palate to our biblical, historical and cultural heritage, and above all delivering on flavour.

The Wild Emmer of Northern Israel

Chapter two

Bread, loaves & artisan bakers

Bread is classified as "food made of flour, water, and yeast mixed together and baked".

Bread has had biblical, historical and political importance across all cultures. Each society has its own type of, and name for, bread, which has nourished and sustained humanity throughout the centuries, making it an essential cultural bond and global currency. Bread is the ancient food of the world.

In 1861, the celebrated English cookery and domestic writer Isabella Beeton, published her book, *Mrs Beeton's Book of Household Management*, a compendium of Victorian cookery and household management. She was clear on her explanation of bread: "...bread has become an article of food of the first necessity; and properly so, for it constitutes of itself a complete life-sustainer, the gluten, starch, and sugar which it contains representing azotised and hydro-carbonated nutrients, and combining the sustaining powers of the animal and vegetable kingdoms in one product".

Bread is the leading global staple, other than in Asia where rice takes pole position. Bread's dominance is due to the natural abundance of cereal crops that have marked the antiquity of agriculture and become our daily nourishment. All staple cereals were named after Ceres, the Roman goddess of harvest, grains, agriculture and fertility, and ultimately bread. Across all religions, bread holds a spiritual meaning to many communities, represented in both devout prayer and superstitious sacraments, to avert starvation. It is in the Lord's Prayer, recited in every Christian church service, that Jesus teaches his disciples to pray for "our daily bread" and when the Israelites were wandering through the wilderness hungry and tired, God said to Moses, "behold, I am about to rain bread from heaven for you, and the people shall go out and gather a day's portion every day, that I may test them, whether they will walk in my law or not" (Exodus 16:4). In both religious teachings, bread is used as a lure to God, so that the people of Israel may be fed and nourished for continued prayer, and the belief that God's hand will feed them in times of plenty as well as in times of famine.

The Old Testament affirms that during the time of the First Temple of Jerusalem (1200–586 BCE) and the reign of King Solomon, bread was sacrificed to God in the form of the "showbread". It was a symbol of abundance given to the Israelites during their exodus from Egypt and as an acknowledgement for keeping them alive. The showbread was principally known as the "Bread of Faces" due to its many facets that perpetually faced God however it was presented. Also known as 'Presence Bread', it was to remain in constant attendance before God in the Temple, "And you shall put on the table showbread before me" (Exodus 25:30) and only replaced with fresh loaves before each Sabbath. There is a clear reference to "the table" that the showbread was to be placed upon, which was required by God to be of specific measurements, gold-plated and made of acacia wood, a symbol of its divine sanctity. "You shall make a table of acacia wood, its length a pair of cubits, its width a cubit, and its height a cubit and a half. And you shall overlay it with pure gold, and you shall make a molding of gold for it, all around" (Exodus 25:23-29). There was further stipulation regarding the details of the bread offering, which was considered a commandment from God as twelve loaves were to be baked and placed on the table in two rows of six, in recognition of the twelve tribes of Israel. "And thou shalt take fine flour, and bake twelve cakes thereof: two tenth parts of an *ephah* [an ancient Hebrew measure equivalent to 0.6 of a bushel] shall be in one cake, and thou shalt set them in two rows, six in a row, upon the pure table before the LORD" (Leviticus 24:5-6). The instructed twelve loaves of non-fermented, unleavened bread were traditionally arranged in two rows on the adorned table, in front of the altar in the sanctuary of the Holy Temple. The showbread remained on the table for a week, until every Friday evening before the incoming Sabbath, by which time fresh loaves were baked and replaced. The bread was eaten the following day by the priests during the holy Sabbath, which in itself was considered to be one of Gods' miracles, keeping each loaf fresh for seven days, as if it had just come out of the oven.

Les Saidel, a South African born, artisan Jewish baker living in Karnei

Shomron in the West Bank, is attempting to revive the showbread from a recipe that has been lost over time. As a devout, practicing Jew, he is of the opinion that each of the twelve loaves should be baked using a semolina flour, which prevents a good rise, and that in a true likeness to the original the loaves are baked in a specific rectangular shaped pan. This he understands to be the precise way it was made during the times of the Temple. He has not perfected the showbread recipe yet and it remains unpublished, however he continues to work on the loaf and pass on the teachings of this significant part of his culinary heritage through baking workshops, in which he revives this ancient symbol of prosperity.

The Eucharist, which also goes by the name of "The Sacramental Bread", connects bread across the Christian and Catholic orthodox religions, following the birth of Jesus. From the ancient Greek word *eucharistia*, meaning "thanksgiving", the bread is eaten as an acknowledgement of gratitude to the many sacrifices Jesus made to his disciples. Bethlehem, which means "House of Bread" in Hebrew, and translates in Arabic to the "House of Flesh", was the city of Jesus's birth, from where he proclaims, "I am the living bread that came down from heaven. Whoever eats this bread will live forever. This bread is my flesh, which I will give for the life of the world" (John, 6:51). Christians still believe that the Eucharist bread confers eternal life, and it also serves as a stark reminder of Jesus's last meal before his death.

Saidel's interpretation of the biblical 'Showbread'

The Last Supper is commemorated in Christianity on Maundy Thursday, the day preceding the crucifixion and resurrection of Jesus. It is said to have been the final meal Jesus shared with his apostles in the Temple of Jerusalem before his crucifixion, circa 33-30 AD. A meal dominated by unleavened bread and wine, at which Jesus insisted the pieces of bread represented his broken body and the wine his blood, validated the religious symbolism attached to the staple.

The Last Supper and the Passover Seder have striking parallels with unleavened bread, a feature of both meals, yet with quite contradictory reasoning for their presence. The Passover story is of the Israelite's hurried exodus from Egypt, with little time for their bread to rise and therefore the unleavened bread, known as "matzah" is eaten to remember their hardship. It is through the adversity and departure of the Israelites and Jesus himself, that links the similarities to both significant meals and the sacrificial bread of affliction, revered in both religions.

Matzah is the symbolic unleavened bread that is eaten during the eight days of Passover, commemorating the Israelites exodus from slavery in Egypt. They were commanded to leave in such haste, that "the people picked up their bread dough before it had risen and carried it on their shoulders in bowls, wrapped up in their clothes" (Exodus 12:34). Matzah is made with flour and water, which according to the culinary rules of the religion, can

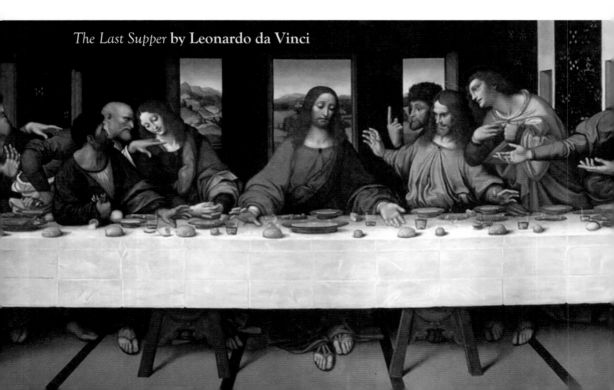

The Last Supper **by Leonardo da Vinci**

only be made from the wholegrain, refined flour of the five ancient grains; wheat, barley, rye, spelt or oats.

Culinary historians and archeobotanists found the Egyptians to be baking with predominantly emmer wheat during that era, as other than the rare citing of einkorn, emmer appeared to be the only available grain, and therefore it is presumed to be the grain used by Israelites for making matzah. Matzah was also referred to as "cakes" which was assumed from their shape rather than their texture.

The lack of bread and a threat of starvation continued to torment the wandering Israelites following their exodus from Egypt, until their plight was resolved by God. "I will rain down bread for you from the sky, and the people shall go out and gather each day that day's portion" (Exodus 16.4). This divine test of trust led to the belief that bread would nourish and support them physically and spiritually, and that it would be proclaimed for ever as "the food of life".

Unleavened matzah © British Museum

Challah bread is integral to the culinary culture of the Jewish religion and a proud symbol of the customary Sabbath and festival table. There is a strong biblical reference to its name as either a loaf or cake, roughly translated from the biblical Aramaic language, but could also have meant "morsel of bread". Either meaning has its own significance to the portion of the dough that Moses was instructed to detach before baking, and present as an offering to the Hebrew priests or *kohanim*. God's instructions are clearly cited: "When you enter the land where I bring you, it shall be that when you eat of the bread of the land, you shall set aside a portion for God. Of the first of your dough, you shall set aside a loaf as an offering; as the offering of the threshing-floor, so you shall set it aside. From the first of your dough, you shall give to God an offering throughout your generations" (Numbers 15:18-21). This tradition has remained in the Jewish religion and is observed as "the separation of the challah". It has become customary in Jewish households to bake two loaves of challah bread as a constant reminder of the double portion of manna, the bread from heaven that fell from the sky shortly before the beginning of the Sabbath, and fed the Israelites during their wanderings through the wilderness, even on the holy day of rest.

Despite the lack of scripture writings describing the braided, enriched dough, the original Sabbath challah bread was said to be a round, flat white bread, to differentiate it from the daily loaf. It was not until the Middle Ages when the Ashkenazi Jews of Eastern Europe developed the braids and twisted shapes, that the shape became synonymous with the rich dough made from eggs. Jews from around the globe who found eggs and sugar scarce, livened the dough with spices and sweeteners, which led the way for the delightful variations of this yeasted, enriched bread, that signifies the culinary culture of the Jewish religion. The challah was purposely made as a dairy-free loaf, so that it could be eaten with meat in a strictly kosher home on the Sabbath and at religious festivals. The simple twelve long braids or strands, that has remained customary over the centuries is yet another testimony to the ancestry of the twelve tribes of Israel, and has become more complex, with the twists of soft dough filled with contemporary flavourings and toppings. However, the essence of the Sabbath bread remains true to its origins with the intertwining of arms linking the love and harmony of family unity, freedom and creation with the sanctity of life. It is believed by devout culinary Jewish observers that the seven basic ingredients of flour, yeast, water, egg, oil, salt and sugar, all have a vital significance to our sustenance, growth and nourishment, both physically and spiritually.

For the Jewish New Year of Rosh Hashanah, the challah dough is typically rolled into a circular shape of a wheel, as opposed to the traditional long braids, symbolising the "whole" of a yearly and seasonal cycle. As customary at this festival, apple is dipped in honey to signify a sweet new year, so the challah is brushed with a honey egg wash and raisins are often added for extra sweetness and, as cited in the blessing to God, for a sweet and fruitful new year.

This is an original recipe from Les Saidel, the master Jewish baker from Israel's West Bank, who has been baking challah for the Sabbath and festivals for many years. This is his festive round loaf, traditionally baked with raisins for Rosh Hashanah, the Jewish New Year, signifying the fluidity of the coming year and representing the circle of life. This is an easy all in one method for a challah dough, requiring a large mixing bowl or electric mixer with dough paddle, the ingredients and some much-needed patience for the dough to rise twice before baking and devouring. It makes wonderful toast for breakfast, with lashings of butter...

Challah Bread with Raisins (Saidel's Bakery)

Ingredients (makes 1 loaf):
2 cups / 280 g strong bread flour
¼ cup / 30 g whole wheat flour
⅔ cup / 150 ml warm water
2 tablespoons instant yeast or 20 g fresh yeast
1 ½ teaspoons salt
⅓ cup / 50 g caster sugar
2 tablespoons / 30 ml sunflower or vegetable oil
for the filling:
1 cup / 125 g raisins
1 teaspoon cinnamon
1 egg

Method:

- ❖ *place the dough ingredients into a large mixing bowl or an electric mixer with a dough paddle & mix until it is all combined but still looks rather flaky, turn it all out onto a floured surface or keep in the mixer with the dough hook & knead furiously for 10 minutes until you have a smooth, elastic dough, place in a lightly oiled bowl or proving basket if you have one & cover with a clean tea towel, leave to rise in a warm kitchen for 2 hours*
- ❖ *transfer the dough onto a well-floured surface & knock back the air from it, roll it out into a rectangular shape approximately 30 x 20 cm / 12 x 7 in, splash the surface of the dough with a little water, then sprinkle the cinnamon & raisins evenly over the top, I used golden raisins, but use whatever you have to hand*
- ❖ *starting with the long end of the rectangle, roll the dough spirally into a cylinder with the seam on the underneath, twist the cylinder into a round, tucking the ends underneath the challah & place on a floured baking tray & leave to rise for a further 2 hours*

Symbolic Round Challah Bread

❖ *about 15 minutes before the end of the second rise, preheat the oven to 180 °C / 350 °F / Gas Mark 4 beat the egg & carefully brush all over the surface of the dough making sure you have an even glaze, place in the oven for 20 to 25 minutes until golden brown & the base of the bread sounds hollow, remove from the oven & if possible, leave to cool before eating...*

Ancient black food fragments, resembling the breadcrumbs that are found at the bottom of a toaster, were unearthed a few years ago by archaeologists in an excavated site in the Black Dessert in Jordan. They were discovered by Amaia Arranz-Otaegui from the University of Copenhagen and carbon-dated back to the origins of bread and the Natufian hunter-gatherers, 14,000 years ago. These charred plant remains were identified by the Institute of Archaeology, London, where these remnants of ancient cereal plants found in the Levant and probably made from emmer, einkorn or barley, were said to have likely been "the oldest bread remains in the world, prepared before the dawn of agriculture".

The Natufian community were among the first people to cultivate cereal plants for edible foods, commencing the shift from hunter-gathers to farmers, and predating the emergence of agriculture. They harvested the wild wheat, barley and oats, and ground the cereals between two large stones, creating a fine dust-like powder, that we now know to be flour. It was then sieved and mixed with water to create a flat paste, which was thrown onto an open fire until hard and charred, resembling a pita or flatbread. It would have been the crumbs of these unleavened breads that were found in Shubayqa, Jordan.

In 3000 BCE, the Egyptians improved upon the Natufian's basic bread making methods and became the first bakers of the more palatable and nourishing leavened bread. Emmer wheat and barley were the prolific crops of Egypt's fertile land, enriched from the flowing Nile and the arid climate. The wheat and barley initially shared an equal status in the production of bread and beer, however, it was with wild emmer that Egyptian bakers sought to make their bread, despite the difficulties they faced turning the tough grains into a soft flour, due to the wheat's long spindly spikelets. It was difficult to thresh the wheat in the fields and to remove the chaff, so once scythed they softened the husks in water and then pounded them with large stones, which released the wheat kernels. The grains of wheat were then dried in the sun and sieved a number of times to remove any remnants of the husk, before finally being ground and milled into flour, using their own invention of the 'saddle quern'.

It was around this time that the Egyptians, as they were refining the milling process of the wild emmer through their own ingenuity, accidently discovered the process of fermentation by mixing flour and water into a paste and leaving it for the natural airborne spores to form and react. This led not only to the Egyptians becoming the region's "super bakers" with the advent of leavened bread, but also the creators of alcohol and the inventors of beer.

The saddle quern was also known as the "handmill" and was essentially two stone slabs. The larger of the stones resembled a saddle with a depression at one end that would hold the grains. The smaller stone was shaped like

Saddle quern

a rolling pin, and would be hand held to crush the grains in a persistent grinding motion from in front of the quern. A tiring and physical method, the chore of grinding grain into flour was often given to women, servants or slaves who saw this as a form of humiliation, rather than an essential part in the daily process of making bread, before animals became the powerhouse behind the querns. The bread making process in all its forms, from farming through to baking, was the work of the Egyptian lower socio-economic class. The farmers who cultivated and harvested the grain were able to store large quantities on their land, which were sold to the richer households for a mere pittance, where the women were then charged with the menial task of grinding the grain into flour and making the bread.

It is well documented that around 4000 BCE the unleavened flatbreads made by the Egyptians evolved into puffy risen loaves. Culinary historians still maintain that the process of leavening was stumbled upon by chance. When baked in the hearth, the bread puffed up as it cooked giving a lighter textured loaf and a more palatable flavour, which was to become the signature bake of the region.

Bread-like products in a hearth

During this ancient era, bread was ornately crafted and decorated, and had a ritualistic role in pagan offerings and was sacrificed to the divine Egyptian gods and goddesses as a symbol of prosperity in life and sustenance in the afterlife. Wheat and barley grains were thought to contain magical symbolic properties, which gave significance to sheaths of wheat and beer jugs being shaped or carved into the doughs, and presented to the deities at the temple altars.

The second century BCE witnessed the baking of bread as a recognised craft with the introduction of the Rotating mill, a device that was also known as the Roman or Donkey mill. As all three names suggest, it milled large amounts of whole wheat into flour through the force of a rotary mill, powered by donkeys. This innovation allowed for a significant increase in the production of flour, from the use of a crank attached to the donkeys who were harnessed to a wooden frame that alternated the large milling stones, piled high with grain. The donkeys would drive the mills for hours at a time, saving the peasants from this arduous and exhausting work. However, the result was a coarsely textured flour, that required further refining, by sieving repeatedly before it could be used to make bread, which naturally fell to the women bakers.

The Romans were one of the the first civilisations to respect the baker and pastry cook, deeming the beautifully carved and decorated loaves and

Ancient Egyptian bread offerings © Oxford Expedition to Egypt

pastries to be a culinary decadence, highly valued by the rich members of the Empire. In the poorer Roman households, a basic hearth with an outlet for a chimney, allowed for bread to be baked on a much smaller scale and became known as "hearth bread". This was a fermented dough that was simply baked on the floor of the fireplace until brown and crisp. This was adequate for domestic use, but not for the Empire's banquets, when larger quantities of baked goods were needed and requiring more sophisticated equipment. This led to the development of the "furnus" or "fornax", named after the Goddess of the hearth, a dome-shaped construction of stone, built on a flat floor and filled with dry twigs. These were burned until the fire was spent, leaving the heat of the glowing embers to bake the bread. The Romans, not renowned for their baking skills, had far more architectural know-how and knowledge of buildings and infrastructure, which gave bakers the ability to create and bake elaborate breads. Ovens with chimneys were built that came to be known as "black ovens", because the remnants of soot remained permanently in the oven chamber even during baking. With further advancements in the milling process and the introduction of the watermill, flour was ground to a finer powder and baking thrived. This led to the first prestigious artisan bakers guild, *Collegium Pistorum*, being established in Pompeii in 68 BCE, which brought about regulations for bread, necessitated by such growing demand.

The amount of bread baked increased and it became the Empire's principal staple as it was affordable to all, but only because different grains were used for the rich and the poor. Black or dark wholegrain bread, although more nutritious due to the contents of bran, germ and endosperm, was harder to digest, cheaper to buy and baked into bread by the poor. The more luxurious fine white flour, ground from the endosperm alone and with all the proteins and fibre removed, was the bread of choice for the richer community, whose loaf was not only softer in texture but beautifully shaped and sculpted by master bakers, and very much more expensive to buy.

Moses ben Maimon was a medieval philosopher, physician and highly acclaimed religious scholar from Sephardic Jewish descent, who became known as Maimonides, or by the acronym "Rambam". He was highly revered for his rabbinical teachings on law and ethics, but his true vocation was in medicine, and he wrote many books on health and nutrition. He was acclaimed as the predecessor of the holistic practice of medicine through his vociferous belief that the health of the body was intertwined with that of the mind, that they were of equal importance and should be medically treated as such. Born into a religious Jewish household in the strict Muslim rule of Spain in 1135, Maimonides left his country of birth during his teen years and settled in Egypt where he became a respected physician, advising the Grand Vizier on all health matters. His writings merged the ethical and spiritual works of orthodox Jewish law with Greek philosophy and Islamic theology. His vast medical knowledge was the source from which came the foundations of dietetics and the holistic aim of eating to create a healthy body and mind. He strongly believed that "no disease that can be treated by diet, should be treated with any other means," a mantra which became the essence of his medicine.

Maimonides proclaimed that bread should be regularly consumed, particularly "if one suffered from asthma". The "healing" loaf should be made from a good quality, coarsely ground whole wheat flour that had not had the bran removed from it. It should also contain salt. He stipulated that the bread should be kneaded well and baked until

Rambam Bread from Saidel
Jewish Baking Centre, Israel

"clearly raised". This method for making bread, he believed, produced "the best of foods". His writings, such as *On the Regimen of Health* and *On Asthma*, concluded that this bread was highly nutritious and easily digested, suggesting that he was aware of the health properties of the whole wheat grain. He supported the eating of fresh, local herbs, including parsley, hyssop (a plant often used in traditional medicine) and fennel in cooked dishes for their nutritional value, as well as eating fresh onions, radishes and green leaves with the bread, to aid the metabolism and digestion of food.

At Saidel Jewish Baking Centre, they follow Maimonides' belief that the perfect, healthy loaf uses the germ, endosperm and bran of the whole grain and should be adequately salted and well hydrated, before baking in an authentic brick oven. Artisan baker Les Saidel built his own commercial brick (earthenware) oven, giving additional flavour and authenticity to his traditional bread, which includes his own recreation of the Rambam loaf. His dough is made from wholemeal spelt to which he mixes organic medicinal herbs, for added vitamins and minerals. Saidel also scores the dough down the middle to symbolise the middle path through life, in accordance with the great physician's philosophy. I was not privy to the actual Rambam recipe, which is a well-kept secret, but Les Saidel delighted in giving me a loaf to savour its flavour and to benefit from its healthy properties.

Breads advanced rapidly through the Middle Ages with the sophistication of agriculture, commercial bakeries and culinary innovations. Emmer and einkorn were often in short supply following the destruction of Rome, so soft textured breads were baked mainly for the upper classes as the basic loaf was no longer affordable to all. Rye was to become the grain of choice throughout Europe, thriving in harsh terrain and a cold, damp climate which made for a heavy, moist bread that was more economical to produce, and therefore a cheaper way of nourishing the poor. Although considered a lifeline to the poor and vulnerable, the rye crops were also highly susceptible to *Claviceps purpurea*, a poisonous fungus that caused the potentially fatal disease ergotism when the affected grain was ingested, this inevitably led to many deaths. A mix of grain was then used to bake a more nutritious and sustainable loaf, still using rye but with a greater blend of other flours that were ground from legumes (a plant from the *Fabaceae* (pea) family grown as a crop e.g., fava beans, lentils) or starchy vegetables that included potatoes and peas, often with the addition of blood from oxen or horses to give a richer taste.

The feudal class system of the medieval era that lasted until the rise of the Ottoman Empire circa 1299, introduced a social acceptance for feasting and dining with bread at the heart of each meal. The edible tableware known as "trenchers" (from the French *trancher*, "to cut") were flat, round loaves of stale bread that were cut in half and hollowed out, creating a centrepiece for serving food, that was usually meat. At the end of each meal, the trencher could be eaten with the meat juices that had soaked into the remaining crumbs, however if they were not eaten by the over indulged gluttons, or trenchermen as they became known, it became the acceptable practice to give the trenchers away as alms to the poor, or sometimes even to the animals, until this innovative plate evolved into a board made of wood, likened to the bread or cheese board.

Bread was starting to be baked in various shapes and sizes, from a base grain of wheat, rye and black rye. The Empire's physicians began to dictate that the refined white wheat flour contained curative properties and should be baked for the upper classes of society who could afford the purity of this luxury, despite the bread being absent of the nutrients contained in the wholesome bran and germ of the grain. Commercial bakers, regulated by the Bakers Guild, therefore produced more white loaves to benefit from higher profits, baking lower priced mixed grain breads only for the poor. Regardless of the bakers' governing body, bread was central to the livelihoods of all classes in society. By the thirteenth century, the rising cost of grain was being passed on to the price of each loaf of bread sold, resulting in the introduction of the law of the Assize of Bread, which was established to control the prices charged for each loaf by individual bakers, and limiting their takings. Bakers were directed to weigh their dough to conform to standard measures, and mark each loaf they produced, initiating the first law of trademarking, which carried the risk of prosecution if not strictly adhered to.

The demand for a purer flour to produce a more refined bread grew significantly throughout the sixteenth century, which stemmed from the baking innovations across Europe using a dough that was boiled before it was baked in wood-fuelled ovens and embraced the introduction of the bagel. The bagel was a solid ring of a yeasted wheat dough, that was initially boiled before it was baked, associated with the Jewish community of

Krakow, Poland. Although initially documented in 1610, a "boiled-then-baked ring-shaped bread" had been mentioned in a thirteenth-century Arabic cookbook, but not given the name bagel, which was derived from the Yiddish *beygl* meaning "ring". According to American journalist and author Maria Balinska this round piece of bread with a hole in its middle replaced the *taralli*, which, as she explains in her book *The Bagel: The Surprising History of a Modest Bread*, was a hard, non-perishable cracker, eaten by pilgrims and soldiers in the 1300s.

Wheat began to take over from rye and barley as the principal bread making grain in Europe by the 1700s, as the development of mechanical mills were being engineered to cope with the increasing requirement for producing flour. There was initially considerable disapproval from the traditional millers, who were reluctant to grind their flour with anything other than

The Roller Mill © Mills Archive.

stones. In the late 1800s, Hungarian engineer Abraham Ganz pioneered the roller mill, that allowed the grains to be passed through sets of spinning cast iron rollers, crushing the grains and separating the bran and germ from the endosperm. This produced a super-fine, white flour.

Roller milling improved its proficiency throughout the nineteenth century, as the mill became powered by steam engines, as opposed to wind, water or by hand. This produced larger quantities of the finely ground flour needed for the increasing numbers of commercial bakeries and bakers. The mills soon needed to take on workers as flour production increased, which became known as history's first fully mechanical manufacturing process.

By the late 1700s or early 1800s, scientists began to understand that the theory of the chemical reaction giving rise to leavened breads was not fabricated or a miracle, but the natural process of fermentation from the spontaneous reaction of airborne wild yeast on cereals. In the late 1600s, Dutch scientist Antonie Philips van Leeuwenhoek, became a pioneer in observing yeast globules under a microscope, and laid the groundwork for global scientists and microbiologists to understand not only the fermentation process, but also the role the micro-organism yeast played, in the making of both bread and alcohol. It was during the mid-1800s, that the work of the French scientist Louis Pasteur transformed the bakery world. Pasteur believed that yeast spores were the responsible organisms for fermentation and leavening, and he proved that yeast could survive both with and without oxygen. This played its part in developing the flavour, texture and aroma of breads.

Saccharomyces cerevisiae was a single-celled micro-organism that was to become known as Baker's yeast, the leavening agent for bread. It had originally been sold commercially by the Dutch as a frothy liquid, before German scientists started producing it in the form of a cream during the nineteenth century. It was made from barm, the foaming scum that naturally formed on the top of fermented brewing liqueur. The liquid was drawn out of the cream which formed a soft, beige solid block, and made the way for commercial bakeries to bake soft, pillowy, well risen bread. Following the Second World War, the North American company Fleischmann's developed a dry granulated yeast which could survive without refrigeration, improving its shelf life and becoming one of the top selling baking products across America. At the same time, yeast was also being sold as a nutritional supplement and promoted as a good source of protein and vitamins, low in fat and salt. In the 1920s Fleischmann's advertisement, 'Yeast for Health', yeast cakes were endorsed as healthy for the skin and an aid to digestion, but this "fad" was short-lived and decreed as misleading by the US Federal Trade Commission.

Following the French Revolution of 1789 and the Napoleonic wars (1803-15), bread became a scarcity in Britain, due to French blockades and the subsequent rise in the cost of grain. Unrest ensued with rioting, as the staple of the nation was rationed. People were hungry and the country was on the verge of famine, as the millers who had any supplies of grain sold them to the highest bidder. The government needed to take back control and brought in the Stale Bread Act in 1801, which banned the sale of freshly baked bread. Bakers were only allowed to sell bread baked in the previous twenty-four hours, under the premise that stale bread was more filling and would stave off hunger. Draconian measures were enforced to ensure conformity, through fines for the bakers who sold fresh bread and

Fleischmann's dry yeast advertisement.

rewards to those who informed them of the offence. The act lasted just a year, as it became too onerous to enforce and grain seemed to be in better supply and back in circulation.

The Bread Act of 1822 saw the regulation of the weight, price and quality of manufactured loaves originally set out in the thirteenth-century law of Assize of Bread. This ensured that the price of grain was fairly set at market prices and more available to commercial and home bakers. Purchasing laws were not a new charter in Britain, as they were known to date back to Medieval England and the reign of King

the Clerks of that Market, and which took place Wednesday laft, the 12th Inft. the following Weights and Prices were fixed, viz.

			To weigh,	lb.	oz.	
The Penny Loaf	{	Wheaten —		o	8	
	{	Houfhold -		o	10	1
Two-penny Loaf	{	Wheaten —		1	o	
	{	Houfhold		1	5	
			To be fold for		s.	
The Peck Loaf —	{	Standard Wheaten			2	
	{	Houfhold ———			2	
Haif Peck Loaf —	{	Standard Wheaten			1	
	{	Houfhold ———			1	
Quartern Loaf —	{	Standard Wheaten			o	
	{	Houfhold ———			o	

N. B. The-Peck Loaf is to weigh 17 Pounds 6 Ounce Half-peck 8 lb. 11 oz. and the Quartern 4lb. 5 oz. 8 dr.

Prices of GRAIN at the Corn-Exchange.

Assize of Bread, *Oxford Journal,*
15 November 1777.

John (1199-1216) when buying provisions for the royal household. The assize laws were placed upon three types of loaf, the Household (made from inferior quality flour, usually by home bakers), Wheaten (made from whole wheat flour) and White, with a fixed scale of costs to determine the weight of the loaf according to the price of the grain, enabling bread once again to be an affordable commodity. This led to the production of the Quarten loaf, which generally weighed four pounds and could be sold in quarters for 1 shilling per piece.

Advances in bread baking surged from the quality of the grain and loaf to the technology of the ovens. Wood and coal burning brick ovens were being replaced by modern gas ovens, increasing productivity but also giving an even rise and colour to the bread. The popularity of the gas oven increased even further in 1923, with the installation of the thermostat that regulated the temperature for an even bake.

Refined white flour remained the flour of choice in commercial bakeries as the bakers still believed it produced a more luxurious and digestible loaf. The white loaf remained in high demand particularly from the upper-class consumer, despite its lack of nutritional value. The removal of the essential vitamins B1 and B3 contained in the bran and germ of the grain saw growing epidemics of beriberi (which affected the heart and circulatory system) and pellagra (which caused dermatitis, diarrhoea and dementia) among the population but still white bread prevailed as the optimal loaf.

The desire for white bread was heightened in the 1920s when the first bread slicing machine designed by the American inventor Otto Rohwedder was exhibited and marketed. It was not only able to slice the loaf, but wrap it too, an invention whose legacy was the idiom "the best thing since sliced bread". The excitement was short lived when in the 1930s scientists discovered the importance of vitamins in the diet and, concerned with the health of the nation, the British Government initially made it law to add the group of B vitamins to white flour. It was to be years before it was realised that grinding the whole wheatberry preserved the nutrients in the grain and produced a whole wheat flour that was healthier than the pure white ground endosperm, and greatly improved the flavour too. This heightened the debate on the adulteration of bread which had been rumbling for many years, with the addition of bitter and often 'poisonous' substances, including the plant-based strychnine, which was said to enhance the taste of manufactured breads. This led to tighter law making and the Food Adulteration Act was passed preventing these substances from entering food products.

It was in the midst of the Second World War, and the rationing of 1942, that there was a shortage of shipping space for the import of white flour, and so Britain introduced the "National Loaf", an unappetising, grey looking, soft bread made with brown wholemeal flour, that was fortified with vitamins and minerals and designed to overcome the health concerns of the nation, in the challenging times of war. The production and distribution of this loaf was given to the newly formed Federation of Bakers, who organised and oversaw the rationing of this product, although as an economical war effort, they prohibited the slicing and packaging of the loaf, and bakers handed it out unwrapped. It was a further decade before this unpalatable loaf was abolished and bread was made with a variety of flours, that by law had to be enriched with calcium, iron and thiamine. During the 1960s, supermarkets opened up and took away the production of bread from the small independent bakeries, as the vast scale that was required to bake and distribute the staple became apparent. Wholesale bakeries were established and the Chorleywood Bread Process came into force, as high energy bread mixes and added chemicals were introduced to speed up the fermentation process, enabling faster production.

In the 1950s, as artificial chemicals were added to the national loaf, many master bakers found the traditional methods of baking breads challenging, and were concerned for their craft. The longer fermentation times of the traditional process, allowed for the natural enzymes in yeast to react with the flour and break down the gluten, which made the bread easier to digest through natural bacteria in the gut. It developed the flavours and textures of each individual loaf, but it came at a cost to their trade. The addition of potassium bromate was used to strengthen the elasticity in the dough, which was essentially to give the loaves uniformity, longevity and whiteness, as well as the mass-produced bread forming a drier crumb and a more closed structure. It was, however, affordable and available to all. It led skilled master bakers to continue with baking healthier, flavoursome breads, kneading and shaping loaves by hand, and baking in antiquated wood-burning ovens, all in the hope that there was still a call for the more natural staple, from the richer, health-conscious consumer.

At the same time, France was becoming known throughout Europe as the *civilisation du pain* with 65% of its highly talented bakers turning yeasted doughs into beautiful breads, rolls, buns and cakes from a variety of grains, including wheat, spelt and rye. These breads and cereals were increasing in popularity due to their health, cultural and historical properties. Simultaneously, the role of the artisan baker was being shaped by the independent bakeries and innovative specialty breads were attracting the healthier eaters. Artisan bakers advocated the baking traditions and practises from bread making across Europe and beyond, to create a "real" loaf, distinctive for its texture, flavour and organic ingredients, not for homogeneity and its pallor. English poet Robert Browning (1812-1889) epitomised the beautifully shaped breads with crusty, golden exteriors and a soft, pillowy crumb that embraced a new era of baking with ancient grains through his poetic verse: "If thou tastest a crust of bread, thou tastest all the stars and all the heavens." It was more than a century later that breads would be crafted with such quality grains and taste of utter heaven...

The latter part of the twentieth century saw the rise in organic agriculture that led to a change in farming practices, and forced the political food agenda to move towards sustainable food systems. Artisan bakers were at the forefront of this campaign, as ancient grains and early pseudocereals began to make their comeback into healthy bakes. Food trends were changing to include "grandma's traditional recipes", using the staple cereals that appeared to have been forgotten over time. This, coupled with the return to nature for food inspiration, played into the hands of the artisan producers and their bread-making craft as the culinary world saw the re-emergence of wholewheat soda bread, spelt rolls, rye breads and the ancient sourdough, believed to have been the earliest form of leavened bread.

The origins of sourdough stretch as far back as 3000 BCE, with the ancient Egyptians, who were bakers of leavened bread and discoverers of natural yeast in the atmosphere, the traditional process of fermentation.

The first 'sourdough' bread is said to have occurred by chance, with the most likely account being of a natural reaction taking place in the atmosphere causing the leavening. The story is that a paste made from wheat flour and water was left outside in the sun to dry before baking, when a chemical reaction from the wild yeast spores, combining with the carbon dioxide in the atmosphere, took place. The dough started to rise from the effect, resulting in a lighter, yeasted bread. With Egyptian breweries and bakeries often housed in close proximity, another possibility is that dough was left out in the sun and yeast spores, blown from the foamy barm in the vats of liquor, may have landed on the dough, giving a considerable rise to the usually flat dough. As both are credible explanations, the sourdough remains attributed to the Egyptians in an era long before commercially produced yeast or baking powder was available.

Sourdough, as its name suggests, has a tartness to the flavour of the crumb, due to the naturally occurring fermentation process between the organism lactic acid and the yeast cells, which breaks down the starches in the flour. It is cultured through a "starter" made simply of flour and water, which is fed daily to allow for the wild yeast to settle on the flour and organically ferment. The beginning of the twenty-first century saw the advent of artisan bakers and bakeries in all corners of the globe perfect this new style of loaf, which brought local communities together with a nourishing affluence. It evoked an interest throughout the food world and saw the beginning of the sourdough craze in both commercial bakeries and domestic kitchens. It became the hobby of men and women alike, starters were discussed and kept like pets and the beautifully crafted patterns on the breads' crust became a new found artistry. Celebrity bakers, chefs and food writers promoted the sourdough, placing it on a pedestal for its flavour, texture and above all health properties, with the beneficial bacteria that naturally occur during the fermentation process helping to promote a healthy gut.

With a high fibre content, sourdough aids the balance of blood sugars, and is associated with lowering the risks of heart disease. It was found to be listed as the choice of bread on restaurant menus made with ancient grains and paired with innovative flavours. Inevitably there was not only a sudden rise in the sales of this ancient bread, but also a real demand for the creative artisan baker to produce a range of speciality breads from a variety of cultures and religions, using traditional baking processes and long-lost ancient grains.

The preparation for any sourdough is in the starter. The process for the wild yeast to ferment the flour initially takes about seven days of "feeding", after which you can begin to make your loaf. Experts will leave starters of all different flours in the refrigerator for months on end, feeding them every now and then, to re-activate the yeast. I am a sourdough novice, but this standard recipe is easy, suitable for all first-time sourdough makers, and makes a great loaf.

Spelt Sourdough for Beginners:

Ingredients (makes 1 loaf):
for the starter:
¼ cup / 50 g white spelt flour initially, followed by ⅛ cup / 25 g per day for 6 days

¼ cup / 50 g wholemeal spelt flour initially, followed by ⅛ cup / 25 g per day for 6 days
½ cup / 100 ml warm water for the initial starter, then ¼ / 50 ml per day for 6 days

for the dough:
3 ½ cups / 450 g white spelt flour
¼ cup / 50 g wholemeal spelt flour
¼ cups / 300 ml warm water + a further ⅛ cup / 25 ml is required for a smooth dough
2 teaspoons / 10 g salt
½ cup / 100 g sourdough starter which is about half the starter, enough to keep feeding it

Method (for the starter)

❖ mix the white spelt flour, wholemeal spelt flour & warm water until smooth, transfer to a container & leave in a warm kitchen with the lid slightly ajar for about 1 hour, place the lid loosely on the container & set aside for 24 hours

❖ each day for the next 6 days, you will need to 'feed' it by tipping away half of the starter & adding 25 g of each white & wholemeal flour with 50 ml of warm water, stir well, replace the lid & set aside, after a few days, bubbles should start to appear on the surface & it will begin to smell slightly sour, by day 7, it will smell a little sweeter & can be used, keep half back & continue to feed the starter for your next loaf

Method (for the dough)

❖ mix the flours, 300 ml of warm water & starter into a dough & leave in a warm place for 1 hour

❖ add salt & the extra 25 ml of water & knead gently together, cover & leave in a warm place for 3 hours, folding the dough onto itself occasionally during the time until the dough has increased in size by about a third

❖ place a clean tea towel in a bowl & flour well or flour a proving basket if you have one, then shape the dough into a tight, smooth ball & place in the bowl or basket, seam side up, dust with flour & place in the fridge overnight until risen by about a quarter

❖ heat oven to 230 °C (210 °C fan) / 450 °F / Gas Mark 8 & place a lidded casserole dish in the oven for 30 minutes until really hot and at the same time, place a roasting tin filled with boiling water at the bottom of the oven, to create steam; after the 30 minutes, carefully remove the casserole dish, *invert the loaf into it and slash the top once with a sharp knife to create a pattern of your choice, cover with the lid & bake for 20 minutes, remove the lid & bake for a further 20 minutes, until the crust is dark & the bottom sounds hollow, serve warm with lashings of salted butter*

NB: the water should be warm to touch each time, as this helps the activation process, and if you don't have spelt flour, use strong white bread flour and wholemeal flour instead

Spelt Sourdough

Chapter three

Lost crops

.

The Near East and Fertile Crescent are regarded by archaeologists, agronomists and culinary historians as the birthplace of agriculture, from which the roots of so many lost or forgotten crops originate. Wild wheats, barley, rye and millet link to our historic and biblical ancestry, widely referenced from as early as the Neolithic era (9000–3000 BCE) and in the numerous books of the Old Testament. These wild grains would be subsequently abandoned in favour of high yielding, cultivated grains. The lost crops connect the land with its natural heritage, having played a vital role in agricultural history, trade and food chains, fusing the culinary connection from our ancient past to the future of sustainable eating. As traditional methods of farming from the Neolithic age were abandoned, strains of wild wheats and ancient cereals disappeared for centuries.

The displaced wild wheats and edible grasses, closely associated with their natural habitats and a basic human diet, are now re-emerging into our food chains with other forgotten ancient grains and pseudocereals, including buckwheat, sorghum and teff, and are increasingly seen as healthy, nutritious and organic staples. For centuries, cultivated grains and cereals, with the addition of fibre, vitamins and minerals, provided nourishment and sustenance to the global diet, while the wild cultivars, rich in their own natural source of nutrients were omitted. The ancient grains and pseudocereals were alleged to have an improved taste, colour and nutritional content, and produced a healthier staple to make bread, flour and beer. This left the food world foraging the land for the lost crops and wild edibles to enhance their diet and health.

Cereals and grains have dominated man's diet since the dawn of agriculture, when hunter-gatherers foraged for wild grains, ground them into a powder which was mixed with water to make unleavened bread. They relied heavily on the natural cycles of plants as their source of food and nutrition until the agricultural industry changed the landscape and introduced the domestication of wheat, barley and other cereals. The introduction of farming took hold, and grains and pseudocereals from ancient civilizations were included in the rotations with other crops such as bitter vetch (a plant from the pea family) and flax (a flowering plant also known as linseed), until such times as they were abandoned for higher yielding, more profitable grains.

The primitive grains of emmer and einkorn became the founding crops of landrace domestication over 10,000 years ago in the Fertile Crescent. Both strains of wheat were genetically similar and able to adapt to the change over the course of time, but created a complex relationship between the cultivated crops and their forgotten wild ancestors, which gave the archeobotanists and plant geneticists valuable insights into the origins of these grasses and cereals.

In Israel's Institute of Evolution at Haifa University, Professor Assaf Distelfeld leads the research on cereal evolution and domestication, focusing on the nutritional value and genetics of wild emmer wheat. Wild emmer thrives in cooler, wetter environments but also adapts and matures in regions of climatic change. The wild wheat grows in swathes over the rough northern terrain of the Golan Heights, where it has established its natural habitat. An artificial selection of wild wheat seeds, containing a richer source of proteins and minerals were identified by Distelfeld and his team of researchers, which was assimilated into other wheat genes, namely spelt, and consumed by those with sensitivities to gluten. They carefully selected seeds from wild emmer that had a high content of proteins and minerals in order to domesticate them with the lesser nutritional modern cultivars, and thereby develop a protein rich, natural mutation of whole wheat which would allow for better gluten tolerance. The wild cultivar was then returned to modern circulation.

Wheat selections were initially made by the farmers, identifying the strains that were easily harvested and showed a favourable yield, rather than chosen for flavour, higher nutritional content or healthier gut properties, which recent research into lost crops have shown the ancient wild strains to contain.

Heirloom grains, which include the unripe green wheat kernels known as freekeh, are identified as lost crops from ancient cultures, passed down through the generations without any genetic modification. They preserve more of their nutrients and contain less gluten, so while heirloom grains may have been abandoned through historical periods, they had clearly not vanished from diets. Traditional agricultural methods from biblical times continued throughout the Middle East, so precious wheat harvests were shielded from the natural elements, allowing for the traditional staples to thrive on through the generations, as a key component in the Levantine diet. Lost to heavy processing and the addition of unnatural chemicals from the years of industrial revolution for economic gain, the ancient grains and pseudocereals have found their way back into mainstream diets and cooking, due to the nutrient rich flavour profile and organic benefits of each whole grain.

Over the centuries, grain and cereal harvests have been lost as much to conflict, as to natural environmental and climatic change, causing substantial food insecurities throughout the world, and in many of the traditional cuisines. The wild crops faced further threats of survival within the early food chains, due to urbanisation, overgrazing and excessive productivity for global economic stability, in an attempt to avoid a surge in poverty and starvation within the communities. Farmers of many rural regions across the Middle East and Africa relied heavily on grain and cereal crops, particularly wheat and barley, which have become the two significant crops of global commerce today and influence the eating habits of so many, with bread at the heart of every meal.

Scientists and ecologists have become responsible for conserving wild habitats and protecting grain and cereal species, preserving the ancient agricultural processes that feed impoverished communities, re-build economies and protect forgotten crops. Food sustainability and crop evolution is paving the way for the culinary trends of the twenty-first century. A growing movement towards a plant-based food diet from a locally cultivated source, coupled with foraging for wild edibles, gives cooking with lost crops from our culinary ancestry a renewed vigour. Emmer, einkorn, spelt and khorasan are being revived in bakeries, as the call for a new healthier diet merges with the ancient cultures and food of past civilisations.

The annual harvesting of freekeh, the young, green wheat grown in the Al-Batuof valley of Israel's lush north, is a deep-rooted agricultural process from biblical times that heralds sustainable farming and the preservation of the natural environment. The reappearance of the ancient "parched" grain has remained a key staple in the Levantine diet and is fast becoming the contemporary grain of the Western restauranteur. Wild emmer, 'the mother of wheat' has survived domestication from over 9000 years ago, and together with wild einkorn and barley, the principal grains during the Bronze Age (3300–1200 BCE in Britain), have made a comeback into global food production and culinary innovation. The healthier member of the farro family, spelt was one of the first grains used to make bread in the Middle Ages, and has become today's common grain of choice among those who require less gluten in their diet to aid digestion. The vanished South American pseudocereal quinoa, originally used as a rich source of food from its leaves and seeds, has also been found and cultivated, and is now appearing again in our salad bowls. It is the rebirth and culinary revival of the biblical, historical and cultural lost crops from traditional cuisines that are rekindling our palates and reappearing in recipes and cookbooks across the globe, as we strive for a healthier diet with an abundance of flavour and a helping of our ancient past on the side.

The Lost Crop of Freekeh

Freekeh

Freekeh is not an ancient grain, it is an archaic process for a contemporary staple.

As ancient as the historical and biblical references to it, freekeh, or "parched grain" as it was originally termed, has been a familiar Levantine staple for centuries. The traditional ancient Egyptian culture of harvesting the whole grain from the immature green wheat sheaves has been inherited from generations of farmers since 2300 BCE, and remains an annual agricultural practice in the fields of the Middle East. The early ripened sheaf of wheat was acknowledged as the first offering to the Roman and Greek gods in classical periods of history and as one of the first fruits presented to God by the Israelites in the First Temple of Jerusalem. "If you bring a grain offering of early ripened things to the LORD, you shall bring fresh heads of grain." (Leviticus 2:13)

This paved the way for the Christian and Catholic faiths to gather the young, green grain as a tax offering following the abundant harvests, which then became a devout celebration of thanksgiving at the beginning of the annual harvesting season. Mosaic law observed by the Israelites during the exodus from Egypt, stipulated in the ancient testaments that the first fruits of grain, whether wheat or barley, had to be blessed by God before the processes of roasting or parching any of the grains for their own consumption.

Wheat and barley have been the dominating grains since the dawn of agriculture in the Neolithic era, and continue to dominate in the Old and New Testament, despite the mention of the "parched grain" or "parched corn" as an accessible and edible cereal. Biblical food experts at Israel's Neot Kedumim – a biblical landscape nature reserve in the Judean Hills – call the traditional young wheat "kali", which derives from the verb *kalla*, meaning "to toast" in Hebrew and *qalah* denoting "to roast" in Arabic. Both names were used appropriately for the immature kernel that was cooked in the fields, symbolising the tradition and culture of processing the wheat, rather than its identity. It was given the name freekeh, pronounced *fri.ka* or *free kah*, sometime between 1100–1300 BCE, when it became popular in the diets of the Islamic caliphs. Derived from the Arabic verb *farik* meaning "to rub". the name seemed appropriate, referencing the method of rubbing the kernel to remove the blackened chaff, following roasting on open fires.

Although kali was inevitably wheat, and believed by the biblical culinary historians to have most likely been young durum wheat, it was likened to a pulse or legume by many of the early Roman poets, which was backed up by the theory that it was in fact corn or maize. "Brought beds, and basons, and earthen vessels, and wheat, and barley, and flour, and parched corn, and beans, and lentiles, and parched pulse." (2 Samuel 17:28)

Heralding from the Fertile Crescent, where traditional farming is still practised, despite the environmental, climate and conflicts of the centuries, today the original ways of harvesting freekeh are still practised in the rural areas of Northern Israel, Lebanon, Palestine and Egypt. Methods of farming are still determined by history and are as important to the Arabic farmers in these regions today as they were in the Akkadian empire, the first ancient empire of Mesopotamia, founded in 2334 BCE.

In her book, *Art, Culture, and Cuisine: Ancient and Medieval Gastronomy*, Phyllis Pray Bober included an ancient recipe entitled Mold of Bulgur & Green Wheat (see below), and noted that "green wheat is freekeh in modern Syria". The recipe shows that freekeh was part of the ancestral diet of the Middle East and Mediterranean Basin, and it remains a key staple of the Arabic diet.

 MOLD OF BULGUR AND GREEN WHEAT: Green wheat is *freekeh* in modern Syria, and may be obtained from Middle Eastern grocers or specialty importers.

> 1 cup green wheat
> 1 cup coarse grain bulgur
> 4 tablespoons ghee
> 1 medium onion, minced
> 4 cups rich stock
> 1/2 teaspoon salt
> 2 eggs, beaten
> 1/2 cup pine nuts or pistachios
> date sauce (see below)
> dates for garnish

Pick over green wheat and wash it in several changes of water (until the water runs clear); mix with bulgur. Heat ghee in a sauté pan and use to cook the onion over a slow fire without browning. Add the wheats and stir for a minute or two to coat the grains. Add stock and salt; cover and cook until liquid is absorbed, about 30 minutes. When almost cool, add eggs and pine nuts, and pack into a greased mold. Bake in a preheated 325-degree oven for about 30 minutes, or until firm. Unmold on a platter and serve with date sauce. Decorate with a few reserved dates.

For the date sauce, mash stoned fresh dates and simmer in pomegranate juice with a tablespoon or so of honey until a syrupy sauce is obtained.

This recipe is my take on the medieval green wheat salad, using spices and dried fruits to bring out the earthiness of the grain. The carrots add colour and vibrancy, complementing the sweetness of the dates, and the citrussy dressing creating a taste of the Middle East.

Freekeh, Heritage Carrots & Medjool Date Salad

Ingredients (serves 6-8):
5 cups / 500 g heritage carrots
½ cup / 120 ml olive oil
2 teaspoons cumin & 2 teaspoons coriander seeds
1 cup / 200 g freekeh
2 cups / 450 ml water
½ cup / 25 g fresh coriander and of fresh mint
⅓ cup / 50 g pinenuts
⅓ cup / 40 g golden raisins
½ cup / 90 g Medjool dates
1 teaspoon sweet paprika
1 teaspoon ground cumin
juice of ½ orange & ½ lemon
2 tablespoons date syrup + extra for drizzling
salt & pepper

Method:
❖ *preheat the oven to 180 °C / 350 °F / Gas Mark 4*
❖ *top & tail the carrots, bring a saucepan of salted water to the boil & place the whole carrots in salted water for 5 minutes until just beginning to soften, drain & place the carrots in a roasting tin, toss the cumin & coriander seeds over the carrots, season with salt & pepper & drizzle over half the olive oil to coat the carrots evenly, cook in the oven for 15 to 20 minutes until soft & beginning to caramelise slightly at the edges, remove from the oven & set aside to cool*
❖ *rinse the freekeh for 2 to 3 minutes under cold water to remove any remaining chaff or grit, drain & place in a saucepan with water; there is so much*

flavour in this salad, that you do not need to cook the freekeh in a flavoured stock; cook on a medium heat for 20 to 25 minutes until the water has absorbed into the grain & the freekeh is tender, but still has a slight bite, place a lid on the pan, remove from the heat & leave to steam for 10 minutes before placing in a serving bowl

❖ *mix the remaining olive oil in a jug with the juice of the orange & lemon, ground paprika & cumin, salt, pepper & date syrup and pour most of the dressing onto the warm freekeh, which will absorb the flavours better whilst warm, add the pinenuts which I like to toast first, golden raisins, coriander & mint, which can be chopped finely or coarsely, according to your preference*

❖ *slice the carrots on the diagonal, pit & chop the dates into quarters, then add them to the freekeh & garnish with coriander leaves & an extra drizzle of date syrup or left-over dressing*

Freekeh, Heritage Carrots
& Medjool Date Salad

The Egyptians have been cooking with green wheat for centuries, with these young kernels taking the place of rice. The stuffing of game and birds has been a feature of their cuisine dating back to ancient feasts of the empire (c.1570–1069 BCE), when the Egyptians were known to breed pigeons in specially built conical towers to satiate their dietary indulgence. Being a delicacy, the squabs were stuffed with fragrantly spiced green wheat and cooked on open fires, a dish called 'Hamam mahshi'. This opulent dish has remained at the heart of this ancient cuisine, despite the controversy as to whether the origins of the green wheat were the unripe grains of durum or emmer wheat. Durum wheat, the hardest of all wheats, is thought to be the most likely wheat for the cracked freekeh as a free threshing, durable husked wheat, however archeobotanists are more of the opinion that wild emmer could have been the early harvested genus, as it was abundant in the Near East during the period of the New Kingdom (15,000–10,000 BCE) and a key staple of the region's diet.

Beit Nefuta Valley, Galilee

The historic tale of the origins of freekeh as a widely cultivated and consumed grain stem from the devastating attacks on the villages and cities of the Eastern Mediterranean region, which, around the first millennium, caused a wave of destruction to crops from raging fires across the fertile land. The unharvested wheat fields were set alight by the piracy of the Sea Peoples of Aegean tribes, causing trade routes and local livelihoods to be demolished. On seeing the wheat burnt to a cinder across the expanse of their land and in storehouses, and realising the enormity of the loss to their communities, the farmers tried to salvage as much of the burnt husks as they could and set about vigorously rubbing at the wheat to remove the charred shells, whereupon a grain with a greenish tinge was revealed. Fearful at the prospect of starvation from the loss of their harvest, the farmers discovered that by laboriously rubbing at the burnt skins of the wheat an edible grain was revealed underneath. They christened the kernels "freekeh", so the process became its Arabic name. The more mythical tale is that green wheat was one of the earliest known insurance policies, that transpired from biblical times, which came out in years of plenty and to protect in times of hardship. In times of flood and drought, a third of the wheat was harvested while young and green, and stored in large stone grain jars until such times of food shortage. These were humorously branded the Bible's 'life insurance policy'.

The historical process of harvesting the immature green wheat has remained a traditional method of agriculture in the rural regions of Israel, Lebanon, Egypt and the surrounding regions of the Middle East, and freekeh has secured its position as an essential grain of Levantine diet. Traditional freekeh stews, stuffing, soups and salads are still made in Arabic kitchens today. Many of these dishes have had very little changes to the original ancestral recipes, as generations of cooks maintain that it is this nutty, herbaceous grain, that gives the food its distinctive flavour.

The freekeh harvest is an important annual agricultural event in the Arabic farming communities of the Levant, where freekeh has remained the main crop, harvested only for the locality. As a cheap store cupboard ingredient, freekeh was initially reaped as the principal food source for the poorer families, often used as a thickening agent for soups or stews or as a stuffing for meat, vegetables or the traditional Middle Eastern dish of grape leaves. For centuries the cracked wheat was the basis of the meal, however, when sieved finely it resembled flour and was often sold cheaply to the village bakeries and turned into unleavened bread for the nourishment and enjoyment of the community. As Palestinian, Lebanese and Israeli chefs, artisan bakers, food writers and health-conscious foodies began to recognise the nourishing qualities and versatility of a locally-sourced forgotten crop, freekeh was rediscovered and started to appear on restaurant menus and in bakeries in the form of freshly made bread, milled finely in commercial flour mills. This Middle Eastern historical grain was to become a trend of the twenty-first century, proudly sitting on international menus and in famed cookbooks, with interesting flavour profiles for meat eaters, vegetarians and vegans, and nutrients that would lift the humble green wheat kernels onto the pedestal of the ancient grain revival.

In the lush Beit Natufa Valley of rural Galilee in Northern Israel, the ancient biblical process of harvesting young wheat to shield and sustain the crop production of freekeh is an annual spring custom. It is performed by local, often elderly, Arabic farmers and their families during late April and early May, when the wheat is still very young and a light green hue. The climate is changeable on a day-to-day basis in the Middle Eastern spring, where the vast swathes of green wheat can be seen in the fertile basin from the roadside. The harvest commences only when the wheat kernel is soft in the glume, dubbed by the farmers as the "milky stage". It is totally dependent on the region's winter and the amount of rainfall as to how early or late in the spring the process begins. The Arabic farmers of the valley rely heavily on their crops of wheat, barley, fava beans and sesame for their income, as well as for food for their families throughout the year. The timing of the first cutting, therefore, is as crucial as the tradition, and comes with years of experience as to when to take the first slash at the stalks.

The freekeh season is invigorating for the landowners, farmhands and cooks, as each member of the family takes on a role of equal importance. If any of the previous harvested freekeh remains in store, it is used up by the community before the harvesting of the new season's crop, by milling it into flour for pitta bread, or for stuffing young grape leaves as they start to flourish on garden vines, and in nooks and crannies along the roadside, rather than using the traditional filling of rice or burghul. This is a legacy from the time of Alexander the Great and the siege of Thebes, when grape leaves were the only available wild edibles, and morsels of food lying around were stuffed into the greenery. This simple, rustic stuffing has been refined, but it remains a soft, gently spiced filling, when served as a starter or part of the traditional Middle Eastern meze.

Freekeh Stuffed Grape Leaves

Ingredients (serves 6-8 as a starter):
18 vine leaves
1 vine tomato
lemon slices & chilli flakes
for the freekeh stuffing:
2 tablespoons / 30 ml extra virgin olive oil
2 banana shallots
½ cup / 75 g freekeh
½ teaspoon sweet paprika
1 teaspoon baharat
1 cups / 250 ml vegetable stock
¼ cup / 15 g mint, finely chopped
¼ cup / 15 g fresh coriander, finely chopped
½ lemon, juiced
salt & pepper

Method:

* ❖ *start with the stuffing as this needs to be cooked and cooled before filling the grape leaves, place the olive oil & finely chopped shallots into a saucepan, use 1 onion if preferred & cook on a low heat for 5 minutes until soft & golden; when previously cooking with Arabic women, they advocated cooking the shallots or onions in cold olive oil, so that the flavour of the oil is absorbed whilst heating up, a tip I now promote in all my recipes too*
* ❖ *rinse the freekeh for 2 to 3 minutes under cold water to remove any remaining chaff, drain & add to the shallots together with the spices, salt & pepper, stir to combine so that the freekeh & shallots take on the flavour of the spices before adding the vegetable stock, I use a stock pot, but use whatever you have to hand, bring to a boil then reduce the heat & simmer for 15 minutes until the freekeh is tender & all the stock has absorbed into the grain, remove from the heat, cover with a lid & leave to steam & cool for 10 minutes, add*

the herbs & lemon juice, mix & set aside until cold; baharat is a warming Middle Eastern spice blend, that complements vegetable or meat dishes and available in most supermarkets

❖ *blanch the fresh or frozen vine leaves in boiling water for 2 minutes & drain; if you cannot get fresh vine leaves, you can buy them in brine ready for use, however, do rinse them thoroughly in boiling water first, to remove the briny flavour before stuffing; place the leaves on a board vein side up & place a teaspoon of the cooled stuffing on each leaf just above stalk, don't be tempted to overfill the leaf as it will explode during cooking, roll up each leaf into a cigar shape, folding the inner leaves in as you roll*

❖ *line the bottom of a saucepan with slices of tomato to prevent the leaves sticking & place the rolled vine leaves in a tight layer on top, seam side down, sprinkle with salt, chilli flakes & lemon slices, place an inverted plate on top & pour boiling water just to the rim of the plate, cover with a lid & simmer on a gentle heat for 25 to 30 minutes, turn off the heat & leave covered until completely cold, refrigerate overnight & serve at room temperature the following day, if you can wait that long*

Freekeh Stuffed Grape Leaves

The Agrigultural Process

The first stage of this ancient agricultural process is to gather the wheat in large handfuls, which are cut at the exact upper part of the ear, where the grains grow from the spikes, using a customary sickle. The younger members of the farming community are usually the reapers, as the work is arduous and the authentic old-fashioned scythe is heavy. The implement is traditionally called a *manjal*, although colloquially amongst the younger Arabic farmers it is known as the *hashushi*, the name they give to the tool that cuts the "smoking" grass...

The bundles of green ears of wheat are tossed into large tarpaulin sacks and pulled away from the threshing fields by the more senior farmers, a chore that was once carried out by oxen. The sacks are placed together and left to parch in the warm sunshine for a few hours, aiding the evaporation of the spring morning dew and assisting with combustion, once alight on the open fires. This method is practiced to shield the tenderness of the young grain while burning in the roaring flames. After a couple of hours drying out, the bundles of wheat are ready to be set alight and roasted. This can be performed in one of two ways, depending on the farmer's preference, agricultural expertise and resources. The ancient biblical way of roasting the wheat is on an open fire, called a *ballan*, made of dry thorny burnet, a perennial indigenous to the Middle East which produces less ash while burning and is quick to die down, reducing the amount of contamination to the grain. Some farmers create a fire with charcoal, wood and cardboard, and place a wooden planter with a wire grate over the top to hold the wheat. Both methods are equally effective in roasting the green wheat, and the choice is often made by following the methods of the previous generation.

Moshe Basson, an Israeli food historian, chef and owner of Eucalyptus, a restaurant in the artist quarter of Jerusalem, is known in culinary circles for his biblical dishes which he cooks using wild edibles foraged from the Judean Hills that were also available during the wanderings of the Israelites. He states that the traditional method of smoking the wheat on a ballan, "kills mice, insects and insect eggs in the wheat", which confirms the thinking that this method was used in biblical times following abundant harvests, and the wheat kept for periods of food scarcity, insuring a constant provision of grain during the ancient agricultural times of uncertainly.

The roasting is finished once all the tarpaulin sacks are empty of wheat ears and the plumes of smoke and large flames fade to glowing red embers. A large wire mesh, often constructed from old bedsprings, is positioned next to the open fire and the blackened, charred wheat is tossed upon it. Netting is cast over the expanse of newly roasted wheat, and it is left to dry out for up to a week, depending on the compassion of the elements. This paves the way for the next stage of this process, the ancient custom of rubbing the chaff from the burnt spikes that affords freekeh its fame and preserves its agricultural integrity.

The rubbing and removing of the scorched, blackened husks was historically an agricultural tradition that was carried out in the fields, using a succession of ancient sieves, starting with a coarse textured sift and continuing until the debris could be passed through the finest of meshes. The burnt thorns and chaff of the husks were separated from the kernels by friction, rigorously rubbing the shells by hand on the surface of each sieve. This was a time-

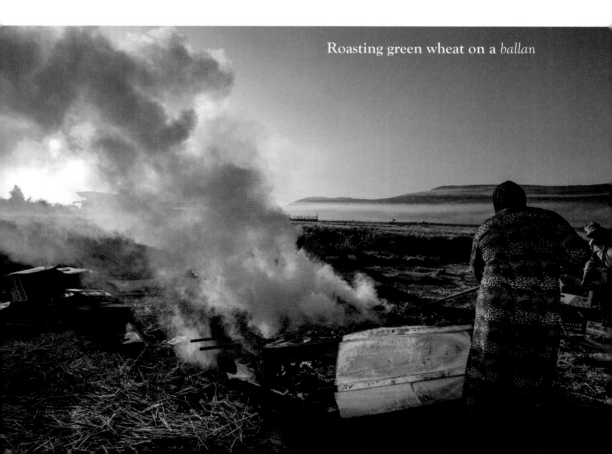

Roasting green wheat on a *ballan*

consuming, dirty and tedious task that was usually performed by women, from the oldest to the youngest, who sifted together in the family fields. The long-lasting blisters on their hands was evidence that they had finished the annual undertaking. Once the kernels had been through the sequence of sieves and the tinge of the typical greenish hue of freekeh appeared, the grain kernels are winnowed for one final inspection. For this last sieve, the kernels are continuously moved around on a large metal tray, ensuring the position of a downwind, to remove any residual ash or chaff before the grains are placed in hessian sacks and stored in cool, dark storerooms for a number of weeks. It is only then that the smoky grains can be milled into flour, or the kernels cracked and eaten in a similar way to rice or burghul.

In 2014, Professor William Burgwinkle at Cambridge University, who was researching the culture, literature and language of the Middle Ages, examined how medieval French manuscripts that had been brought to the Eastern Mediterranean during that period affected the language associated with ancient cultural practices. Chafing, meaning "to rub", takes its meaning from the sixteenth-century Middle French word *friction*, derived from the Latin verb *fricare* meaning "to rub down". This

Mechanical winnowing of freekeh in Beit Hatufa Valley

influenced the theory that the aptly named parched grain in the Bible, acquired its name *fri.ka* or *free kah* from the cultural perspective of an ancient language.

However, with advances in agricultural machinery and a younger generation of farmers, many Arabic communities throughout the Levant harvest their freekeh using a custom-built, heavy duty sieving machine attached to a tractor. Large amounts of netting cover the rest of the ground, where the farmhands trudge back and forth with crates of the parched ears. An experienced farmer, covered in protective clothing that shields him from the dust and brittle particles, stands on a wooden plank at the back of the apparatus, ready to receive the grain.

Crates of sun-dried wheat heads are carted to the edge of the machine and handed individually to a farmhand standing waiting to tip each one onto the lower ledge of the rudimentary appliance, before manually steering each one along to the cleaning shaft, a long metal cylinder that separates the hard husks and spikes from the delicate grains. Once forced along the trough, the semi cleaned husks are propelled down a chute and onto a bulky metal sieve, which has a second chute attached to the undercarriage of the mesh. At the end of the channel, a big hessian sack is attached to collect the filtered grains. A second farmworker crouches down by the side of the sack to catch any of the grains that fall through the mesh, pushing the remnants of the husks and spikes to the side, for burning at a later stage. This is a filthy task as the brittle, blackened husks are discarded and blown around in the air, clinging onto the hair, skin and clothes of the workers. But the rewards of seeing the first grains of freekeh appear are well worth it.

The greenish tinged wheat kernels, the size of long grain rice, tumble into the sacks still slightly blackened from roasting, and as the smoky debris falls with them the air is filled with the smell of a wood burning fire that has burnt to cinders. The sacks, overflowing with the new season's grain, are loaded onto an awaiting tractor and taken to the local flour mill, where again it is vigorously threshed to remove any dirty particles still mixed in with the freekeh.

In the north of Israel, close to the thriving wheat fields, two of the original stone ground flour mills remain, both having maintained the traditional milling processes from over hundred years ago. In Nazareth, the Elbarbour Mill is one of the original steam powered mills, built in 1870 by Melchior Wagner, who belonged to one of the first communities of German settlers known as the Templers. Wagner used steam to power the stones to mill the grain, that had been driven previously by animals, wind or water. By the 1930s a local named Jarjoura Kanaza bought the flour mill, realising the prosperity in grain, and although he kept the original grinding stones, he replaced the steam power with diesel, then electric, over the years. In nearby Haifa, close to the port, the Grand Flour Mill continues to produce tons of flour on a daily basis, using the same stone ground milling process of the previous century. The initial mill merely cracks the wheat into coarse grain, leaving the millers to decide which wheat will continue its journey to become finely milled flour, in accordance with the old Palestinian saying "All roads lead to the mill."

The majority of freekeh is milled into very coarsely cracked kernels, although some of the freshly harvested grains are set aside for the production of young, whole wheatberries. The milling process often takes a number of days, before the grain is picked up by the farmers and taken to their local stone houses, where it remains for four to six weeks to fully dry out in the cool, dark conditions, optimal for the grain's freshness and flavour.

Winnowing is defined as "blowing a current of air through grain in order to remove the chaff". It is the traditional agricultural method used by many ancient cultures for separating grain from straw and a crucial element in the harvesting of freekeh. At the very end of the harvest, the women were traditionally allowed back into the fields "to glean" the discarded grain, usually as their form of payment. Gleaning leftover crops that were not commercially viable for the landowner became a "legally enforced entitlement" to the women and poor who worked in the fields in the Middle East during the Christian reign. According to the Old Testament, Ruth asks Naomi to "let me go to the fields and glean heads of grain" (Book of Ruth 2:2) so that she may provide for her mother-in-law and herself, and sustain them with a nourishing porridge or gruel. This privilege is still bestowed on the women of Arabic communities in the Levant, who glean the freekeh fields to gather the smoky green wheat and fill their store cupboards, enabling then to feed their menfolk and families from the annual harvest.

Hanadi Higriss is the environmental planning manager of the Towns Association for Environmental Quality (TAEQ) in Sakhnin, Northern Israel. She has responsibility for projects that initiate environmental leadership and sustainable development in the agricultural community, where freekeh is annually harvested. She is a strong believer in promoting co-existence between the Palestinians and Israelis of Galilee, through working together for a common purpose. Through the neutrality of food, I was fortunate enough to have cooked out in the fields with her and Amal Badarny, a local Arabic cook using this year's newly gleaned freekeh. The freshness was apparent, when placing handfuls of grain into the pan, from the smell of the smoke left on the grain. Using finely ground grain, we made the traditional freekeh soup, simple, fragrant and refreshening, and often the first taste that these women savour at the Iftar meal following the fast of Ramadan. With the coarser milled grain, we made a local Arabic salad, soaking the freekeh in boiling water to soften the kernels, in a similar way to bulghur wheat.

Cooking Freekeh with Hanadi Higress and Amal Badarny, Sacknin.

S horba is the Arabic word for soup of any kind. Although traditionally, freekeh soup is known as Arabic chicken soup, my freekeh shorba is made with vegetables and za'atar, the earthy condiment made from the dried wild herb of the oregano family, dried sumac and sesame seeds. Wild za'atar, with its soft, green leaves, has become a protected species in Israel, due to over foraging. Arabic cooks often use water for the soup broth, which gives a smoky and nutty flavour to the soup from the freekeh itself. This is a light, nourishing soup and very delicious...

Freekeh & Vegetable Shorba

Ingredients (serves 8):
1 cup / 150 g fine freekeh
4 tablespoons / 60 ml extra virgin olive oil
1 red onion
2 leeks
3 sticks celery
3 carrots
3 garlic cloves
2 courgettes
1 teaspoon za'atar
8 cups / 2 litres vegetable stock or water
1 piece parmesan rind
2 tablespoons oregano or thyme
salt & pepper

❖ *place the freekeh in a bowl, cover with cold water & set aside to for the grains to soak for 5 to 10 minutes, drain in a fine mesh sieve so that the little grains don't escape then rinse well under the cold tap so that all the grit & chaff is removed, set aside*

❖ *prepare all the vegetables, use whatever combination you have or want to use up, and cut into cubes or slices, peeling along the way if you so wish, I like a more rustic approach that is similar to the authentic Arabic cuisine, set aside in piles*

❖ place the olive oil into a large saucepan together with onion, leek, celery & carrots & heat all together on a medium heat, stirring to ensure all the vegetables are coated in the oil, I learnt this from the Arabic cooks who heat the olive oil from cold with the vegetables, so that the flavour of the 'amber nectar' is imparted into the dish

❖ leave the vegetables to sweat for 10 minutes, until beginning to soften, then add the garlic which I simply peel & smash to release the flavour, courgettes & za'atar, which although available in all supermarkets, use mixed herbs or dried oregano if you haven't got any, cook for a further 10 minutes

❖ add the freekeh & mix well into the vegetables, add the stock, parmesan rind, for that savoury umami flavour, fresh herbs, salt & pepper & leave to simmer for 45 minutes until the freekeh has softened, but still has a nutty bite... a word here about vegetable stock, I use stock pots, which are quick & easy, but use what you have, when cooking freekeh for a salad or pilaf, water is usually used and then flavourings added afterwards

❖ remove the parmesan rind & serve bowlfuls of this warming soup with crusty bread

Traditional Freekeh Soup

Wholewheat grains have been shown to be a healthier dietary option than refined grains, through the high fibre and protein content in the bran and the germ. Between 2014 and 2017 scientists reported in the journals of Cereal Foods World that harvested immature wheat preserves more of its proteins, vitamins and minerals than the processed ripened wheat, providing greater health benefits if eaten as part of a nutritionally balanced diet. Freekeh may be young and immature, but it is a valuable ancient whole grain, containing a resistant starch that functions as a soluble fibre which aids digestion and ranks much lower on the glycaemic index. This allows for a more balanced sugar level, presenting less glycaemic acid in the blood. Rich in iron and high in fibre, this nutty supergrain is also regarded as a prebiotic food for healthy bacteria in the gut.

With the catchphrase "the new, old grain" freekeh has affirmed its global status as a supergrain, knocking quinoa off pole position as the number one nutritional whole cereal. Due to the individuality of each region's culinary traditions, the diversity of Middle Eastern food has set the palates of internationally acclaimed chefs alight with this cracked grain, which has become the growing food trend of the twenty-first century. Nutty, smoky and fresh-looking with an olive-green tinge, freekeh has a versatility in savoury dishes and is beginning to be accepted when paired with sweeter flavours. This Levantine grain has conventionally been cooked in a simplistic way to extract the optimum flavour from the wheat kernel itself, however, Palestinian, Israeli and Lebanese chefs are now creating innovative recipes for nutritious main dishes, salads and accompaniments, to place on their restaurant menus while experimenting with freekeh for cakes and desserts, often similar to rice pudding or a breakfast porridge, for increasingly popular plant-based diets.

Whole, cracked or milled into flour, the young wheat grain has a culinary use for all, although refining freekeh flour for a commercial product is seemingly rare in the agricultural communities of the Middle East. Expensive to produce and package for small economic return, farmers tend to wait until the end of the freekeh season to decide on its yield and whether the annual harvest has gleaned enough to turn a percentage into flour.

Erez Komarovsky, an Israeli chef and pioneer of the country's artisan bread movement, has been recognised over the past decade for adding seasonal and locally grown ingredients to his innovative breads, changing the face of dough forever in this bread loving nation. Living in the small village of Mattat, in one of Israel's most northern settlements bordering Lebanon and overlooking the Druze village of Hurfeish, Komarovsky is ambivalent about the re-emergence of ancient grains back into the world's diet, having never ceased to use them in his baking. On this topic he says, "evolution has indeed made wheat tastier, but wild wheat is not practical as a baker". The discussion moves through the individual grains and cereals to his famed freekeh bread, that he is proud to share.

This recipe is from Komarovsky's *The Baking Book*, which is currently available in Hebrew only. Freekeh flour isn't easily available to buy in England, however, I have simply ground the easily accessible cracked kernels in a coffee grinder to the required consistency of fine flour. This is a textured bread, with a nutty flavour from the toasting of the wheat. Freekeh loses a little of its smokiness when mixed with other ingredients and baked, but remains a delicious, soft textured bread and even better when eaten with soft cheese, butter or a relish.

Freekeh Bread

Ingredients (makes 2 loaves of bread):
250 g freekeh, medium ground, washed and drained
750 g strong bread flour (or 375 g strong bread flour & 375 g whole wheat flour)
20 g fresh yeast or 7 g dry yeast
1 teaspoon ground allspice
500-550 ml water
1 heaped tablespoon salt

Method:
❖ *soak the freekeh in boiling water for 10 minutes, drain & cool*
❖ *sift the flour into a bowl, add yeast and stir to blend, add the freekeh &*

allspice, before gradually adding water, to make a dough

- ❖ knead for 8 minutes, either in a mixer or by hand, before adding the salt, knead for another 5 minutes, then transfer the dough into a clean, lightly oiled bowl
- ❖ cover & leave to prove for 1 ½ hours in a warm, dry place
- ❖ knock back the dough lightly to release some air, cover and refrigerate for 7 hours (this is best done in the afternoon/evening, so the second proving will occur overnight)
- ❖ place the dough on a lightly dusted floured surface & divide the dough in half with a sharp knife, shape each one into a thick, circular, pita-like form, before folding the dough over without pressing on the edges
- ❖ place the loaves on parchment paper, cover and leave for 1 hour for the final rise
- ❖ preheat the oven to 230 °C / 450 °F / Gas Mark 8, place baking tray on the lower shelf of the oven & a small tray on the bottom, filled with ½ glass of water
- ❖ slide the parchment paper with the loaves onto the baking tray & bake for 20 minutes before lowering the heat to 210 °C / 400 °F / Gas Mark 7 & baking for another 15 to 20 min or until the crust is golden & the base sounds hollow when tapped
- ❖ remove from the oven & leave to cool

Erez Komarovsky's Freekeh Bread

Freekeh is one of the connecting staples from our ancient past to our culinary future, and as a sustainable ingredient, we are hungry to understand its journey from the land to the plate, and its benefits to our modern diet. As current trends define the importance of food to heal and sustain life by linking to its indigenous roots, freekeh unwittingly steps into the forefront of these culinary vogues. As scientific methods promote the health and well-being of its immaturity and the tenable ancient agricultural practices, the harvesting, cooking and eating of freekeh in global culinary circles has kept this whole wheat grain alive through historic and biblical traditions and beliefs.

With so much awareness put on what we eat to maintain the well-being of our body and mind, and to protect the natural environment, there is an increasing appreciation for including ancient whole grains, pseudocereals and legumes into our daily food intake, benefitted by the Levantine and Mediterranean populous for centuries. Most of these nutritious cereals originate from these countries, where they are produced for global export, and we are beginning to see them in Western supermarkets and on the shelves of whole food and health shops.

This whole wheat supergrain, with its nuttiness and smokiness, is an asset to our diet, and it has the same versatility as rice, bulgur and maize. So many of the ancient recipes call for ghee or meat fat, which added flavour to the grain when boiled in meaty stocks, and although this was luxurious and delicious, it was perhaps not ideal when trying to promote healthy eating. I have taken inspiration from generations of Levantine cooks for my freekeh recipes. which I have given a modern, nourishing and seasonal twist to, replacing ghee with extra virgin olive oil, and using ingredients that are easily accessible to all. Influenced by Middle Eastern cuisine using fresh vegetables, fruits and herbs, my recipes exclude meat, but maintain the pairing of this young grain with the cultural flavours and textures of this region, in which freekeh is anything but forgotten or a lost crop.

Chapter four

Wild wheats

The earliest beginnings of wild wheat have been traced back to the Fertile Crescent and the Neolithic era of 10,000–4500 BCE, where Triticeae grass was gathered by primitive hunters and used for food. Dame Kathleen Mary Kenyon led a team of archaeologists to Tell Es-Sultan, an excavation site of the ancient city of Jericho during the 1950s, where she unearthed storage jars of burnt grain, carbon-dated to that ancient era. Wild grasses of wheat, barley and other cereals were reputed to have been the ancient staples of the Levant, as they flourished in the temperate climate, and from the natural flowing water of the Jordan river. The early hunter-gatherers found that the seed heads of the wild grasses were brittle and shattered easily, and that only a few seeds clung to the glumes, making threshing and harvesting a difficult task and the reward of food slim. However, through agricultural advances over the centuries, the self-seeding wild grasses naturally established themselves, and became the cultivated wheat grain that is now the chief crop and predominant global food source.

Wheat is classified by the genus *Triticum*, of which ten species belong. There are four wild wheat species and six that have been cultivated over the centuries. Wild wheat was given the biblical Hebrew name of 'hittah', the first of the seven species that God blessed the Israelites with (Deuteronomy 8:8).

The taxonomy of wheat remains a matter of debate among scientists and botanists, as some of the species, notably the wild wheats, are known by identical names that can only be distinguished through their sub species. Early classifications of wheat categorised them into two groups, depending on whether they were hulled or free-threshing. In 1913, the German botanist, August Schulz classified the groupings of wild wheats into three natural species: Emmer, Einkorn and Dinkel.

Emmer and Einkorn were wild hulled wheats, and given Latin names. The wild emmer prototype was given the name *Triticim dicoccoides*, and wild einkorn, *Triticum monococcum*, sub species *aegilopoides*. However, in 1958 with advances in plant and cereal research and a far better knowledge of the wheat genus, more species of wild wheat were discovered and named, including the red wild einkorn that was given the name *Triticum urartu* by the Russian wheat botanist Moisej Markovic Jakubziner. The specific morphology of these original wild wheats was found to have notably toughened glumes encasing the grains and brittle stems that shattered effortlessly upon threshing, however they would always bear insignificant annual yields.

Wild emmer has been growing in the northern foothills and rural regions of the expanse of the Middle East from Israel to Iran since ancient times, despite its ancestors' origins being reported to have been genetically discovered on the slopes of the shield volcano, Karaca Dağ in Eastern Turkey.

Triticum dicoccoides was discovered in excavations and ancient tombs in sites close to the Sea of Galilee and the Jordan Valley, carbon-dated to thousands of years before its domestication. In one of the most preserved archaeological sites from the Palaeolithic and Neolithic Stone Ages, evidence of the pre-agricultural era and identification of wild emmer was discovered in 1989 at Ohalo II, located on the edges of the Sea of Galilee by a team of Israeli researchers led by Dani Nadel, from the University of Haifa. Significant amounts of charred wild emmer seeds and other wild grains and grasses including barley, were found at the site, which provided them with insight into the diet of the hunter-gatherers and the organic foods that sustained them. Sickles, flints and grinding stones were also excavated, suggestive of the agricultural and culinary practices, employing the wild cereals. In an article entitled, 'Small Grained Wild Grasses as Staple Food at the 23,000-Year-Old Site of Ohalo II, Israel', Nadel and his fellow archeobotanists concluded that the site contained fully ripe grains that were gathered "after the plants turned dry and brittle". They stated that the wild cereals were of the "small-grained species", which led them to the assumption that "wild barley and wild emmer wheat, together with acorns of Mount Tabor oak, provided the major carbohydrates" for the hunter-gatherers' diet.

From the stone grinding slab that was also excavated, we can assume that the charred seeds had been ground into flour, which was the basis for a dough. Blackened and carbonised, the assumptions were made that the emmer seeds had been initially dried in the heat of the sun or toasted on an open fire. Fragments of small seeds were recovered clustered around flat stones that had been traditionally used to cook the basic mix of flour and water into wild emmer flatbreads.

It is well documented that emmer wheat had a significant status in the ancient Egyptian economy and was an extremely sacred plant to the gods. According to Sara El Sayed, a food sustainability writer for Egypt's *Heritage Review* (RAWI), as many as forty different types of breads, mostly containing wild emmer wheat were discovered, dating back to the Fifth Dynasty of Egypt from early 25 BCE to 24 BCE, including remnants from the traditional flatbread, Aish baladi, found in the preserved tomb of Ti, in Saqqara. In the original Egyptian recipes, bakers had to "crush the emmer grain with sticks, using a grindstone to crush the grain still finer until you have a heap of white flour". *Aish* means "life", a fitting name for the staple bread that sustained and nourished everyone indiscriminately.

Charred wild emmer seeds excavated from Ohalo II in 1989.

This is a traditional recipe for Egyptian flatbread, simply using emmer wheat flour, yeast, salt and water. Easy to make, these flatbreads have a dusting of wheat bran for added flavour and texture. Breads of all shapes and sizes, leavened or unleavened were cooked in wood fired or stone ovens, which can still be found in bakeries throughout the Levant, where flatbreads or pitta breads are baked daily.

Aish Baladi (Ancient Egyptian Flatbread)

Ingredients (makes 8 flatbreads):
2 ½ cups / 300 g emmer wheat flour
½ tablespoon / 7 g yeast
½ tablespoon salt
1 ¼ cups / 300 ml warm water
wheat bran for dusting

Method:

❖ *in a large bowl, mix together the flour, yeast & salt, add the warm water & mix it all together with your hand or a dough whisk until a soft dough is formed, cover the bowl with cling film & leave for 1 hour*

❖ *preheat the oven to 225 °C / 450 °F / Gas Mark 7 & set a baking stone or baking tray on a middle rack of the oven*

❖ *turn the dough out onto a lightly floured surface & divide the dough into 8 equal pieces, cover with oiled plastic wrap*

❖ *sprinkle two pieces of parchment paper with wheat bran, working with one piece of dough at a time, roll each into a ball & then flatten each into a 10cm/5" round & sprinkle the top of each piece with more wheat bran*

❖ *cover with tea towels & rest for a further 30 minutes while the oven is heating, until the flatbreads are puffy*

❖ *using a pizza peel or a baking tray, transfer the parchment sheets to the baking stone, one sheet at a time & bake for 8 minutes, remove from the oven & transfer to a wire rack to cool briefly, serve hot or warm*

Traditional flatbreads cooking in an ancient wood fire oven

Wheat was deemed the most important cereal of ancient Egypt. It was their main source of nutrition, health and financial stability, although barley came a close second and was occasionally substituted for emmer as a cheaper, more available grain. The ancient Egyptians were strong believers in the afterlife and became obsessed with the importance of burial rituals and customs. These involved placing wheat based foods, mainly loaves of bread, in the tombs of the deceased. The loaves, often containing crushed emmer and dried fruits or spices, took the shape of trussed oxen, fish, or a round silhouette, symbolising the sun. The baked dough was traditionally placed inside the tombs as a premeditated offering, which it was believed would keep the deceased fed during the journey to the afterlife.

The ancient Egyptians' staple grain for baking bread was wild emmer, according to Dr Mennat-Allah El Dorry, an Egyptologist from the Ministry of Antiquities, whose main focus of research centres around food and culinary anthropology. She believes that remnants of charred crumbs that were found on the archeological sites of Wadi el Natroun in Northern Egypt along the Nile Delta were emmer, determined by the morphology of the grass. This evidence came from Stefanie Jacomet at the archaeobotany laboratory in Basel University, who in 2006, produced a comparison study of the emmer grain, identifying cereal remains from archaeology sites throughout the region, which clearly defined the variances between the ancestry of the wild and cultivated species of *Triticum*, based solely on the structure and characteristics of this ancient grain.

There still appears to be a controversy among archeobotanists as to exactly when and where wild emmer was domesticated. However, despite the uncertainty surrounding the time and place of cultivation, there is agreement that emmer was the grain most used in ancient Egyptian bread making, closer to the wild genus than any of the domesticated wheat species that are baked with today.

Wild einkorn has been hailed as the oldest and most primitive of the wild wheats and the main crop used for food prior to its domestication in the Fertile Crescent, approximately 7500 BCE, around the same time as

Trussed oxen shaped bread from the Tomb of Kha © Museo Egizio, Turin.

emmer. Einkorn's status began to wane, as emmer succeeded as a higher yielding crop, worth more to Egypt and the surrounding region's economy from the Bronze Age, circa 3000 BCE. The earliest find of emmer was from the Faiyum Oasis, west of the Nile, an area of rich fertile land and ideal for the farming and production of their primary crop.

Wild wheats tasted better than the domesticated equivalents we eat today although difficult to produce for large-scale production, the wild species also contain more proteins and minerals. Wild wheats are indigenous to the remote habitats of the Levant, as they appear to adapt better to the severity of the climate as well as drought. Self-seeding across the rugged terrain, the wild wheats cannot be cultivated for edible use as the obvious botanical difficulties obtaining the quantities of grain from the brittle spikelet makes it uneconomic. There is still however a positivity from artisan bakers and culinary historians throughout Northern Israel and beyond, that in this food era we can expect a resurgence of wild wheats into our diets due to their health properties and increased flavour profiles. With innovative recipe ideas for salads, soups and stews together with breads and cakes using these ancient grains, chefs, cooks and foodies around the globe are looking to embark on a regenerated culinary journey of wild wheats.

The identification of charred remants of emmer © Stefanie Jacomet.

Characters and images of (pre)historical finds of emmer (*Triticum dicoccum*): grains

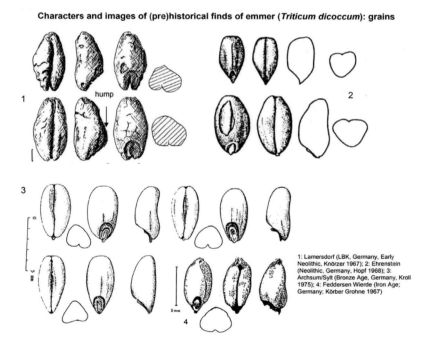

1: Lamersdorf (LBK, Germany, Early Neolithic, Knörzer 1967); 2: Ehrenstein (Neolithic, Germany, Hopf 1968); 3: Archsum/Sylt (Bronze Age, Germany, Kroll 1975); 4: Feddersen Wierde (Iron Age; Germany; Körber Grohne 1967)

Emmer

Emmer, *Triticum turgidum* subsp. *dicoccum*, is an ancient hulled wheat that is also known as farro in the historical region of Garfagnana, Tuscany. The term farro has been coined biologically and anthropologically from the way the combination of the three species of wild hulled wheats, emmer, einkorn and dinkel which is more commonly known as spelt, have been affected by their environment with each wheat species being distinguished in size. In Italian, they are known as *grande, medio* and *piccolo*. Emmer was given the title of *farro medio*, and was dubbed the "true farro" due to the superior quality of its grain for cooking.

Emmer is a hulled wheat with strong husks that hold the grain and a brittle stem, making free threshing unmanageable for this strain. It is typified as an awned wheat, with a bristle attached to glume, requiring a milling process to release the grains from their hold. Wild emmer, *Triticum turgidum* subsp. *dicoccoides,* has the ability to self-cultivate in their natural habitat due to the awns on the shaft of the wheat sheaf, that becomes erect in the increased humidity of the night, and draws the bristles together while pushing the grain from the glume into the soil. As the night-time humidity drops, the awns relax, preventing the grains from dropping. The main difference between the two species is that when ripe, the wild emmer plant head shatters when scattering the seeds into the atmosphere, while the domesticated plant head remains unbroken and therefore a harvestable grain.

The evolution from wild emmer to the domesticated species is due to the genetic profiling of the tetraploid wheat, which contains twenty-eight chromosomes as opposed to the forty-two of its modern relation. Dr Assaf Distelfeld and his team of genetic researchers in Haifa University, Israel is currently leading the Wild Emmer Wheat Genome Sequencing Consortium, establishing a reference genome for this wheat species, and looking at the nutritional relevance the ancient wild grain has on human consumption compared to the common domesticated kind.

The evidence of wild emmer domestication was with a hybridisation of the wild plant of *Triticum dicoccoides*, the durum wheat species *Triticum durum* and barbed goat grass *Aegilops triuncialis*, an invasive weed indigenous to the Eastern Mediterranean habitat. A hardy grain with a good yield on poor soil made the transition to the cultivation into a bread wheat, high in proteins and fibre, rich in minerals and a healthy and tasty wheat. However, the process of selecting seeds for a natural mutation and germination in terminal climatic conditions, allowed for the identification of specific genomes to develop into this cultivated grain that has left emmer a relict crop.

Wild wheat at the foothills of Ramat Hagolan, Northern Israel

In 1906 when Romanian born botanist Aaron Aaronsohn found wild emmer growing while on a field trip to the Upper Galilee of Northern Palestine, it was deemed an outstanding discovery for agriculturalists and historians alike. It created such global interest, that he secured financial backing from the United States of America to continue research into this ancient cereal crop. Aaronsohn reported to scientists, that Palestine's wild wheat was "a hardy plant in the sense of being able to exist under a wide range of natural conditions", and whose distribution extended from the snow-covered

Aaron Aaronsohn

mountain tops of Mount Hermon to the scorched land of the Dead Sea Valley. Sceptics wanted evidence from Aaronsohn that his discovery was a "wild" prototype of this wheat strain, as studies of geographic origins of cultivated crops and its history of domestication had previously been studied and documented by the French-Swiss botanist, Alphonse de Candolle. Candolle had made this discovery thirty years earlier, which was considered a marked contribution to understanding the relationships between plants and their geographical demarcation, between the past and the present.

Aaronsohn verified his findings, defining the fragile rachis of emmer as "undoubtedly one of the characters of this wild prototype" and claiming that a rigid rachis as "an acquired characteristic, developed by man under cultivation and having a tendency to destroy the plants natural capacity for dissemination." The brittleness of the rachis commanded the wheat to be harvested before maturity, due to the close hold on the grains in the toughened glumes that could not allow for free threshing. He maintained that a system of milling this type of wheat, was traced back to the ancient Egyptian tombs of Menna in the Theban necropolis, where domesticated emmer husks were found in abundance and chronicled extensively on the tombs.

A key focus of Distelfeld's genetic research is around the core genes responsible for the fragmenting spikes of the wild genus which do not function in the domesticated species and provide a preference for the seed selection for cultivation. In January 2020, Professor Terrence Brown, at the Department of Earth and Environmental Studies at the University of Manchester, published new findings to suggest that the origins of domesticated emmer were genetically complex, formulated from wild and farmed wheat selections from opposing elements of their natural habitat in the Fertile Crescent. Artificial selection was through natural mutations dependant on the wheat's adaptation to terminal drought in the summer months and abundant rainfall in the winter.

Emmer is undoubtedly one of the world's oldest crops and has been a primary source of protein and energy throughout the ages. As a basic grass, it was the main component of the plant-based diet of the hunter-gatherers and shaped the foundation for the cultivation of this ancient grain. Although it is now regarded as a low yielding minor crop and agriculturally uneconomical, emmer remains of valuable interest to the archeobotanists and culinary historians whose fascination for this ancient and heirloom wheat species is key to the global culinary agenda of sustaining plant based nutritional diets.

All wheat grains contain gluten, albeit to a greater or lesser extent. The gluten structure of the ancient wild emmer was lower than its modern equivalent, from its natural hybridisation with other wild grasses, such as wild goat grass. With less gluten, it is slightly more tolerable to those with the protein sensitivity, however, it cannot be consumed by those who suffer from the medical condition, coeliac disease, and who can only digest gluten-free wheats. Emmer grain, like all wheat grains, contains proteins, carbohydrates and vitamins, components providing the necessary nutrients for all diets. The ancient grains have a higher protein content than the modern wheats, richer in fibre, antioxidants and micro nutrients, which when consumed in conjunction with legumes and nuts, provide a high protein plant-based diet for sustainable eaters. Promotors of gut health favour the ancient supergrains, as the insoluble fibre that is concentrated in the bran of whole grain wheat appears to act as a prebiotic, feeding our beneficial bacteria.

As bread remains the global staple food in our diet and cultivated wheat the single most important crop worldwide, there is an ever-increasing connection between our agricultural and culinary history and the food of our biblical ancestry, as emmer makes its revival onto our plate as the healthier and tastier wheat. Emmer wheat has many culinary uses, including the whole wheatberry in salads and soups, pearled wheat for risottos and stews, most commonly used in Italy, cracked emmer which makes a nutty tabbouleh salad or porridge, and ground into flour for cakes and breads. With the addition of yeast or a starter, emmer produces a soft wholemeal crumb on a risen loaf, however the leavening agent of bicarbonate of soda, first used as a leavening agent in the early 1800s, creates the denser crumb and the hard crusted soda bread.

The precursor to bicarbonate of soda was "pearlash", a purified potash of potassium carbonate, used by native Americans to leaven quick breads. Soda bread is traditionally made with a low gluten flour and buttermilk, which contains lactic acid that reacts with the bicarbonate of soda to form carbon dioxide particles which leavens the bread. I love the earthy flavour of this Middle Eastern biblical herb which when paired with salty feta cheese, is very satisfying with a bowl of warming soup.

Emmer Soda Bread with Za'atar & Feta

Ingredients (makes 1 loaf):
3 ½ cups / 400 g wholemeal emmer flour
1 teaspoon salt
1 teaspoon bicarbonate of soda
2 sprigs za'atar
50 g / ½ cup feta cheese
1 ¼ cups / 300 ml buttermilk

Method:

❖ *preheat the oven to 200 °C / 400 °F / Gas Mark 6*

❖ *finely chop the za'atar leaves & set aside, the fresh herb za'atar is related to marjoram and oregano with a very similar flavour profile, and much easier to access, rosemary and thyme also work well in this recipe, so use whatever fresh herb you have in your garden or fridge*

❖ *place the emmer flour, salt, bicarbonate of soda, chopped herb & feta, finely crumbled in a large bowl & mix to combine, grated parmesan or gruyère cheese are also delicious options if you prefer*

- ❖ pour in the buttermilk & mix gently with a blunt knife until the ingredients are evenly incorporated and the dough is beginning to come together, this dough does not need to be kneaded or overworked, buttermilk is often not an ingredient readily to hand, but simple to make by mixing 2 cups / 500 ml of milk with 2 tablespoons of lemon juice or white wine vinegar & leaving to stand for 10 minutes or so, until thickened and slightly curdled, any white lumps will be lost when mixed in the dough and cooked and any amount left over can be kept in the fridge for another loaf
- ❖ shape the dough into a round loaf with your hands & place on a lightly floured baking tray or baking stone, if you have one, with a sharp knife, score a deep cross half way down the sides, so that it will tear easily into quarters, once baked
- ❖ place in the preheated oven for 20 minutes until golden brown & a metal skewer inserted into the middle of the loaf comes out clean, allow the bread to cool for 10 to 15 minutes & serve warm with butter, soft cheese or dipped into a pot of hummous

Emmer Soda Bread

Einkorn

Einkorn is said to be "man's first wheat" and the world's most ancient grain. Its name, from the German for "single grain", is a true reference to the individual spikelets of wheat that contain the solitary grain. Einkorn falls under the classification of primary hulled wheat farro, that is grouped with emmer and dinkel. Einkorn was given the title *farro piccolo* and classed as the smallest and most primitive grain of the three. *Farro piccolo* remains a rare grain that is not easily accessible to modern cooks, as it is a unique cultivar and grown in only a number of select global farms, harvested in the summer months and only after emmer and dinkel.

It is characterised in both wild and domesticated forms; however, einkorn is primarily known by its domesticated title, *Triticum monococcum*, as its wild form *Triticum boeoticum*, has become a lost crop and no longer cultivated for culinary use. Genetically, einkorn resembles emmer as a twenty-four chromosome, diploid species of hulled wheat, with hardened glumes that firmly encases the single grain.

Remnants of einkorn from the Chalcolithic Copper Age of 3400 BCE were found as recently as 1991 in the stomach of a naturally preserved mummy, Ötzi the Iceman. Discovered accidently by hikers on the Italian Val Senales Valley glacier, archaeologists carried out extensive research on Ötzi's body and together with archeobotanists reports from the historical era, authenticated Ötzi as a hunter-gatherer and einkorn as his food source. The staple grain, was primarily ground and made into paste like a dough. Particles found in Ötzi's stomach were analysed and carbon-dated, and were thought to have been part of the last meal, eaten shortly before his death.

In biblical times, wheat was one of the two most prominent grains referenced as food for both man and beast, and the oldest documented grain was assumed to be einkorn. It is reputed that when Noah was instructed to build an ark for his family and two kinds of every living creature to escape the perils of the floods, einkorn was the grain of choice to accompany them, due to its longevity as a stored cereal, after an abundant harvest.

There has always been evidence that the domestication of wild einkorn and wild emmer played a key role in the transition from hunter-gathering to early farming and that the crop husbandry of wheat was of great significance in the first agricultural revolution of the Neolithic period of 10,000 BCE. However genetic research from DNA fingerprinting (Manfred Heun, et al.) identified evidence that einkorn, found close to the mountainous region of Kacaradag, south east Turkey, in the Fertile Crescent, was farmed for human consumption in the 3,000 years preceding. These findings are supported by archaeological excavations from the Neolithic agricultural settlement of Göbekli Tepe, located in the same region of the Levant, where wild wheats were native to the terrain and einkorn originated. As one of the oldest remaining temples, Göbekli Tepe is believed to have been the cultural haven for the transition of gatherers of nature to farming cereal crops and from where cultivated wheats stem.

In 1967, Jack R Harlan (1917–1998), an American Professor of Archeobotany from Illinois, whose main research interest was the origins of crop domestication, wrote a paper entitled 'A Wild Wheat Harvest in Turkey' in which he examined the complex history of the domestication of einkorn and emmer in the rocky volcanic plane of Kacaradag, also known as the Black Mountains. On examination, it turned out that "over much of Karaca Dağ the grass cover consists of vast strands of wild wheats, together with a few wild barleys and other grasses. By far the most abundant are the wild einkorn (*Triticum boeoticum* var. *thaoudar*) and the little weedy goat grass, *Aegilops speltoides*." Einkorn, although identified as one of the wild cereals first used as food by man, as a primitive non threshing form of wheat, never materialised as a major domestic crop. Harlan, along with with other archeobotanists, was of the opinion that brittle rachis of the wild wheats would easily shatter if harvested with a sickle, the process that precipitates the onset of domestication.

Einkorn is classed among the cluster of "covered wheats", a name given to the ancient wheat species whose kernels do not manage to break free from their glumes when threshed, requiring each grain to be hulled from its husk, after harvesting. This wild species has smaller kernels and a brittle rachis that shatters naturally when ripe, causing the seeds to disperse through self-pollination and germination in its surrounding wild habitat. The realisation for farmers that wild wheats were unmanageable and low yielding, led to their cultivation, which started with the domestication of einkorn, recorded around 7500 BCE in the Fertile Crescent.

The domestication of einkorn came as a result of the hybridisation of the wild wheat with the goat grass weed, which produced a softer and slacker glume, which when threshed allowed for a slicker, stronger and less brittle rachis, and kept the wheatberries intact. This paved the way for a more practical process of harvesting and benefitted a greater yield than if the cereal wheat was allowed to self-pollinate. This new wheat species, which became known as "the common wheat" *Triticum aestivum*, appeared to be well suited to the continuing changes in the agricultural industry and the advances in the machinery that was used for its cultivation and growth. However, this led to the decline of the hulled wheat and the extinction of einkorn. A possible reason for its near extinction was that einkorn remained a pure wheat that was never hybridised, and although it grows to an above average height among modern wheats, it still only manages to produce grains a third of its size.

Wheat genetics has gathered pace recently with landrace species developed to create stable gluten structures and prolific yields for the global demand. Geneticists have found einkorn to be absent of the D wheat genome, which detects the presence of gluten, so although we know that einkorn has a nominal amount of gluten, it is evidently not as stable as the modern wheat grain, and tends to produce a denser, less risen bake. Innovative recipe ideas are creating an interest in using einkorn in cooking and baking, as with a lesser gluten content it is more easily digested and can be used as a whole wheatberry or ground into flour. Einkorn can be substituted for whole wheat or bread flour; however, it requires less kneading to develop its minimal gluten structure. Packed with nutrients, vitamins, minerals and proteins, it is an excellent choice of grain for pasta and risottos, adding a rich nutty flavour to the dish.

Uri Mayer-Chissick is a culinary historian and expert on the wild edibles of Israel. He is a specialist in the field of nutrition and medieval dietetics, with an extensive knowledge of local wild ingredients from his natural surroundings in Northern Israel. He hosts cooking workshops from foraged ingredients and locally sourced produce, and this recipe of his highlights the ancient einkorn grain with two of the country's other main staples. These rolls are delicious eaten with foraged salad leaves, hummous and a glass of cold wine.

Einkorn Rolls with Tahini & Date Syrup

Ingredients (makes 8-10 rolls):
2 ¼ cups / 200 g wholemeal einkorn flour
1 teaspoon active dried yeast
1 teaspoon salt
1 cup / 195 ml warm water
1 ½ tablespoons date syrup
1 tablespoon tahini paste
60 ml extra virgin olive oil

Method:

❖ *place the einkorn & dried yeast in a large bowl, add the warm water & date syrup and leave for 5 minutes to froth, date syrup is the naturally refined sweetener from pulverised dates, dark, rich and deliciously sweet, it is a great alternative to sugars*

❖ *add the salt, tahini & olive oil & mix well form a smooth dough, it will feel quite wet, but will come together well, tahini paste is simply ground hulled sesame seeds and eaten in abundance in the Middle East, makes a great dressing too and gives a nutty taste to all your cooking*

❖ *lightly dust a work surface with einkorn flour and turn the dough out & knead for 10 minutes, until soft & elastic, dust a large bowl with a sprinkling of einkorn flour and place the dough in the centre, cover and leave in a warm place to prove for 1 hour, or until the dough has doubled in size*

❖ *divide the dough in 75 g equal pieces & roll into balls, place on a baking sheet lined with baking parchment & leave uncovered for a further 30 minutes*

❖ *preheat the oven to 190 °C / 375 °F / Gas Mark 5*

❖ *place in the preheated oven for 15 minutes until golden brown & the bases of the rolls sound hollow when tapped*

❖ *serve warm with hummus, fava bean dip, cheese or simply butter...*

Uri Mayer-Chissick's Tahini
& Date Syrup Einkorn Rolls

Spelt

Spelt *Triticum aestivum* subs. *spelta*, is also known as *Dinkel* in German. It is thought to be related closely to the wild wheats of emmer and einkorn that were found during the Neolithic Era in the Near East and Fertile Crescent, the ancestors to modern wheat. However, the actual origins of spelt are more widely debated by archeobotanists, with one hypothesis relating to the geographical location of its earliest archaeological evidence, discovered in Transcaucasia, a region bordering Eastern Europe and Western Asia around 5000 BCE. As this ancient wheat started to spread throughout Europe and became the primary species of wheat grown in Germany and neighbouring countries during this historical period, this assumes the more accurate theory.

In 2011, an article written by environmental archaeologist Meriel McClatchie, found large amounts of spelt wheat deposits in Baysrath excavation in County Kilkenny, southeast Ireland, when a new road was constructed. Spelt grains and chaff found at the site in a T-shaped drying kiln were carbon-dated to around 400–1150 AD, a rare find in Ireland from that era, and more common in Roman Britain. Identifying prehistoric cereal remains required expert understanding in the archaeobotanical field and in particular with charred grains of spelt, as their distorted shape and size closely resembled emmer.

From evidence gained at this site it seems that spelt was introduced into Ireland as a cereal crop during the Bronze Age, a long time after emmer and einkorn. Regardless of its potential uses for food and animal fodder, spelt historically remained one of Ireland's minor crops, despite the ancient grain's ability to produce good yields on poor soil and in adverse weather conditions. McClatchie concluded in her article that "the discovery of a large quantity of spelt remains at Baysrath is an important find, providing new evidence for the use of this cereal type thousands of years ago".

Another indication of spelt's ancestry can be found in Greek mythology and the legends of Demeter, the mother and goddess of grain, harvest and agriculture. Many festivals took place throughout the agricultural year, and at each celebration spelt was offered up to the goddess as a token of thanksgiving for the sowing, sprouting and harvesting of this fruitful grain.

Spelt, like emmer and einkorn is a hulled wheat, requiring the arduous process of removing the inedible husks to release the grain, giving it a longevity and resistance to disease, unlike the free threshing modern grain.

Charred spelt grains from Baysrath

5mm

Therefore, in all likelihood, spelt too appeared in the Bible and was eaten as a staple grain, or made into a form of bread. There are a number of references to *kuccemeth*, the ancient Hebrew word for spelt, in the Books of Exodus, Isaiah and Ezekiel. It was always believed that most of the wheat found in Egypt and around the Fertile Crescent, referenced as one of the seven species, was in fact emmer, however it cannot be ruled out that spelt was also found to be growing in the region, although archeobotanists do not advocate that it was *Triticum spelta* in its true form, but a hybrid species of *Aegilops tauschii*, the common wild goat's grass.

The Book of Exodus tells of the ten plagues unleashed on the Egyptians following the cruel suffering of Moses and the Children of Israel at the hands of the Pharaoh. The seventh plague of hail struck down all the crops, but we know that the vast swathes of wheat were spared, due to later harvesting. "Now the flax and the barley were ruined, for the barley was in the ear and the flax was in bud; but the wheat and the emmer were not hurt, for they ripen late" (Exodus 9:31-33). Here it is clearly defined as two crops, with "the wheat" assumed to be the *kuccemeth* or spelt, however other explanations from biomedical scientists, have concluded differently. Parallels have been drawn between the plagues and natural ecological events causing destruction and devastation.

There is a more specific reference to spelt by the prophet Ezekiel during the last days before the Babylonians destroyed the Temple of Jerusalem in 586 BCE. In order to prevent starvation in times of famine or destruction, the prophet says "take wheat, barley, beans, lentils, millet, and spelt. Put them into one vessel and bake them into bread" (Ezekiel 4:9).

Ezekiel bread was made with the lower quality grains available to the poor, one of which was spelt, but today it is considered a nutrient rich loaf and one of the best-selling health breads in America, with spelt as its main ingredient.

Dr Tova Dickstein, Israel's leading authority on ancient biblical foods and curator of Jerusalem's Biblical Landscape Reserve, explains that "in Hebrew, bread means man's main food" and that Ezekiel bread was in fact "a stew made of many grains and cereals and mopped up with a barley bread". She likens the stew to an ancient Cretan dish called Palikaria, which was made from a mixture of seeds and cereals. This thick stew became a ritual dish that was consumed at religious festivals by the

Minoans, the ancient inhabitants of Crete from around 11,000–3000 BCE. The Minoans left Crete for Egypt sometime during the end of that period, but refused entry by the Egyptians they settled along the shores of Palestine and became known as "the Philistines from Crete", bringing with them their legendary dish.

This is Tova Dickstein's basic recipe for Palikaria, which she has based on the original biblical recipe for Ezekiel bread. It does not in any way resemble a dough or a loaf, but a stodgy mix of wheat, legumes and vegetables, a little onion and seasoned with some salt, pepper and dill. The Minoans ate Palikaria served with the cooking liquor as a soup, or sometimes drained and served as a salad. Cooked in water this recipe lacks flavour and texture, however it remains a nutritious and filling dish, true to Ezekiel's original instructions.

Ezekiel Bread

Ingredients:
½ cup / 100 g whole spelt kernels
½ cup / 100 g fava beans
½ cup / 100 g millet
½ cup / 100 g lentils
½ cup / 100 g peas
dried onion
dill
olive oil
salt & black pepper

Method
❖ *soak the fava beans overnight*
❖ *fill a pot with a large amount of water & cook the spelt for 30 minutes, add the fava beans, millet, lentils & peas and continue cooking for a further 45 minutes until soft, season with salt & black pepper*
❖ *add some olive oil, chopped dried onion & dill*

'The Bread of Life' Essene, Ezekiel or Manna Bread

Another interpretation of a stew full of ancient grains and legumes using the façade of bread is Manna bread or Essene bread, which was considered to be the oldest bread known to man, described in an Aramaic manuscript from 100 BCE, entitled 'The Essene Gospel of Peace', where the "bread of fuel" took one of its many names. It was during 600–500 BCE, when the Jews began their exile in the wilderness, that they were given the edible manna as a form of sustenance, which was also written in the Bible as *kuccemeth* or spelt.

Manna bread and Essene bread, like Ezekiel bread was made using a variety of sprouted grains and cereals. It took a number of days to make and was baked over hot rocks in the sun. It was nutritionally balanced to heal the body and mind, as the long, slow process of baking this bread helped to maintain the food enzymes in the germinated wholegrains and legumes. This increased their health properties from incorporating the entire kernel of the bran, germ and endosperm. Jesus wanted his disciples to be sustained with Essene bread, as is written in these ancient scriptures, "Happy are you that hunger for the truth, for I will satisfy you with the bread of wisdom". This bread, which we know included spelt became known as "the bread of life", a name that has been preserved throughout history in most religious communities.

Ezekiel bread has recently become a health food phenomenon in America, and a hot commodity for plant-based foodies. It is a made using sprouted or germinated wheat kernels that cause biochemical reactions in the grain, and increases the number of healthy supplements in the kernel, while decreasing the antinutrients which prevent the healthy nutrients from being absorbed into the gut. Sprouting whole grains of spelt, wheat or legume kernels favour warm, damp conditions, where they are able to rapidly germinate. On culinary trend, sprouted breads have overtaken whole grain loaves and are set to become one of our most popular home baked loaves, for both flavour and health.

Gaius Plinius Secundus, better known as Pliny the Elder was a Roman author of natural history and philosophy, during the early Roman era. His last and probably most famous work, the *Naturalis historia* (*Natural History*), took the form of thirty-seven books which made up an encyclopedia of natural history. This compendium drew on his vast knowledge of the subject, backed up by archaeological findings from the fields of botany, technology and agriculture. Pliny alleged that the Romans preferred to eat wheat as a grain, rather than barley which was favoured by the Greeks, and stated that spelt was the finest grain that emanated from the Gauls: "The Gauls have also a kind of spelt peculiar to that country: they give it the name of 'brace', while to us it is known as 'scandala': it has a grain of remarkable whiteness. Another difference, again, is the fact that it yields nearly four pounds more of bread to the modius than any other kind of spelt."

The Romans were not as renowned for their bread making as the ancient Egyptians, however, their use of spelt as their wheat grain of choice was clearly documented over emmer. Spelt was regarded as the esteemed grain of the emperors and the foundation of their diet, whilst barley, rye and oats were considered only fit for consumption by soldiers, slaves and animals. Spelt was used in a variety of ways, including as flour for breads and a thickening agent for sauces or soups. It was also used in its whole form as kernels or groats for porridge or gruel, a traditional Roman dish known as *puls* that was usually flavoured with cheese. Pliny quotes his contemporary and fellow author, Marcus Porcius Cato, also known as Cato the Elder, whose historical prose acclaimed Latin as a language in its own right and the native tongue of Rome. As an agriculturalist, Cato wrote *De agri cultura*, translated as 'On Farming', which is his only surviving manual from circa 160 BCE. Cato's spelt recipe for *puls* has survived over the centuries as a very basic dish that was traditionally served with venison. This recipe is an early version of a freekeh or bulghur dish where the grains have absorbed their cooking liquor and softened in the process, before being served with meat, fish or vegetables as a good source of carbohydrate. The addition of milk gives the wheat a richness, which personally I would substitute with a deep flavoured stock, if pairing with meat or game:

> *86. Make durum wheat granea as follows. You place ½ lb. clean durum wheat in a clean mixing bowl, wash well, thresh well and rinse well; then you place in a cooking pot with clean water and cook. When cooked you add milk gradually until the liquor thickens.*
>
> *Cato: On Farming*, edited by Andrew Dalby, p. 163

Marcus Gavius Apicius, a self-professed gourmet from the Roman Empire's aristocracy, often held lavish dinners for the emperors and foreign dignitaries, illustrating through the finest and often most exotic ingredients, the art of the Roman cuisine, with dishes that included peacock, flamingo and dormouse. In 100 AD, he compiled *De re coquinaria*, twelve compendiums of recipe books on 'The Subject of Cooking' and although he does not specifically document breads using spelt, he included a recipe for a pudding, called *apothermum*, an opulent dessert with almonds, raisins and sweet wine, similar to a rather luxurious rice pudding. The recipe calls for pearled spelt, which was often polished using clay to brighten the kernels a shiny pearl white. It was called *alica*:

> *2.2.10. You make a cold dessert like this: boil alica with pine nuts and almonds which have been soaked in water and skinned and washed in some 'silver' chalk so that they are all equally white. Add to this raisins, caroenum*

or passum. Sprinkle ground pepper over the top and serve in a dish.
Apicius: A Critical Edition, C. Grocock and S. Grainger (eds.), p. 153

Traditionally made using spelt flour, Roman slipper bread was named after its flat, oval shape. It was also known as the Roman army bread. Following a slow rise, the wetter dough produced a good crumb structure and gave the bread a long shelf life, allowing the troops to take the loaves into the battlefields with them, and led to the ancient spelt grain inheriting the legendary name of the "marching grain". Recipes for the slipper bread has been adapted by bakers over the centuries from the original writings of Apicius, who baked with wholegrain spelt flour.

Roman bakers would vigorously mix their dough until smooth which often took up to fifteen minutes, however, this recipe adapted from Doves Farm Organic Flour Specialists needs only a few minutes kneading to develop the gluten. Enriched with olive oil and honey to add flavour, once baked it remains rather flat, like a slipper, remaining true to its ancient name. I am not so sure it keeps that well, as if made with wholemeal spelt flour, extra virgin olive oil and a good quality floral honey as I did, it was devoured almost as soon as it came out of the oven and was demolished after one meal with good cheese and a cold glass of crisp white wine.

Roman Army 'Slipper' Bread Recipe

Ingredients:
1 cup / 225 g whole meal spelt flour
1 teaspoon salt
1 ½ teaspoons / 7 g dried action yeast
¾ cup / 200 ml warm water
1 ½ tablespoons extra virgin olive oil
1 teaspoon honey
wheatgerm for dusting

Method:

- ❖ place the flour in a large mixing bowl with the salt
- ❖ mix the yeast into half of the warm water & add to the flour, followed by the oil & honey, which will form a soft and lumpy dough, mix well for 15 minutes with a wooden spoon or a dough hook attached to an electric mixer, unless you want a morning workout
- ❖ form the dough into an oval 'slipper' shape & place on a floured tray, dust with extra wholemeal flour or wheatgerm if you have some and prefer an extra crunch to the crust & leave to rise for 30 minutes in a warm place in the kitchen
- ❖ pre heat the oven to 180 °C / 375 °F / Gas Mark 6
- ❖ once the dough has sufficiently risen in size, bake the 'slipper' in the pre-heated oven for 20 to 25 minutes, until golden brown and the bottom sounds hollow, when tapped, leave to cool slightly before eating, if you can...

Wholemeal Spelt Roman Slipper Bread

During the Medieval period, Saint Hildegard von Bingen (1098–1179), a German Benedictine abbess, wrote a number of medicinal treaties, perhaps the most acclaimed of which are *Physica* and *Causae et Curae*, which championed the wonders of monastic herbal medicine. Favouring her native tongue, her remedies and recipes were mainly written in German rather than Latin, and aimed at treating various health conditions, aiming to unify the mind, body and spirit. Her medicinal writings struck a chord with women and men of all social classes across Europe, who took her plant, cereal and herbal remedies as visionary in healing the body and the soul.

Hildegard's recipes referred only to dinkel wheat and never spelt, and she strongly believed that dinkel was indeed the perfect grain, packed full of nutrients to aid the healing process. She wrote: "Spelt is the best grain, warming, lubricating and of high nutritional value. It is better tolerated by the body than any other grain. Spelt provides the consumer with good flesh and good blood and confers a cheerful disposition. It provides a happy mind and a joyful spirit. No matter how you eat spelt, it is good and easy to digest."

Despite her unwavering belief in the nutritional value of dinkel, she also wrote favourably about the other ancient wheats, emmer and einkorn, as well as rye, yet she always seemed more focused and gave specific recipes for prescribing the benefits of dinkel when debilitated by illness. "When someone is so weakened by illness that he cannot eat, then simply take whole spelt kernels and boil them vigorously in water, add butter and egg (and a pinch of salt). This will make the food tastier and the patient will want to eat it. Give this to the patient and it will heal him from within like a good healing salve."

Saint Hildegard wrote many other healthy recipes containing the nutritious dinkel, including her most famous bread, Hildegard's Spelt Bread as it later became known. She combined wholemeal spelt flour with whole spelt flakes which was mixed to a dough with a combination of water and milk. Her leavening agent was always yeast, not a sour starter and she added a touch of lemon juice and sunflower oil for flavour, although I doubt it made too much difference, as the ancient recipes appeared to add a scant amount of each. Her bread is still made in bakeries and homes across Germany, adapted from a recipe that dates back hundreds of years, and makes quite a dense and filling loaf. She also wrote recipes for porridge, that was called Habermus, which she made using the whole grains or flakes of spelt, occasionally with the addition of ground flour. She avidly believed that Habermus aided digestion and remedied ill health. Her porridge was similar to oat porridge when spelt flakes were used and more like a risotto when made with whole grains. With the addition of flour, it was similar to semolina, as they were all cooked or mixed with milk or water, to give the consistency of porridge.

Saint Hildegard von Bingen always recommended starting the day with a warm cereal of dinkel wheat. She advocated that it provided all the necessary healthy nutrients to start the day. Her original recipe, rather surprisingly called for the addition of galangal, a root said to strengthen the immune system and "a couple of pinches of Bertram powder", a plant similar to chamomile, that aids digestion. Adapting her recipe, you can mix up the spices to your taste, substitute fresh root ginger or fresh turmeric for the Asian galangal, add dried fruits or frozen berries to the apple and to make it even more luxurious, a touch of warm milk or cream...

Hildegard's Habermus (Breakfast Porridge)

Ingredients (serves 2-4):
1 cup / 200 g spelt flakes
2 cups / 400 ml of water
1 teaspoon ground or freshly grated ginger
1 teaspoon ground cinnamon
grating of fresh nutmeg
4 tablespoons wild flower honey
½ cup / 50 g whole almonds
2 apples

Method:

❖ *place the spelt flakes in boiling water for 5 minutes to soften, drain & place in a saucepan with the water, bring to the boil, cook on a medium heat for 5 minutes stirring occasionally before turning off the heat, place a tight-fitting lid on top of the saucepan & leave the spelt to steam & soften for 15 to 20 minutes*

❖ *remove the saucepan lid and loosen up the flakes with a fork & add the ginger, cinnamon, nutmeg & honey, before returning to the heat for a further 10 minutes until you have the consistency of porridge*

❖ *toast the almonds in a dry pan over a medium heat for about 5 minutes, tossing the nuts every minute or so until golden brown or roast in the oven at 180 °C / 350 °F / Gas Mark 4 for 6 to 8 minutes, remove from the heat, cool slightly & roughly chop, wash, core & dice the apples, set side*

❖ *divide the habermus into bowls and serve sprinkled with apples, almonds & a sprinkling of extra cinnamon*

In spite of spelt being closely related to the ancient wild wheats of emmer and einkorn, its genetic makeup is quite different. It is a hexaploid wheat, bearing six sets of chromosomes as opposed to the tetraploid emmer and the diploid einkorn. The heritage of this hulled wheat is closer to that of the common wheat or "club" wheat, which possibly accounts for the belief that spelt was derived from multiple hybrids of the domesticated free threshing wheats and their hulled wild relatives from the Fertile Crescent. Wild spelt *Triticum spelta*, can be found growing in the Galilee of Northern Israel, but has only been domesticated for modern use in Europe and parts of America, where is appears to have acclimatised to the colder environment of a winter wheat.

In 1890, spelt made its way to the United States, where it took hold predominantly in the mid-west state of Ohio. *Triticum spelta* requires a large surface area of land to grow but yields less grain from each ear than many of its wheat relatives, making it an expensive crop to farm. However, it is more resilient to disease and variable climatic conditions than the common wheat species due to tougher glumes that protect the kernels from insects and crop damage. At the beginning of spelt's American Dream, farmers only looked at cultivating a few species including spelt, that did not seem to establish themselves in the highly fertilised soil, and so was abandoned as a fruitless crop. It wasn't until the middle of the 1900s, when organic farming gained global popularity, that agriculturalists realised that the spelt crops required less fertiliser to produce not only a greater yield, but also a healthier grain and it soon regained its reputation as a wheat substitute for the artisanal bakers.

Erez Komarovsky, Israel's pioneer in artisanal breads and advocate of sustainable eating, states that "spelt is a good ingredient against the globalisation of food", as due to its availability, growth and price, its supply cannot be sustained for the ever-increasing demand of this healthy alternative to common wheat. By the beginning of 2000, spelt appeared more popular throughout the world, in part due its nutritional components, but also due to the prevalence of vegetarian and veganism. Many countries including the United Kingdom sought to grow spelt to meet the demand, however it only survived in certain regions in Eastern Europe and America, so large shortages were reported, which in turn increased demand for it from bakers, chefs and healthy eaters. Spelt is mainly imported as whole grains from Europe to the Middle East, the Mediterranean countries and England, and only milled into flour by commercial millers for supermarkets, wholesalers and individual bakeries.

Spelt cannot be classified as a gluten-free grain, but it has a significantly reduced gluten content. It is unsuitable for sufferers of severe wheat allergies and coeliac disease, however, it is a good grain for those who are wheat 'intolerant' as the differing amounts of proteins and carbohydrates in the grain's molecular structure, has not been modified from its original state and therefore it is less reactive on the gut. As a water-soluble grain, it has a fragility to its constitution, making it easier to digest and significantly reducing bloating of the stomach. This is also in part due to the different amino acids that spelt contains over whole wheats, which allows for a smoother absorption into the gut.

Spelt contains a lower glycaemic value and therefore is a preferable grain in the diet of diabetics. With an increased iron, fibre and protein content, the sugars are released into the bloodstream at a slower rate, and together with higher levels of niacin and other B vitamins, it produces more energy in the metabolism and, some claim, a higher level of immunity

In Germany and Austria where spelt has become the more customary grain to use when baking many types of breads and rolls, and have become known by spelt's Germanic name collectively as *dinkelbrot*. It is widely available in supermarkets and bakeries and dinkel flour is as common as the UK's plain flour, used for cakes, bakes, roux, batters, and as a binding agent or thickener. *Grünkern* or "green grains" are the young, unripe dinkel grains that are threshed before the dinkel is fully ripe and eaten once dried, which is likened to the ancient process of freekeh, but without the symbolic roasting of the grain to create a smoky flavour.

Spelt has gained a firm hold in the Israeli bread market since 2007, when Keren Ziv Rabovsky, a novice baker from the north of Israel, started making and selling 100% spelt products from her home, to combat increasing health issues involving the gut that she was experiencing from eating wheat. The Middle Eastern cuisine traditionally serves a wheat-based bread with each meal, however with the advent of artisan sourdoughs and the rise in vegetarian and vegan diets in Israel, Keren herself a vegan, took the opportunity to start baking using only spelt flour to create a healthy business with the nutritious grain. "Pitputim", which was called after the playful meaning of the Hebrew words "chit-chat and a slice of bread", has over the years expanded from her domestic kitchen to a large bakery in the Dalton Industrial Estate in Safed.

Pitputim is the only 100% spelt bakery in Israel, delivering their products all over the country with the added benefits of only incorporating vegetarian and vegan ingredients into their foods, and creating a greater following from the increasing number of the country's followers of the plant-based diet. Keren and her team have adapted all their recipes to suit the composition and structure of spelt, which she says "depends on the species of the grain, which is imported from Germany or the Ukraine, as it is not grown commercially in Israel." Every Friday, they bake hundreds of spelt challah loaves, the traditional Sabbath loaf, a popular product as more and more

Israelis are backing sustainable healthy diets but demanding the same level of flavour in their food. Other innovative products include bourekas, a popular filled pastry from Sephardic Jewish cuisine, made using boureka dough, phyllo dough, brik pastry or puff pastry.

Pitputim's Spinach & Cheese Spelt Bourekas

Ingredients (makes approximately 16 bourekas):

for the pastry:
1 cup / 130 g white spelt flour
1 ½ cups / 195 g wholemeal spelt flour
¼ teaspoon salt
1 cup / 220 g butter, softened
1 cup / 250 g cottage cheese
1 tablespoon soured cream

for the filling:
1 ½ cups / 300 g hard cheese, Cheddar, Emmental or Gruyère, grated
1 egg white
½ cup / 100 g frozen or fresh spinach, chopped
1-2 egg yolks, for egg wash
black or white sesame seeds, for topping

Method:
❖ place the flours, salt, softened butter, cottage cheese & soured cream in a large mixing bowl or an electric mixer with a dough paddle, beat all the ingredients together until smooth and a soft dough is formed, refrigerate for 3 to 4 hours or overnight
❖ make the filling while the dough is refrigerating by mixing the spinach, grated cheese & egg white together in a bowl until combined, refrigerate until ready to use, if using fresh spinach, pour boiling water over the leaves and drain well before chopping and mixing with the cheese, you can use any hard cheese of your choice, or a combination if you prefer
❖ once the pastry dough is sufficiently chilled, remove from the refrigerator & cut into 16 equal portions, roll each one into a rectangle approximately 30 x 12 cm / 12 x 4 in, remove the filling from the refrigerator too & cover each piece of rolled dough right to the edges in a thin layer with the

filling, taking the long edge of the dough, roll it up tightly then taking one of the short edges, roll it into a tight spiral, tucking the end of the dough underneath the bourekas to secure it, repeat with each piece of dough, you can shape the bourekas in triangles, crescents or any shape you like, but I like the spirals, as it shows the spinach and cheese filling through the pastry

❖ *preheat the oven to 180 °C / 350 °F / Gas Mark 4 & line a baking tray with non-stick baking paper*

❖ *brush each bourekas with the egg yolk, sprinkle some sesame seeds on the top, you can use nigella seeds or poppy seeds if you prefer & bake for 20 minutes, until golden brown, remove from the oven and leave to cook for 10 to 15 minutes before eating*

Pitputim's Spelt & Spinach Bourekas

Spelt is undoubtedly a relict crop, that can be found growing wild in the foothills of the Galilee alongside emmer, although not for domesticated use due to the hot, arid climate of the Middle East. Pitputim and other artisan bakers import whole spelt grains which are milled into flour in the country. Despite its growing popularity as a healthy, ancient grain, it has become an expensive commodity, mainly due to the huge expanse of land needed to grow spelt and the requirement for organic farming to sustain the health of the soil and retain the nutrients in the grain, yet its comeback continues as we wish for more sustainable eating.

Spelt was not always considered to be a grain of opulence, in fact culturally and in ancient literature it was quite the opposite. Satires originally written by the Roman poet Horace (65–8 BCE) found their way into the compendium of children's tales retold by the Greek storyteller Aesop, called 'The Town and the Country Mouse'. The story recounts in Latin that the poverty-stricken country mouse ate merely "*esset ador loliumque*", which translates to "grains of spelt and darnel", while his city guest dined upon better parts of the banquet, namely wild peas, long oats, a dried raisin, and bits of bacon.

Spelt, like all ancient wheats, has assumed many culinary uses. Innovative chefs, bakers and food writers are creating delicious recipes for breads, risottos, cakes and salads which can be found on restaurant menus, enticing a variety of eaters. As the grains are water soluble, bakers adapt recipes using up to 10% less liquid, particularly with bread and cakes, ensuring a good rise and soft crumb structure. When cooking or baking with the whole grains, they are soaked initially for twenty-four hours to soften the hard husks and make the grain more palatable. Although spelt contains a reduced gluten content, it is only once the grain has germinated that the gluten is present, as whilst sprouting and immature, the seed is gluten-free.

Full of flavour and versatility, the ancient spelt grain or Germanic dinkel wheat, is fast becoming the grain of choice in our modern diets, replacing the plain white, all-purpose flour and modern bread wheats, for a more nutritious wholegrain that is accessible to all and easy to use in contemporary cooking and baking.

Khorasan

Khorasan wheat (*Triticum turgidum* subsp. *Turanicum*) is also known as Oriental wheat but is better known commercially under its brand Kamut, trademarked in 1990, and meaning "wheat", a name derived from the ancient Egyptian language.

John Percival, an English Professor of Botany whose early research in 1921 into grains and cereals was documented in his monograph *The Wheat Plant*, concluded that khorasan was an ancient wheat species, native to the Fertile Crescent and Mesopotamia and related to both emmer and einkorn. Khorasan was originally named after the largest province of Persia (which became modern day Iran in 1935), where agriculture dominated. Percival's research was conducted on a wheat species believed to have been an earlier genus of khorasan, that was sent to him by English Brigadier General Sir Percy Molesworth Sykes, who travelled extensively throughout Persia and the surrounding region, recording in manuscripts the descriptions of his travels, the country's history and its rich landscape and natural bounty. This particular variety of wheat differed from emmer and einkorn only in its colouring of much darker awns, which he documented as "jet black". This was thought to have been a wild variety of khorasan wheat, as the domesticated khorasan possessed white glumes.

However, over the centuries and owing to the similarities to its wild relatives' emmer and einkorn, khorasan remains classed as an ancient grain, unchanged from its heritage and cultivation, and often used instead of the hard, durum wheat to make pasta and bread. Genetically the *Triticum turgidum* subsp. *turanicum* is a tetraploid wheat, with four times the number of chromosomes in its nucleus at 48, and is a much larger kernel that any of the other ancient or modern wheats. Khorasan appears more comparable in its structure to durum wheat than any of its other cousins, suggesting a possible natural hybridisation between *Triticum polonicum*, Polish wheat and *Triticum durum*, according to plant genetic research carried out in Cambridge University in 2007, using DNA fingerprinting to determine its taxonomy.

Despite being named an heirloom grain, khorasan resembles the composition of modern wheats with shorter, tougher glumes and larger kernels. Khorasan's seeds are characteristically about three times bigger than most modern wheat strains, marked by an elongated, golden 'hump'. Peasant farmers from Turkey and Egypt likened these distinctive kernels to the long dirty cream teeth of their camels, and so khorasan was given its humorous nickname of the "Camel's Tooth", which seems to have stuck with the grain, particularly in the Middle East where it is still grown.

In 1949, it was evident that khorasan was first introduced to America by US airman Earl Dedman who when stationed in Egypt, was given the large edible grain by an Egyptian claiming to have recovered it from an Egyptian tomb. Although Dedman considered the story to be more likely to have been bought for a few Egyptian pounds in a street market in Cairo, he sent thirty-six kernels to his farming family in the state of Montana, in the hope that it would be a profitable crop. Dedman's father planted the seeds and gained a small yield of fifteen hundred bushels, which he named "King Tut wheat". The novelty began to wear off believing this grain had little culinary use in America's main diet, until twenty-five years later when it was rediscovered in the same state by two intrigued farmers, who believed it was worth cultivating and bringing into the global food market, as one of our ancestors' healthy, staple grains.

Father and son, Mack and Bob Quinn worked on organically cultivating a specific variety of khorasan, researching its genetic and health properties in conjunction with its farming capacity for commercial yield. After ten years they made the decision to register the protected cultivated grain *Triticum turanicum* QK-77 under the trademark Kamut®. The word was found in an Egyptian hieroglyphic dictionary compiled by Sir Ernest Alfred Thompson Wallis Budge, a nineteenth-century Egyptologist, where it was defined as 'grain or wheaten bread'. As the word was considered to belong to a dead language it was granted the status of a trademark.

In line with trademark standards, Mack and Bob had to ensure that all the products registered under Kamut® fulfilled the desired agricultural, botanical and culinary conditions, as well as ensuring the labelling was clear and accurate, with no misleading or unethical information about the product. As khorasan had not been put through extensive breeding or hybridisation programmes, it had retained its original nutritional and health properties of an ancient grain, and could be classified as such with the Kamut® trademark protection.

The nutritional value of khorasan wheat fascinated Bob Quinn who advocated new research into this ancient grain versus modern wheat and its effects on the human body. His initial small study showed that his trademarked Kamut® may be a contributing factor in the lowering of cholesterol, as well as reducing levels of bowel inflammation and wheat sensitivity due to its lower levels of gluten. This research led scientists at Careggi University Hospital in

Khorasan: The Camel's Tooth

Florence to conduct a wider clinical trial in 2013 to determine whether the ancient grain's effects on the wider clinical picture had a more preferable outcome than those from modern wheat grain products, particularly on the cardiovascular, endocrine and gastro intestinal systems.

Following a randomised trial, findings published in the *European Journal of Nutrition* concluded that "a khorasan wheat-based replacement diet improves risk profile of patients with type 2 diabetes mellitus (T2DM)" by lowering the LDL cholesterol, otherwise known as "bad" cholesterol, as well as blood insulin levels. As with all wheats, whether ancient, wild or a modern hybrid, khorasan contains some gluten, but less than the commercialised products, making it more digestible for those with sensitivities, but not for those who suffer from gluten intolerant diseases such as coeliac disease. A like for like substitute for all wheats, khorasan has become a popular choice with those bakers who wish to promote healthier products, backed by clinical research and practising nutritionists.

With a high nutritional profile, khorasan has a high calorie count, providing more energy per calorie than its modern counterpart. Higher in protein than many other wheats, khorasan is considered an excellence source of protein for a meat-free diet. The whole grain contains high levels of the daily fibre content required to prevent obesity and bad gut health. Essential vitamins and minerals in this staple grain play a key role in maintaining healthy tissues and digestive tract, and are strongly recommended by nutritionists as part of a healthy diet.

Golden in colour, these large kernels have a distinctive nutty and slight buttery flavour with a firm texture, similar to other whole heirloom grains. Khorasan thrives in arid conditions, yielding annual quantities in its native habitat of Iran, Israel and Egypt where it can easily exceed that of durum wheat. When milled into flour it is less elastic due to its gluten structure and composition, requiring more kneading for a bread dough and more leavening agents in cakes and batters, as it doesn't have quite the same ability to rise as modern all-purpose flours. Low in fat, it is becoming a healthy alternative to flatbreads as well as tea breads, pastries and shortbreads, all which pair well with fragrant Middle Eastern spicing of za'atar, cinnamon and rosewater.

According to Anomarel Rotem Ogen, an artisan sourdough baker in the ancient Arab-Israeli town of Abu Ghosh, west of Jerusalem, there is a growing trend in both the Jewish and Arabic cultures to interpret and bake breads using ancient grains from the cuisine's heritage. Khorasan, like emmer, einkorn and spelt remains unchanged through selective genetic breeding over the thousands of years since their discovery, and still rely on their natural flavour to add so much nutritional value to our modern diets, in many innovative and exciting ways.

Tea bread is very English, dating back to the 1800s and the Victorian era of afternoon teas. Traditionally made with dried fruits that were soaked overnight in black tea, the tea loaf was cooked on a low and slow heat, before being sliced and served with butter. I have added a hint of warm spice to the nutty khorasan flour, sunflower and pumpkins seeds for crunch and there is added freshness from simmering the fruits in a tart apple juice. A throwback to tradition with the modern flavours, a real treat with a cup of Earl Grey or English Breakfast tea.

Date, Apricot & Walnut Khorasan Tea Bread

Ingredients (serves 8-10):
1 ¼ cups / 170 g dried apricots
8 fresh Medjool dates
½ cup / 100 ml cox's apple juice
3 tablespoons / 45 ml water
¾ cup / 180 g unsalted butter
⅓ cup / 60 g light muscovado sugar
1 large egg
1 teaspoon vanilla essence
zest of 1 orange
1 cup / 200 g khorasan flour
1 teaspoon / 5 g baking powder
1 teaspoon ground cinnamon
½ teaspoon mixed spice
grating fresh nutmeg
pinch of salt
½ cup / 50 g walnuts
3 tablespoons / 45 g pumpkin seeds
3 tablespoons / 45 g sunflower seeds

Method:

- ❖ *preheat the oven to 180 °C / 350 °F / Gas Mark 4*
- ❖ *grease & line the base & short sides of a 20 x 12 cm / 8 x 5 in loaf tin with baking parchment*
- ❖ *pit the dates & quarter the apricots & place with the apple juice & water in a small saucepan & bring to the boil, reduce the heat & leave to simmer for 10 to 15 minutes, stirring occasionally, until the liquid has evaporated and the you have a thick, almost puréed consistency, remove from the heat & set aside, don't worry if there are still whole bits of fruit, as I like the texture of biting into a piece of apricot or date, once cooked*
- ❖ *melt the butter & add to the fruit with the sugar, beaten egg, vanilla essence & orange zest, place all the dry ingredients together in a bowl, roughly chopping the walnuts & mix to combine, stir in the wet fruit mixture & mix gently, place in the prepared loaf tin & into the preheated oven for 45 minutes*
- ❖ *remove when a skewer inserted into the middle of the cake comes out clean, place on a wire rack & leave to cool completely before serving in thick slices with lashings of butter and for a real treat, a dollop of lemon curd...*

Date, Apricot & Walnut
Khorasan Tea Bread

The resurgence of ancient wild wheats in our diets is contributing to a more sustainable way of eating, one that protects the environment and promotes a healthy way of living. More consumers are looking for healthier staples, made from natural, organic and locally grown ingredients, selecting whole wheats over refined grains, and more farmers are committed to environmentally friendly practices, benefitting from a nourishing and richer soil for future crops.

Modern wheat is the world's most consumed crop and amounts to around 20% of global dietary protein (H. Braun et al, 2010), being easily digestible in readily available and affordable products. However, in the modern wheat kernel, gluten makes up between 7–19% of the gliadin protein which causes an adverse inflamatory effect on the bowel

Wild Wheat Sourdough Breads

tissue, leading to toxicity and interference with absorption which if severe, causes coeliac disease, but more likely a sensitivity or intolerance. Described by American cardiologist William Davis as "wheat belly", this has led to a rise in gluten-free or gluten-reduced products and a food market worth over $1.5 billion. As wild wheats have significantly less gluten in their composition, from less chromasomes than the modern varieties, this is widely believed to be the reason for their resurgence in our diets and a possible solution to the widespread gluten allergies. Linked to research that the lacto-fermentation process may lower the gluten levels in bread, sourdoughs made with ancient wheat flours are heavily influencing commercial and home bakers to produce more loaves from emmer, einkorn, spelt and khorasan, in a concerted effort to improve gut health.

Eli Rogosa, an Israeli researcher and author, helped to establish the Heritage Grain Conservancy in Massachusetts, the aim of which is to protect wild wheat species from extinction, and preserve heirloom

Spelt Twisted Bagel

grains for modern diets. Rogosa considers that ancient grains provide a healthier and more ecologically sustainable solution to the problem of world hunger, as well as being more nutritious and tastier than their modern counterparts.

Chapter five

Ancient grains

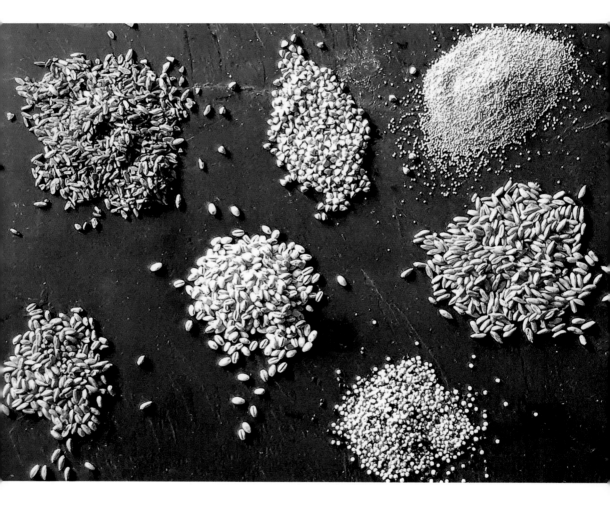

Ancient grains farmed in historical times, and known from biblical stories are making a comeback as superfoods, as we aspire to sustainable eating and a return to the staples of our hunter-gathering ancestors.

The popularity of ancient grains has re-emerged from the largely unchanged agricultural customs and practices of the Neolithic era, the start of the use of wild wheats and cereals. Grains were revered foods used in worship, as rations for armies and sailors of legendary land and sea crusades, and they gave sustenance to the ancient Israelites during their wanderings through the wilderness.

According to the Oldways Whole Grain Council of Boston, USA, ancient grains are defined as "whole grains, containing the bran, germ, and endosperm present in the same proportions as at harvest". These ancient grains vanished into obscurity when they were replaced by other crops, only to be rediscovered as healthier alternatives to modern hybrids of domesticated grains.

Concerns over international development and global efforts to banish hunger dominate the political and culinary agenda, leading to the rediscovery of old alternatives. Through sustainable agriculture in the world's poverty-stricken countries, the ancient grains of the past have established a renewed habitat in poorer soils and ever-changing climates. Crucial to economic growth, the farming of these ancient crops is fast becoming a powerful tool in the advancement of many underdeveloped countries, where hunger and famine remain a major problem.

In the 1800s major advances in the genetics of ancient wheat grains led to the Green Revolution, headed by Nobel Peace Prize winner, Norman Borlaug, who reformed both the milling and yield of cereal grain to feed "a hungry world". Also known as the Third Agricultural Revolution, various technological, agricultural and scientific initiatives from the 1900s increased global farming of wheats, cereals and rice, to provide food security in the underdeveloped, poorer countries. Despite his sterling efforts in saving over a billion people globally from hunger, Borlaug who was given the title of "the father of the Green Revolution" was often criticised for expanding the agricultural infrastructure using hybridised crops, pesticides and synthetic fertilisers to increase yields, which led to modern "dwarf" species replacing the genetic composition of the ancient tetraploid and diploid heirloom wheats. These in turn created cheaper, higher returning staples, without the nutritional value of the traditional wild genus. This was the modern trade off; more grain, less nutritional value.

Geneticists, nutritionists and archeobotanists continue to debate whether the nutritional benefits of ancient grains outweigh their modern peers. However, they are unequivocal that ancient whole grains, with their proteins, vitamins and minerals in the bran and germ, contain additional health properties that are absent or minimised in refined wheats and cereals. As a result, ancient grains are seen by chefs, bakers and food writers as a "good carb" in the modern diet, as opposed to common, cultivated wheat, which is comprised mainly of starch from the residual endosperm and results in the complex carbohydrates of processed white flours.

Most ancient grains have a much-reduced gluten content, with a structure that allows for easier digestion and considerably less bloating of the stomach, although very few of the ancient grains are completely gluten-free. Anyone with a medical gluten intolerance, such as sufferers of coeliac disease who are unable to digest gluten proteins could possibly handle a diet including some ancient grains.

Ancient grains thrive on organic but often poor-quality soil, an inclement climate and require lower levels of irrigation, helping in the quest for a pesticide-free environment. There is little doubt that the natural heirloom grains aid digestion. Benefits include the promotion of gut health, boosting immunity through their antioxidant properties, lowering cholesterol and the levelling of the glycaemic index which lowers blood sugar.

Nutty, earthy and smoky with added textures of puffed and cracked, these whole grains have a versatility in contemporary cuisine. Cakes, energy bars, biscuits, leavened and unleavened breads, salads, risottos, soups, breakfast granolas and porridges are just some of the ways these ancient grains come into play on restaurant menus and in domestic kitchens, as they become an essential store cupboard ingredient for our cooking and modern diets.

Breakfasts in the Middle East are a savoury affair; eggs, chopped salads, hummous and dips fill each plate with hunks of bread to mop up the juices. A bowl of granola with natural labane, usually made from sheep's milk, seasonal fruits and lashings of the naturally sweet date syrup, is my alternative. This recipe can include as many or as little ancient grains as you wish, or have stored in your cupboard, just stick to the dry/liquid ratio. I have used a combination of barley, wheat and spelt flakes, buckwheat groats and puffed quinoa, which gives great texture as well as flavour. The nuts and seeds are your choice too and whether you prefer them whole or chopped. The addition of tahini paste, a staple of the region, adds a sesame kick to the authenticity of the 'ancient' cereal.

Ancient Whole Grain Granola

Ingredients (fills 1 kg kilner jar of cereal):
4 cups / 350 g ancient grains
1 ½ cups / 225 g nuts
½ cup / 75 g seeds
½ cup / 50 g desiccated coconut
1 teaspoon cinnamon
½ cup / 100 ml date syrup
¼ cup / 60 ml tahini
¼ cup of honey
4 tablespoons extra virgin olive oil
salt

Method

- ❖ heat the oven to 150 °C / 300 °F / Gas Mark 2
- ❖ line a large baking tray with baking paper
- ❖ in a large bowl, mix the grain flakes, groats & puffed cereals with the nuts & seeds of your choice and availability, together with the desiccated coconut & cinnamon, adding more or less of either depending on personal taste, I roughly chop the nuts and leave some whole for a textural contrast to the granola
- ❖ mix the liquids together in a jug, adding a pinch, a bit, ½ a teaspoon or no salt to the mix, according to your personal stance on adding salt, pour the wet mixture onto the dry ingredients & mix until every flake, nut & seed is evenly coated with the dark, sticky syrup
- ❖ place the mixture onto the lined tray in a smooth, flat layer & bake in the preheated oven for 30 minutes, turning every 10 minutes or so to ensure an even brown throughout,
- ❖ remove from the oven & leave to cool, the granola will still be soft initially, but will harden as it cools, using a tablespoon or fork, break up the granola clumps while it is still warm & malleable, and place it in a large kilner or cereal jar with a good air tight lid, only once it is cold,
- ❖ it should keep for 2-to 3 weeks if you haven't eaten it all by then and not just for breakfast, it is delicious sprinkled on yoghurt or ice cream or simply delve into the jar for a healthy snack; it is my guilty pleasure when I get the 'munchies' late at night, I just can't resist the satisfying clusters of crunchy nuttiness of these ancient grains

Ancient Grain Granola

Barley

Barley (*Hordeum vulgare*) is a cereal grass that was first cultivated in the Fertile Crescent around 8000 BCE. The wild progenitor *Hordeum spontaneum* was characterised, together with wheat *Triticum*, as one of the seven agricultural species from the land of Israel in the first book of the Old Testament. Barley is cited throughout the Bible as one of the two grains that Moses offered up to God as the first fruits of the ripened crop. In the Book of Leviticus, Moses is asked to instruct the Israelites to "bring a sheaf of the firstfruits of your harvest unto the priest: and he shall wave the sheaf before the Lord" (Leviticus 23:1), which according to archeobotanists would have been a sheaf of barley, as the grain matures and is harvested earlier in the season than wheat. It has since become a significant grain during the offerings at harvest festivals, in both the Christian and Jewish religions.

Barley was given the title of "the poor man's grain". Its low gluten content and high-density texture meant that when made into bread it was as heavy as "a lump of brick". In the Book of Judges, Gideon overhears a friend recalling his dream, which reiterates this: "A round loaf of barley bread came tumbling into the Midianite camp. It struck the tent with such force that the tent overturned and collapsed." (Judges 7:13).

In the Book of Ruth, when Ruth and Naomi return to Bethlehem looking for work during the spring harvests, barley features as the prominent staple. An adaptable crop, barley thrives in a temperate climate and can survive in long periods of drought. Although we are unsure of whether the barley was a wild or domesticated cultivar, it has the ability to ripen more rapidly than wheat and therefore gave the landowner an even amount of grain throughout the year.

The Jewish festival of Passover commemorates the Exodus from Egypt when God freed the Israelites from slavery and instructed Moses to journey with them to the Promised Land. Symbolic of this week-long festival is the eating of unleavened bread called Matzah which, because of the haste in which the Israelites were instructed to leave, did not have enough time to fully rise.

American Jewish culinary author Joan Nathan, who wrote *The Foods of Israel Today* (2001), suggests that the matzah was made from roasted barley grains, picked from the early spring cereal: "The barley was ground with a flat stone; the stone was then heated with a flint stone until it was hot enough to cook the bread." For centuries, matzah made from barley was eaten during the festival, symbolising the original unleavened cakes of the Israelites. Passover was and still is in some communities known as the Festival of Spring, a likely connection to the barley harvest.

This is an ancient recipe for barley matzah, which although easy to make and not unpalatable, produces a solid, heavier cracker than the light wafer that is produced commercially, and bought for the festival. The Israelites would undoubtedly have mixed the flour with just salt and water and cooked the dough outside on hot stones, which gave the same texture, but probably with even less flavour.

Barley Matzah

Ingredients:
1 cup / 125 g barley flour
½ teaspoon salt
2 tablespoons vegetable shortening
5-6 tablespoons water

Method

❖ *mix the flour & salt in a bowl, cut in the shortening & mix in enough water to make a soft & elastic dough*

❖ *divide into four & roll out each one to about 16 cm / 8 in square and place on a hot griddle until brown, turn over & brown other side, remove, set aside & repeat until all are cooked*

❖ *keeps well if in an air tight container*

Archaeologists and culinary historians place barley with emmer and einkorn, as the first cultivated grains for human consumption. We believe wild barley grasses were discovered as far back as 1500 BCE.

American anthropologist and archaeologist Henry Field (1902–1986), began working for the Field Museum of Natural History in Chicago in 1926 on the excavation of Kish, an ancient city in Mesopotamia that was part of the Babylonian Empire of 5000 BCE and made up of around forty 'tells' or inhabited mounds. It became of great archaeological importance during the 1920s, as Field examined and documented flora and faunal remains in and around Kish. It was from his discovery of remains of charred and blackened grain in excavated pottery jars, that he formed the opinion that it was a "type of barley" judging "by the appearance and shape of the crease (slightly twisted in some kernels), flattened backs, boat-shape of kernels, and germ shape, all of which are more or less common to our modern barleys". This discovery shed light on the early domestication of barley, as cited by Dr Berthold Laufer, curator of the Museum of Chicago and a distinguished German anthropologist himself.

In the lower region of Mesopotamia circa 2500 BCE between the Tigris and the Euphrates, lay Sumaya (Sumer), where agriculture was first thought to have developed. Barley was one of the first main cereal crops to thrive on this land and become a key staple of the Sumerian diet. Barley was also fermented and turned into an alcoholic ale, the precursor to beer. Sumer was known, rather beautifully, as the "cradle of civilisation".

The origins of brewing are fragmented, the earliest records of fermenting an 'ale' dating back to around 1000 BCE. An ode to brewing, known as 'The Hymn to Ninkasi' was found etched in clay tablets in Iraq, believed to be written by an anonymous poet in praise of Ninkasi, the Sumerian goddess of beer. Ninkasi, was said to have brought a "blissful mood and happy liver" to the whole community, which represents the early signs of intoxication from the joy of drinking alcohol. The tablet is currently in the British Museum in London.

In 2018, researchers from Stanford University together with archaeologist Dani Nadel, from the Zinman Institute of Archaeology, Haifa, discovered what was controversially claimed to be "the oldest brewery" from the late Epipaleolithic era (20,000–10,000 BCE), distinguished by the Natufian culture of domesticating and farming the land. At the ancient burial site of

The Hymn to Ninkasi, an ode to brewing ©British Museum.

Raqefet Cave, Northern Israel, they found "the earliest archaeological evidence for cereal-based beer brewing by a semi-sedentary, foraging people". In among the wild barley seeds, they found residue on stone mortars containing malted barley and wheat fibres from beer served in ritual Natufian feasts. The evidence was meagre and so microscopic that carbon dating to the exact historical period was virtually impossible, but it was substantiated by other findings at the site. Remnants of wild barley were found which indicated that beer was probably consumed at these ceremonial wakes.

It was during the Iron Age (1200–332 BCE) that barley was made into bread by combining it with other wild wheats, producing a dough with a structure that would rise. The main structural protein of wheat, barley and all of the other cereal grains is gluten, with each one containing a greater or lesser amount of the individual proteins of gliadin and glutenin in the whole grain. Barley contains less of both of these proteins, and therefore produces a denser and harder textured bread, but nevertheless was regarded as one of the staple components of the Iron Age diet.

The bread was made by grinding barley and wheat together in a rotary hand quern to form a powdery flour. It was common practice for the bakers

Ancient Natufian Burial Site.

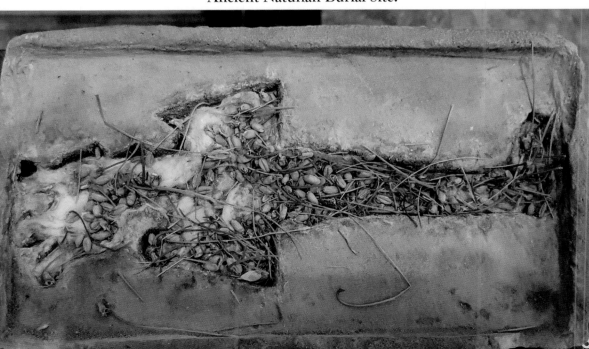

to skim off the surface foam from the fermentation process of brewing beer, which they added to the flour to create the dough, before leaving it to rise naturally in the atmosphere. It was then baked in a clay oven. Barley was also the grain of choice for porridge or gruel and malt that was made from the germinated hulled grains. The barley was left to germinate from the atmospheric moisture and sprouted in the natural environment, probably by chance, however barley is well documented as the grain used in the first beer making process, and was deemed the earliest form of the alcoholic beverage.

In an article in *Vegetation History and Archaeobotany* in 2017, Mikael Larsson, an archaeology and ancient history researcher, analysed the size of hulled barley grain discovered in Uppåkra in southern Sweden on historical Iron Age sites. He concluded that "Cereal remains from the hall-buildings show not only a strong dominance of barley, but also a tendency for large grain, a pattern that is observed already during the early phase of the house-sequence, the early Roman Iron Age." In part, this was due to the increasing popularity of cultivating barley in Scandinavia during the Bronze Age (3100 BC–300 BC), as it was known to grow well in colder climates and harsher winters. It was also known to out yield wheat, the dominant crop throughout Europe and the Near East.

During the early Medieval period, barley became significantly inferior to wheat, and cost considerably less to buy. It remained the main source of sustenance particularly for the deprived and vulnerable, who made soups, gruel and basic doughs with this wholesome cereal. Unbeknown to the poorer community, barley was a natural remedy for many disorders and contained many health benefits. Pliny the Elder wrote that "barley is one of the most ancient aliments of man" (*Natural History*, Volume IV) and he believed in its medicinal properties for curing stomach ulcers and other disorders involving the stomach, liver and blood. It was also understood that the Roman physician used barley to cure boils by taking "nine grains of barley, and traces three times round a boil, with each of them in the left hand, and then throws them all into the fire, he will experience an immediate cure".

Throughout the Middle Ages, barley flour was used by the Greeks, Romans and Arabian Empires to bake cakes and rusks, breads and fermented condiments.

Paxamus was a Greek author of the first century, whose comprehensive culinary writings endorsed barley baked rusks as the staple diet of Crete.

Paximadia were hard, round, slow baked biscuits, that were consumed by farmers, soldiers and priests, all of whom were unable to bake bread on a regular basis. Cheap, nutritious and easy to make, these biscuits had a long shelf life and sustained the poorer classes. Baked outside in ovens traditionally heated with olive wood, the paximadia were placed in the ovens for fifteen days after the ashes and embers had been swept away, producing a lower heat to dry out the bread, which was preserved by the second bake.

Galen of Pergamon, the Greek physician and influencer of nutrition and dietary medicine, modified Paxamus's recipe into a prescription of a laxative biscuit for the wealthier members of society, using pure white flour instead of the "dirty" barley flour that was consumed by the underprivileged. Taken from Andrew and Rachel Dalby's book, *Gifts to the Gods: A History of Food in Greece*, this prescriptive recipe lists the natural ingredients in drams, a measurement used by apothecaries and which equates to nearly two pounds of grain. Galen's recipe is a natural herbal remedy, using the powdered root of the greater bindweed plant, the sap or resin from the mastic tree and the leaves of the polypody fern, all which gently help to relieve constipation from enzymes in the plants that soften stool. His recipe was very basic, but believed to be rather effective...

Galen's Laxative Paximadia

take 2- or 3-drams scammony (bindweed)
3- drams mastic
2- drams celery seed
4- drams polypody (fern)
1-dram cinnamon
1-pound dough using white flour
mix and add the dry ingredients and knead carefully

Paximadia continue to be part of the traditional cuisine of Crete and can be found in bakeries throughout Greece, adapted from Paxamus and Galen's original recipes. They are made with whole grain barley flour and baked with both sweet and savoury flavourings, depending on the baker's choice and local seasonal ingredients. With the savoury version, olive oil is drizzled over the rusk to soften the hard baked biscuit, and eaten with soft, creamy cheese, tomatoes or olives. Sweet paximadia are likened to biscotti where nuts and spices can be added and served with a warm drink.

Paximathakia is the Greek name for the Cretan barley *biscotti*, the twice baked, almond biscuits of Tuscan origin, that are traditionally drunk with a glass of the Italian liqueur Vin Santo. Sweet Paximadaia are delicious when dunked in a heady cup of spiced cardamom coffee or strong cup of English tea. The flavours of orange, aniseed and pistachio in my recipe are Mediterranean flavours that complement each other with the nutty barley flour, and are not overly sweet, which is to my liking, but do try other flavour combinations to suit your taste...

Orange, Aniseed & Pistachio Paximadia

Ingredients (makes 24 biscuits):
¼ teaspoon bicarbonate of soda
½ cup / 80 ml freshly squeezed orange juice
zest from 1 orange
⅔ cup extra virgin olive oil
juice of ½ lemon
¼ cup / 40 ml warm water
½ teaspoon aniseed
3 cups / 400 g barley flour
1 teaspoon baking powder
¼ cup / 50 g caster sugar
¼ cup / 40 g pistachios

Method:

❖ *zest an orange & set aside, juice 1 or 2 oranges until you have 80 ml, dissolve the bicarbonate of soda in the orange juice & leave to react & fizz for a few minutes*

❖ *place the olive oil, lemon juice, orange juice with bicarbonate of soda, warm water & aniseed in a large mixing bowl & mix well for a couple of minutes with an electric mixer, aniseed gives a slightly spicy flavour of liquorice to the dough, however, fennel seeds, cinnamon or cardamon will work equally well*

❖ *add the barley flour, baking powder and sugar into the bowl & mix gently to form a dough, the dough will be soft & slightly oily, so don't be tempted to add more flour, barley flour has been traditionally used in paximadia, and gives an extra nutty flavour to the biscuits, but plain flour can be substituted*

❖ *turn out the dough onto a lightly floured surface and knead for a few minutes to begin to stretch the gluten, paximadia do not need a full rise, so only a few minutes is required to form a soft, elastic dough*

❖ *heat the oven to 190 °C / 375 °F / Gas Mark 5 & place a piece of parchment paper over a large baking tray, cut the dough into two pieces & flatten either with your hands or a rolling pin each piece to a rectangle of 30 x 10 x 1.5 cm / 12 x 4 x ½ in*

❖ *on the slant, cut each piece half way through the dough into 12 slices & bake for 15 minutes until golden on the top and hard on the bottom, remove from the oven & with a non-serrated knife, cut through each biscuit whilst hot, then leave on the tray to cool, the centre of each biscuit will remain soft, but as the paximadia will be baked twice, this will firm up on the second bake*

❖ *once cold place each biscuit cut side up & return to the oven 100 °C / 225 °F / Gas Mark for 1 ½ hours, until the biscuits are hard & dry, leave to cool before dunking*

Orange, Aniseed & Pistachio Paximadia

Barley bread was distributed widely through the Roman army, to sustain the soldiers during their battles, but as it was less nourishing than wheat products it became known in the ranks as "punishment rations". The malt from barley was by contrast more palatable and used in the army's beverage for all ranking servicemen. Following the fall of the Roman Empire, barley remained the inferior grain and was surpassed by rye, with its only real use by the wealthier classes as trenchers, hollowed out bread bowls that were used for mopping up soups and the juices from fragrant stews that drenched and softened the otherwise heavy, flavourless bread. The Roman gladiators believed that the barley grain bread was a good source of energy and gave them stamina and an increased strength to fight, so they in turn devoured more of the dense loaf than any other product and subsequently they were given the nickname "the barley men".

During the Byzantine Empire (395–1453) the process of natural fermentation of barley grains was utilised to add flavour to otherwise bland dishes, particularly among the poorer households, who lacked the finance for tasty, fresh ingredients. This era heralded the early Islamic cuisine that took inspiration from the Roman and Greek culinary influences, which when fused with Persian and Arabic traditions, shaped the profile for Middle Eastern flavours.

Al-murri, commonly referred to as murri or almouri, was a condiment used in 1200, made from fermented barley. It was often described in both taste and smell as that of "rotting" food. The word murri is thought to have stemmed from the Latin word for brine, salmuria, and the Greek for salty, halmyris both ancient processes that were similar to the early making of Chinese soy sauce, the salty condiment for intensifying flavour.

In his book Medieval Arab Cookery, Charles Perry describes murri as a North African condiment, which is made in a two-step process. The first process resembles making a "starter dough" from ground barley groats, which was kneaded into a paste with water and known as budhaj. This was followed by the unleavened barley dough being wrapped in fig leaves, that according to the original recipe required "male fig leaves" due to their longer, thinner fingers than those of the females. Twigs were then inserted into the dough and left for 40 days to ferment or rot and produce an intense dark paste. It was then pounded down to crumbs and a variety of spices were added, including carob, fenugreek and aniseed and placed in a large jar, which was filled with water and left in the sun for a further 40 days to allow the solids to separate and the *murri* to develop its flavour in a treacle consistency. This is the *murri* recipe, as written in *Medieval Arab Cookery*:

> Take, upon the name of God, the Most High, three pounds of honey scorched in a kettle [*nuqra*]; 10 loaves of bread scorched in the brick oven and pounded; half a pound of starch; two ounces each of roasted anise, fennel and nigella; an ounce of Byzantine saffron; cellery seed, an ounce; half a pound of Syrian carob; 50 peeled walnuts; half a pound of syrup; five split quinces; half a *makkûk* of salt dissolved in honey; and 30 [viz. 100] pounds of water. Throw the rest of the ingredients on it [viz. on the water], and boil it on a slow flame until a third of the water goes away. Then strain it well in a clean, tightly woven nosebag of hair. Put it up in a greased glass or earthenware vessel with a narrow top. Throw a little lemon from Takranja on it. If it suits that a little water be thrown on the dough and that it be brought to the boil and strained, it would be a second [infusion]. The weights and measurements of the ingredients are given in pounds and weights Antiochian and *zahiri* [as] in Mayyafarqin.

This traditional way of making *murri* was long and very laboured, so a faster less complex method was prepared using pine seed milk. This was called *kamakh* and also required barley flour to make a loaf. This too was pounded into crumbs and left to soak in water for 24 hours as opposed to 40 days, when it was strained and boiled with carob, a number of spices and the milk, until the condiment was thick and flavoured with spice. A century later, *murri* was no longer a favoured seasoning in the Islamic culinary culture and hadn't appeared to catch on in Europe as a tasty sauce to enhance the flavour of food, which culinary historians and researchers assume was due to the of time it took to make.

Charles Perry suggests that due to the lengthy process of fermenting the barley, the savoury condiment contained aflatoxins, the poisonous carcinogens that can be found in mouldy plants, cereals and vegetables, a possible reason for its demise from the ancient cuisine. He also suggested that it should not have been eaten on its own, just used as an additional flavouring, akin to seasonings like sumac, soy sauce, fish sauce and barberries.

It was during the late Middle Ages that barley became one of the most farmed crops in Europe. Barley grew well in the cooler climates of England and Scotland, however due to severe and often unpredictable weather conditions, barley harvests were often meagre, leaving many communities starving and in need of some basic sustenance. Monks, cooks and peasants became highly resourceful and devised a bread from barley groats. This became known as Hunger Bread or Horse Bread. The basic grain was ground into a coarse powder, mixed into a paste with water, before seeds, cereals or legumes such as peas or fava beans were added, as they all grew prolifically, were accessible and cheap to buy. They significantly increased both the nutritional content and density of the bread. Although it was eaten by the poor in times of famine, it really was only fit for horses.

Medieval monks began to brew ale from malted barley and used this as a key ingredient in their dough. Grown around their monasteries, they combined barley flour with ale and honey from their apiaries, which they then baked into a barley bread, resulting in a rich source of protein, fibre and energy, with an added sweet, floral flavour.

Shakespeare used the word "cobloaf" as an insult in *Troilus and Cressida,* when Ajax ridicules Thersites and his misshapen head. An old agricultural term to describe a round mass of grain, this crusty cob is rustic and full of traditional malt flavours from the barley flour and ale. This recipe is for a soft textured, nutty loaf, a far cry from the dense, tasteless hunger bread.

Walnut, Ale & Barley Cob

Ingredients (makes 1 loaf):
2 cups / 225 g barley flour
4 cups / 450 g whole wheat flour
1 teaspoon salt
1 ½ teaspoons / 7 g dried yeast
2 teaspoons honey
⅓ cup / 100 ml Newcastle brown ale
1 ½ cups / 450 ml warm water
½ cup / 50 g walnuts

Method:

- ❖ in an electric mixer with a dough paddle, place the barley flour, whole wheat flour & salt & mix to combine
- ❖ place the yeast in a small bowl & add 1 tablespoon of the brown ale to it, which will instantly activate the yeast, add the remaining ale, honey & all but 50 ml of the warm water, mix for 2 to 3 minutes into a smooth dough, adding the remaining water if needed, turn out onto a floured surface & shape into a round cob
- ❖ lightly dust a large bowl with some flour & place the dough inside, or into a proving basket if you have one, cover with a clean tea towel & leave to prove for about 1 hour in a warm kitchen, until doubled in size
- ❖ roughly chop the walnuts before removing the dough from the bowl and on a lightly floured surface, knock back the dough, knead the walnuts into the loaf then re-shape into the traditional round cob shape, place on a lightly floured baking tray & leave for a 2nd prove for 30 minutes
- ❖ preheat the oven to 200 °C / 400 °F/ Gas Mark 6
- ❖ place in the preheated oven for 30 to 35 minutes until golden brown crust is formed on the top and the base sounds hollow when tapped, remove from the oven & allow to cool before serving with a delicious mature cheddar or crumbly Cheshire cheese... and a pint of ale.

Walnut, Ale & Barley Cob

Frumenty comes from the Latin word *frumentum* meaning grain, and was a dish of porridge eaten as a daily staple throughout the Middle Ages, a period of frequent feasts and famines, depending on the grain harvest. Although wheat was usually the most popular choice of ingredient amongst the wealthier of society, with the lesser grains of barley and maize left to the poor, it was customary to serve frumenty at the lavish feasts hosted by the king and nobleman. Frumenty was originally a savoury dish of pottage; an old English soup or stew, spiced with saffron which accompanied game, usually venison. It was also made with milk or stock and served with fish, especially porpoise.

The Forme of Cury, the first English manuscript of recipes, compiled in 1390 by the head chef of King Richard's II court, describes how it was made, in the old English language:

To make frumente. Tak clene whete & braye yt wel in a morter tyl the holes gon of; seethe it til it breste in water. Nym it up & lat it cole. Tak good broth & swete mylk of kyn or of almand & tempere it therwith. Nym yelkes of eyren rawe & saffroun & cast therto; salt it: lat it naught boyle after the etren ben cast therinne. Messe it forth with venesoun or with fat moutoun fresch.

If cooking a savoury, contemporary version, this recipe would translate to a pilaf or risotto, where the grains are cooked slowly in a good stock or broth, flavoured with saffron and served with slices of venison, probably without the fat dripping...

Peasants and servants, whose diet sadly did not include venison or porpoise, would make a cheaper version of frumenty using barley simply boiled in milk or a watery stock, without any spicing or meat added to it. It was less luxurious than the frumenty pottage, yet remained a nourishing and fulfilling dish that has been given a modern makeover by contemporary chefs and food writers such as Heston Blumenthal and Sam Bilton, using dried fruits and nuts, plant-based milks and warm fragrant spices.

Florence White (1863-1940) an English writer of cookery and household subjects, and who established the Association for English Folk Cookery, described frumenty as England's "oldest national dish", although she did not advocate making it with whole barley groats, but with pearled grain, both of which softened when soaked and simmered in plenty of flavoured liquid.

I have likened this recipe of sweet frumenty to an old childhood favourite of mine, rice pudding, substituting creamy pearl barley grain for pudding rice. The barley absorbs the lighly spiced almond milk as it gently simmers and with the addition of double cream, gives the dish a rich, sumptuous texture. Toasted flaked almonds, sweet pomegranate kernels and golden raisins mascerated in a little Amaretto liqueur only add to the luxuriousness of this delightful dessert.

Pearl Barley Frumenty

Ingredients (serves 4):
1 tablespoon / 15 g butter
½ cup / 100 g pearl barley
¼ cup / 50 g vanilla sugar
3 cups / 600 ml almond milk
½ teaspoon almond essence
a good grating of fresh nutmeg
2 to 3 cardamom pods
2 slices lemon peel
½ cup / 100 ml double cream, optional
toasted flaked almonds, pomegranate kernels & Amaretto macerated golden raisins, to garnish

Method:

❖ *mix the pearl barley & vanilla sugar together in a bowl & set aside*

❖ *melt the butter in a medium saucepan & add the pearl barley with the sugar & mix well to coat all the grains, add the almond milk, almond essence, lemon peel & spices & bring to the boil, lower the heat, cover with a tight-fitting lid & simmer for 50-60 minutes stirring now and again, until the barley is soft & the milk has fully absorbed into the grain, then remove from the heat when the frumenty is thick & creamy,*

❖ *add the cream, if using very slowly when off the heat, not everyone will want the extra rich double cream added, but I am a glutton for punishment and love cream but you may wish to add coconut cream instead, which will add another flavour dimension to your pudding*

❖ *once added, return the barley to a gentle heat for a further 5 minutes, stir continuously until the cream is fully incorporated and the frumenty is warm, thick & unctuous*

❖ *serve in individual bowls with macerated raisins, toasted flaked almonds, pomegranate kernels & some thyme leaves or edible flowers for decoration, a nice crunchy biscuit will add a textural dimension to this dish too*

Pearl Barley Frumer

Wild barley is a self-pollinating diploid grass of 14 chromosomes that thrives in natural habitats and diverse climates throughout the Middle East, Asia and Africa. Ripening in early spring, wild barley has similar brittle spikelets to the wild wheats that shatter in seed dispersal, yielding only small quantities from the pick. Wild barley is arranged in two rows, with only the central spikelet of the wild grass becoming fertile on maturity. Domestication started to take place around 1200 BCE, as the climate in the regions where barley grew wild destroyed the fragile spikelets, and the farmers feared that the barley harvests would become straw, rather than ripe grain.

Farming of wild barley led to modifications and mutations of the cultivars and the production of six-row barley, which gleaned a higher protein grain, but with less fermentable sugars than the two-row barley. However, the cultivated two-row barley still flavoured traditional English ale and malted German beers. Ancient domestication of barley revealed a form of hulless barley, termed 'naked' barley, which had the husk removed from the kernel and allowed for easier digestion due to a change in the nutritional content. The grain was then polished a lustrous white which became known as pearled barley.

It was towards the end of the Middle Ages that barley was used as the main source of animal feed, rather than a basic dietary staple. The wealthy discarded barley from their diet completely in preference for wheat, while the poor turned to eating rye, which survived in colder European winters and was therefore much cheaper to buy. From the beginning of the 1600s barley was introduced to America for the purpose of brewing beer. Six-row malting barley crops were first grown in New England, due to its temperate climate. The chosen cultivars had a high level of nitrogen, producing low protein levels but high starch levels for malt.

From then on, barley became a main agricultural crop, used solely for beer production. The cultivars migrated to New York and by the end of 1900s, spread west to California. Malting barley commanded a higher price than two-row cultivars, despite a lower yield and susceptibility to disease and mould, but this variety undoubtedly produced a better flavour, which created one of Americas biggest industries. Two-row cultivars also became traditional crops for European beer production, particularly in England and Germany, where beer still remains the most consumed alcoholic beverage.

Barley flour or meal has been an ancient staple ingredient in the baking of breads or as a thickening agent in stews, gruels and soups for thousands of years. Dried, ground barley groats produce a coarse textured flour that is light brown in colour, whereas the whiter, finer flour is ground from the whole barley grain that has been polished white and had most of the brown fibrous bran layer removed. As barley contains almost half the amount of gluten as wheat, barley bread was traditionally denser than wheat flour breads, which made it more suited to the unleavened flatbreads of Middle Eastern, African and Asian cuisines. Barley flour can also be substituted for an all-purpose flour and makes a nutty, flavoursome pastry for savoury or sweet pies and tarts.

Pot barley, also known as scotch barley is the crude grain with only the outer husk removed, leaving the kernel with a nuttier flavour but a chewy texture, when cooked. Pot barley formed the basis of the customary stew, Cholent, traditionally eaten on the Sabbath, amongst the poorer communities of Ashkenazi Jews of eastern Europe. When meat was unavailable or unaffordable, the cholent was considered just as hearty and nourishing when made with potatoes, carrots and pot barley, and with the addition of spices and herbs, full of flavour. Hamin, the Sephardic version of cholent, sustained the Mediterranean and North African Jews over the Sabbath and festivals, using pot barley in the same way.

The refined pearls of barley, polished to remove the dark bran layer, remains the most common form of barley in today's kitchens. Pearl barley forms the basis of the Italian *orzotti*, which is cooked slowly in wine and stock, and famous in the north eastern region of Italy as the alternative to risotto. Barley water and barley tea make for healthy drinks from these grains, which are supposed to reduce cholesterol and provide antioxidants in abundance, and when flavoured with lemon or lime, make a refreshing drink.

Full of flavour, texture and packed with proteins, vitamins and minerals, the ancient barley grain is a healthy, unrefined carbohydrate, that is high in fibre and an excellent source of energy for a balanced, natural diet. Barley can be adapted to so many culinary dishes and is returning to our diets as the affordable grain.

Black garlic is aged and darkened by the Maillard process, a chemical reaction between the amino acids and sugars that gives it the dark, coaly distinctive colour and rich umami flavour. Sweet and slightly bitter in taste, the black cloves offset the toasty barley kernels, nutty sesame tahina in the dressing and aniseed from the fennel perfectly. This is best served warm as an accompaniment to a protein, or for a filling lunch with a glass of wine.

Toasted Barley with Caramelised Onions & Black Garlic

Ingredients (serves 4-6):
¼ cup / 60 ml extra virgin olive oil
2 onions
1 fennel bulb
1 tablespoon fennel seeds
1 tablespoon black sesame seeds
1 teaspoon cumin seeds
5 black garlic cloves
1 cup / 200 g pearled barley
2 cups / 450 ml hot vegetable stock
1 handful of flat leaf parsley & of mint
salt & pepper
micro beet leaves, for garnish

for the yoghurt dressing:
½ cup / 125 ml natural yogurt
1 tablespoon tahini paste
½ lemon, juiced
½ teaspoon salt
iced cold water to mix

Method:

❖ *finely slice the onions & fennel & place in a saucepan with 50 ml of olive oil, cook on a medium heat for 10 to 15 minutes until really soft & caramelised, if brave enough, take them to a rich brown colour, then season with salt &*

pepper, remove from the heat & place into a bowl, scraping all the juices with the vegetables, cover & keep warm

❖ *place the fennel, black sesame & cumin seeds in a small pan & dry fry them for 2 to 3 minutes until the oils start to release & the seeds begin to toast & colour, filling your kitchen with spicy aroma, remove from the heat, add the whole black garlic cloves & tip into the caramelised onion & fennel mixture, cover & set aside*

❖ *add the remaining 10 ml of olive oil to the saucepan that had the onions, add the pearled barley, cook on a medium heat for 5 minutes, mixing continuously to toast the grains, cover with the vegetable stock, I use a good quality stock pot, but you could use whatever you have to hand, cook on a medium heat for 20 minutes until tender, but still has a bite, drain & place in a serving bowl*

❖ *chop the parsley & mint, as roughly or finely as you like & add to the warm spiced onion & fennel mixture, spoon into the softened barley & mix well, adding more salt & pepper if needed & an extra drizzle of the olive oil*

❖ *make the dressing by mixing the yoghurt with the tahini, lemon juice & salt & add cold water, a little at a time to thin it down to double cream consistency, drizzle over the barley salad & add micro herbs for garnish, serve warm or at room temperature*

Warm Salad of Toasted Barley with Caramelised Onions & Black Garlic

Rye

"When he hath made plain the face thereof, doth he not cast abroad the fitches, and scatter the cummin, and cast in the principal wheat and the appointed barley and the rie in their place?" (Isaiah 28:25)

It is in Isaiah's prophetical writings that rye, or *rie* as it was first written, is mentioned in the Bible as a lower class of grain to the heralded wheat and barley. The grains were defined by superiority in order of planting, with rye on the outer borders surrounding and shielding the proud rows of the prominent crops. The ancient Hebrew word *kussemeth* was given to a variety of grains and grasses that were not specifically wheat or barley, which in the Book of Isaiah, translates to mean a "bearded grain". The same noun has been used in many other biblical translations to denote any inferior cereal to wheat, including rye and spelt.

Rye (*Secale cereale*) is botanically classified as a grass, but agriculturally grown as a grain. Wild rye (*Secale montanum*) was thought to have been indigenous to Asia Minor in the Anatolia region that is modern day Turkey, as a "weed" that flourished in amongst fields of grain crops. As a perennial grass, it did not initially produce edible seeds so was cut back in its first season, only to regrow and produce the grain seeds that became a vital food source. *Secale cereale* is not to be confused with Ryegrass (*Lolium*) which is a definitive grass genus grown on fallow ground and cultivated solely for animal feed and hay.

Evidence of the domestication of rye was discovered by David French (1933–2017), an expert in Anatolian archaeology at the Neolithic excavation site of Can Hasan III, Central Turkey in 1969–70. Remnants of grain and seed were found and "carbonized grain was discovered in an oven" which was analysed and discovered to be rye. According to an article in the Journal of Vegetation History and Archaeobotany in 1992, Karl-Ernst Behre, a German Archeobotanist, recognised that unlike most other cereal grains, rye was distinguishable not only by its carbonised impressions, but also by is sizable curvy pollen and so the findings were authenticated and verified.

The discovery of rye domestication in the late Neolithic period circa 4500–300 BCE was also made in the Carpathian Basin in Central Europe, on the findings of the Alföld Linear Pottery at the excavation, which connected the Anatolian culture with the Balkan Peninsular. A winter hardy crop, rye was farmed in this harsh terrain and became the main cereal crop across the belt of its central, eastern and northern regions by the beginning of the Middle Ages.

There remains uncertainty as to exactly when rye migrated from the Anatolian region and the Balkan Peninsular into Northern and Central Europe. Here, it grew in popularity among many communities, despite the aversion to the cereal expressed by Roman authors and physicians, who were of the opinion that rye was "a very poor food and only serves to avert starvation". Many of them felt that it should be mixed with emmer "to mitigate its bitter taste, and even then, it is most unpleasant to the stomach" (Pliny, *Natural History*).

During the later years of the Bronze age, rye overtook the cultivation of wheat and barley to become a dominant grain in the area that became known as "the rye belt", stretching from northern Germany through to Russia. Rye thrived in the climate of Europe, preferring the colder, harsher conditions and the highly nutritious soil from the fresh waters of the Danube, where the cereal crop was largely and profitably farmed. Rye was mainly cultivated for bread during this era, where the traditional breads were being baked only from rye, and would become the culinary culture of the poorer communities, with denser, fulfilling loaves.

However, rye was not cultivated without its challenges. As a "weed grain" it overtook and dominated the wheat fields and brought with it an outbreak of ergotism, a poisonous fungus that led to a crippling epidemic of this deathly disease. The damp, weedy rye was so poorly harvested, milled and stored by the farmers, that the grain became highly susceptible to the mould ergot. The ingestion of infected rye caused its victims severe burning sensations in their extremities, which led to an onset of blackened gangrene, an infection so severe that it resulted in death. This was considered a punishment from God and from where it received its name *ignis sacer* or "holy fire".

The first documented outbreak of this plague in the *Annals Xantenses*, circa 800, afflicted the inhabitants of the Rhine Valley and eastern France and took thousands of lives on route, "a great plague of swollen blisters consumed the people by a loathsome rot, so that their limbs were loosened and fell off before death."

Dr Elinor Lieber, a physician and medical historian at Oxford University, wrote an article for the *Bulletin of the History of Medicine* in 1970, entitled 'Galen on Contaminated Cereals as a Cause of Epidemics', in which she noted that Galen attributed *ignis sacer* to "unwholesome cereals". The article also cites Rudolfus Glaber, a French monk best known for his chronicle *Historiarum*, which recounts the epidemic of 994 AD and describes how "a hidden fire burnt up their limbs in a single night and caused them to drop off". This clearly referenced ergotism and with the epidemic worsening, a hospital was set up in the community of Vienne by the order of St Anthony, dedicated to care for the victims of this terrible plight, which became historically known as St Anthony's Fire.

Medieval Europe saw the rise in maslin bread, a dough that combined both rye and wheat grains, which produced a better-quality loaf from the combination of both flours. It became an acceptable staple for the lower class of society, who were able to afford more than just bran, oats and legumes, the ingredients that made up the unpalatable hunger bread that afflicted the poor, yet was avoided by the wealthy consumers of white bread, made from the higher quality wheat. It was undoubtedly cheaper to produce a combination flour, with rye cheaper than wheat, and it was a much healthier and more nutritious bread too.

William Rubel is an American culinary historian who specialises in the history of bread. In a seminar relating to maslin bread, Rubel, together with Tony Shahan a milling historian and director of the Newlin Grist Mill in Pennsylvania, suggested that the bread reflected the growing flour trade between America and England in the 1800s. They also proposed that this loaf containing both rye and wheat could have been a precursor to the sourdough starter, which was known as the pre-ferment stage when left for the natural airborne yeasts to rise the dough.

This is William Rubel's eighteenth-century maslin loaf, presented at the seminar on bread history for all the participants to bake. The initial step in making the dough produces a barm, which is a foam or sponge that is formed in the fermenting or leavening process, authentic from that era and suggestive of a sourdough starter. Once you get your head around the measurements, and have decided on the flour ratios for your loaf, the recipe is pretty straight forward. I used the *gros métail* ratio with a higher proportion of rye flour and substituted the white flour for wholemeal flour, which gave a rather good flavoured and textured maslin loaf.

Maslin Bread

Ingredients:
500 g all white flour
or: 440 g white flour + 60 g rye flour – blé rame
or: 330 g white flour + 170 g rye flour – gros métail
375 g warm water
5 g dried yeast, add to the flour
5-10 g salt (Eighteenth-century bread recipes called for a higher level of salt, but often it depended on the baker's taste)

Method:
❖ *place the flours in a bowl with the salt, make a well in the centre & add the yeast before adding about ⅓ to ½ of the warm water, stir to form a thick batter, cover with some dry flour & cover with a tea towel to let rise until*

'the sponge' has risen & forms cracks in the flour on top, circa 1 to 2 hours *

- ❖ *when the sponge is active and has risen, probably between 1 and 2 hours, mix in the remaining water, mix thoroughly & place the dough on a work surface and knead until the dough is smooth and elastic, place back in a bowl, cover & let rise until at least double in size*
- ❖ *knock back the dough by gently pressing down on the dough, form into a round or oval shape, cover & prove again until the bread has risen again, circa 30 to 40 minutes*
- ❖ *preheat the oven at to 185 °C / 365 °F / Gas Mark 4 whilst the bread its on its last prove*
- ❖ *bake for 25 to 30 minutes, the top should be golden & crisp & the base hollow when tapped*

* This is the pre-fermenting stage. Period instructions state not to leave it so long that the risen sponge then collapses back into itself.

Maslin Bread using the *gros métail* **ratio of rye to wholemeal flour**

Rye became the staple grain throughout Europe in the Middle Ages, as it was cheap to produce and affordable to all. Its culinary versatility became a traditional symbol of many of the region's cuisines, particularly in the making of rye breads.

Bread was the most reliable and long-lasting source of food during the crusades, and made up the basic rations and majority of calories for soldiers and sailors. It was vital that the rations lasted the duration of the battle or voyage, so a hardened biscuit was baked made out of rye flour, salt and water. They were called "ship's biscuit" or "hardtacks", as the sailor's slang for food was "tack" and these biscuits were so hard from days of being left out to dry after baking. There are references as early as 1190 to Richard 1 sailing from England with supplies of "biskit of muslin", made from a mix of the lowest quality flours, most commonly rye, barley and bean with added cornmeal. These dense, tasteless biscuits were part of the daily rations for all lower ranks, with the higher-ranking officers and ship's captain naturally fed a more plentiful and nutritious diet, with bread or biscuits made only of wheat.

The recipe for Ship's Biscuit is an authentic reproduction from American artisan baker Jeff Pavlik that consists only of a low-grade flour, namely rye and water, baked to a hardness and then dehydrated even beyond the biscotti to prolong its shelf life, and decrease its flavour. I tackled his recipe to understand the food rations these men endured. The simplistic dough of rye flour and water was totally lacking in flavour and once baked and dehydrated was totally inedible, unless dunked in a hot coffee or tea for a few minutes to soften. The pattern of holes was the distinctive mark of these biscuits, and certainly the best part of this otherwise dismal bake. These biscuits were inevitably the precursor to the American cracker, the savoury dry baked biscuit made with wheat or grain flour.

Ship's Biscuit

Ingredients:
3 cups / 385 g rye flour
1 cup / 235 ml + 2 tablespoons of water

Method:

- ❖ *preheat the oven to 190 °C / 375 °F / Gas Mark 5*
- ❖ *combine flour and water (this is a stiff dough, so allow to rest for 10 minutes so the flour can soak up the water, if too stiff. To mix by hand, add another tablespoon of water, give it time to incorporate & the dough will form)*
- ❖ *knead the dough for a few minutes until it is smooth (the amount of kneading is less than when developing gluten in yeasted dough, but the time & effort needed for this is often the same, as a stiff dough, it will become easier as the water soaks into the flour)*
- ❖ *divide the dough into equal pieces & hand roll each one into a smooth roll, press down on each roll with the palm of your hand until it is about 8 mm / ½ in thick (if the dough cracks on the edges or splits, then more kneading is required)*
- ❖ *make a number of holes about 12 mm / ¾ in apart from each other, covering the surface of each biscuit, but not all the way through the dough*
- ❖ *place the biscuits on a baking tray and bake for 1 hour at 190 °C / 375 °F / Gas Mark 5, opening the oven door once or twice during the baking to allow the steam to escape*
- ❖ *remove biscuits from the oven and place them on a wire rack to cool, leave to dehydrate uncovered, for up to 5 days*

Ship's Biscuit or 'Hardtack'

Over the centuries, rye bread has become synonymous with many cultures and cuisines, particularly in colder regions, where the grain thrives and is the country's main crop. It was through the "rye belt" that the affordable traditions for black bread, pumpernickel and the Jewish rye bread developed, due to its availability but ultimately its flavour, and has lasted through the generations, remaining the principal staple throughout.

The "Jewish" rye bread is an inherent slice of Ashkenazi cuisine, reflective of the colder regions of its inhabitants. Through the migration of Jewish immigrants after the Second World War to Israel, America and Australia, rye bread kept its place on the bakery's shelves, despite the agricultural decline of rye in warmer climates. From the poorer regions of Northern and Eastern Europe, rye was the affordable grain for Jewish families to make the Sabbath bread, originally called *kornbrot*, *korn* being the Yiddish for rye.

Made from a sour rye starter, the women often added stale bread, known as an *alte brot* to the dough, which added a deeper flavour and darker colour to the fresh loaf. It was considered not only economical to add the older bread rather than to throw it away, but some suggestion made by religious scholars, stated it was symbolic of preserving the sacred circle of life, in one's daily loaf. The Jewish rye bread has become famous throughout American delicatessens today, with two thick slices sandwiched between hot salt beef and mustard. The bread is usually baked with the addition of caraway seeds and depending on the shade of the baked loaf, more or less rye to wheat ratio, is placed in the dough.

The ubiquitous Russian black bread was as much part of the culture of Russia as its religious belief in the Eucharist bread, despite the challenge from the Russian Orthodox Church that the bread offerings should be pure and baked using only white wheat flour. Black bread became the staple of the Russian peasantry, not only because of its affordability but with rye being highly nutritious, maintained the poorer community's health, preventing vitamin deficient diseases, such as beriberi. Black bread has since developed into a speciality bread, with subtle flavours of sweetness from molasses, a slight acidity from the apple cider vinegar and an earthiness from the caraway seeds, a traditional pairing with rye, and served in Russia today, with butter and caviar.

The hard, thin slices of Germany's pumpernickel bread, was referenced as far back as 1500 and its particular association with the north west region of Westphalia. It was habitually made using a sour starter of a coarsely ground rye flour, which was given a longer baking time in a steamer, producing a thinner, softer crust and a tighter structure. The origins of the name of Germany's traditional pumpernickel are not entirely without humour, the word translating as "farting devil". German linguists and language historians have taken both parts of the word to form this translation from *pumpern* meaning flatulence and *Nickel* from the name Nicklaus, familiarly associated with medieval trolls and the devil. Coupled with the breads' apparent indigestibility from the starch in the rye flour, the name seems to have languished with its tradition.

Nordic bread culture has utilised rye in their doughs since the time of the Vikings. With bread being considered to be the most important part of any meal, the poorer households often only ate one meal each day, consisting of a ration of bread. In Nordic countries rye still features as their main grain, from which many types of loaves, crackers and crispbreads were made. Over the centuries, the rye grain was used as a sour dough starter, having been left over time to ferment with other staples, such as pea flour, moss or barks added to the rye for longevity or to simply bulk out the dough in times of famine. Sweet additions such as malt, molasses or sugar have become a favourite in Nordic doughs which are now often fried and eaten with smoked fish. The Nordic *limmpa* or *limmpu* is the common name across the countries for the soft, pillowy, round rye loaf.

The old, dark, lowly rye grain has lasted through the centuries feeding the poor, the warriors, the pirates and the prisoners with a dense, tough and unhealthy dough. Rye contains less gluten than wheat, and is much richer in fibre, vitamins and minerals than many other grains. It is thought to be a promising addition to our diets and beneficial to our digestive health. With a fuller flavour, rye makes the basis for a rich, crumbly pastry, soft pancakes and spiced cakes. Hand in hand with caraway it makes for a delicious, shortcrust savoury onion tart and paired with ginger and honey in easy to bake cakes and traybakes.

There is nothing like a savoury tart with melting, crumbly pastry and a soft filling bursting with flavour, which when served with a green salad and a glass of cold wine, ticks all the boxes for a light al fresco lunch. Sweet caramelised onions, earthy, nutty pastry and a mild bitterness from the caraway works wonders together and with a slight saltiness from the Gruyère, this rye tart will not disappoint with the flavours of Eastern Europe.

Caramelised Onion, Caraway & Rye Tart

Ingredients (serves 6-8):
1 ½ cups / 175 g whole rye flour
1 teaspoon salt
½ cup / 100 g unsalted butter
1 egg yolk
2 to 3 tablespoons iced cold water

filling:
¼ cup / 50 g unsalted butter
2 large white onions
1 teaspoon caraway seeds
2 eggs, beaten
¾ cup / 200 ml double cream
a grating of fresh nutmeg
½ cup / 50 g Gruyère cheese
salt & pepper

Method:

❖ *lightly flour a 25 cm / 10 in round tart tin*
❖ *place the whole rye flour, salt & butter into a mixing bowl & using your fingertips rub the butter into the flour until it resembles fine breadcrumbs, or as I do for ease, place in a mixer & mix for a minute or two, before adding the egg yolk & 2 to 3 tablespoons of iced cold water, mix to bring the pastry together into a smooth dough, wrap in clingfilm & chill in the refrigerator for 30 minutes*
❖ *preheat the oven to 190 °C / 375 °F / Gas Mark 5*

❖ roll out the pastry to ½ cm thick & line the tart case, prick the base all over with a fork, line with baking parchment & fill with baking beans, before placing it in the preheated oven for 10 to 12 minutes, remove the baking parchment & beans and cook for a further 5 minutes, remove from the oven & set aside & turn down to 180 °C / 350 °F/ Gas Mark 4

❖ make the onion filling while the pastry is chilling, peel & slice the onions, melt the butter in a frying pan & add the sliced onions, caraway seeds & some salt, cook on a medium heat for 10 to 15 minutes until the onions are soft & golden brown and starting to caramelise, remove from the heat & set aside to cool and until the pastry case is cooked

❖ mix the eggs with the cream & nutmeg & season well with salt & pepper

❖ place the all the onions into the pastry case, pour over the egg mixture & grate the Gruyère over the top of the mixture, sprinkle with a few extra caraway seeds, place in the oven for 25 to 30 minutes, until the custard has set & the cheese is golden & melted on the top, remove from the tin & serve warm with a green salad & that customary glass of wine

Caramelised Onion, Caraway & Rye Tart

Sorghum

Sorghum (*Sorghum bicolor*) is a multipurpose, gluten-free, cereal crop from the Poaceae grasses genus, that is cultivated for grain, molasses, animal feed and biofuel. Ranked among the world's top five cereal grains and central to global food production, it is one of the most consumed staples across America, Africa, India and Australia, where it thrives in the arid climate. According to American archaeobotanist and plant geneticist Jack Harlan (1917–1998), who carried out extensive research on wild plant cultivars from the Near East and their early domestication, "sorghum is one of the really indispensable crops".

A 1966 article published by the Oklahoma Department of Botany and Plant Pathology cites extracts from Hugh Doggett's *Sorghum*, "very little was known about the antiquity of sorghum as the crop was absent from the ancient tombs of Egypt and from the excavated early farming sites in the Near East".

Nabta Playa is situated in Egypt's Nubian desert, south of modern-day Cairo. It was excavated in the early 1990s, and revealed charred remains of sorghum from the early Egyptian Neolithic era, circa 7500 BCE. Remnants of wild sorghum were identified at the excavation by the size of the grains, being almost half that of wheat kernels, as well as by the brittleness of the rachis. The evidence suggested that while wild sorghum was located in this region, it was domesticated more than 2000 years later, near the Niger River, in West Africa. Anthropologists corroborated the existence of pastoral communities in the region who practised animal husbandry, and lived off wild sorghum, which they stored for their own consumption as well as for their herds.

However, in their studies on this ancient crop, Doggett and Harlan concluded that the only cultivated species, *Sorghum bicolor*, had been domesticated directly from its wild progenitors *Sorghum bicolor* subsp. *verticilliflorum* around 4000 BCE in West Africa, and not in the Near East, as once thought. This was substantiated as the domesticated *Sorghum bicolor* followed the global silk trade routes from Africa through to the Middle East and by 2000 BCE travelled onto routes into India, where it acquired its important role in agriculture and has since become the region's second largest cereal crop.

In Pliny the Elder's *Natural History*, sorghum was referenced as a generic plant of seeded grasses, and resembled millet due to the similarity in size of its kernels. However, despite making its way from India to Rome, little archaeobotanical evidence suggested that these remnants of millet were from the same ancient plant genus, but managed to have attached a significant importance in the Roman agricultural and culinary culture whether as millet or sorghum, and became the widely used grain in their cuisine. Oribasius, the ancient Greek personal physician to Emperor Julian the Apostate, described the medical benefits of millet soup, declaring "the grain was applied hot in a linen bag for aches and pains" (*Medical Compilations*, 4.7.21). The confusion of the actual name lies here as Oribasius's description of the grain was given the name of "sorghum", taken from the Latin, *suricum granum*, "Syrian grain" and the Italian *sorgo*, however this perplexity has continued, for sorghum is still known as "great millet" in Africa and "Indian millet" in Asia.

Sorghum was evidently grown in Egypt during the Neolithic era, but does not appear to have a biblical reference other than as millet. It is mentioned by the Prophet Ezekiel, who told the people of Jerusalem to use this grain with wheat and barley to make bread for their sustenance, prior to the destruction of the Temple. Millet was also used as a trade between Judah and the Land of Israel "exchanging for your goods, wheat from Minnit, millet, honey, olive oil and resin for healing" (Ezekiel 27: 17), which when deemed on a parr with wheat, honey and olive oil, stood out as a discernible grain. The ancient Hebrew word for this grain was *dochan*, a similar sounding word to *dokhan* which is Arabic for pearl millet and sorghum, a common cereal used in their cuisine for bread making and suggestive that it was originally grown in the Near East, for vital nourishment.

By 1500, sorghum was grown in China and used for both culinary and medicinal purposes. In one of the most comprehensive compendiums of the era, written by Chinese physician, Li Shizhen (1518-1593), his fifty-two volumes of *Materia Medica* extensively documented natural medicines and remedies using cereals and grains, including sorghum, boasting their scientific and medicinal qualities in healing. Shizhen travelled the country for his research, interviewing farmers and gatherers of the cereals and collecting ancient herbal therapies and "folk recipes" to include in his work. He described sorghum as two kinds of grains: "sticky ones that can be used as bait to brew wine with glutinous and un-sticky ones that can be used to make gruel or pudding."

Sorghum bicolor, which is also known by the name of "Broom corn", was introduced to the United States of America in the mid-1700s by one of its Founding Fathers, Benjamin Franklin, reportedly having made its way into the country with the West African slave trade. Broomcorn was aptly named, from the proud grain kernels that protruded from the end of the long and very upright stems. When harvested and allowed to dry out, the stalks became wiry and coarse, so the farmers bound them together to form the heads of brushes and brooms. Sorghum was then grown throughout America, favouring the arid land of the central region dubbed the "sorghum belt". Grown predominantly for animal feed and ethanol for renewable fuel, sorghum has become one of the America's largest exports and is now being produced for the emerging health food market, as a plant-based ancient grain.

A "sweet" sorghum was cultivated in some of America's southern states from the 1850s as a cheaper alternative to sugar cane and molasses. When the American south was under naval blockade during the American Civil

War, the erratic importation of cane sugar from the Caribbean was a scarce commodity, which led the farmers to grow sweet sorghum for its syrup, by extracting the juice from the crushed stalks, which was then steamed to produce the syrup. Although a very labour-intensive product, it soon became part of the sweet southern food culture, however farming declined across the south following the Second World War, and sadly the production of sorghum syrup slumped with it. Sorghum syrup and molasses are still produced and sold commercially in the Southern regions of the United States, and served traditionally as a breakfast syrup on pancakes, waffles and grits.

As another modern "superfood", the ancient sorghum grain is packed full of nutrients to boost energy levels and fight off disease, maintaining a healthy equilibrium in the body. As a cereal crop from the Poaceae grass family sorghum is favoured as a gluten-free grain, and avidly promoted as the alternative in cooking and baking for all medical sufferers of gluten intolerance, who are physiologically unable to digest the proteins in gluten. With an abundance of plant compounds, sorghum contains antioxidants that lower the risks of chronic disease. This nutritionally heavy, ancient grain contains high levels of fibre, proteins and iron as well as being packed full of vitamins and minerals, and is rapidly finding its way onto restaurant menus for plant-based diets and sufferers of gluten intolerance.

A versatile grain, sorghum has many facets including a pearled grain, flour and a molasses or syrup, giving rise to its many uses in cooking and baking. Often used as a breakfast cereal, this nutty pearled grain can be cooked as a porridge, although cooking time is much longer than barley or wheatberries and the end result is a smoother consistency, similar to millet or semolina. A true breakfast cereal, the finely ground sorghum makes delicious light batter for pancakes, waffles or crepes. As with freekeh, pearled barley and spelt, the whole grain lends itself well to a healthy salad when mixed with seeds, nuts and herbs, warm vegetable risottos or added to bulk and enhance the texture and flavour of soups. It is considered a dense textured flour for cakes, breads and puddings, but if mixed with another gluten-free flour, such as almond or coconut flour will lighten the sponge and also makes for a crumbly, short pastry, suitable for sweet or savoury pies and tarts. Sorghum can also be popped when heated in a dry pan or microwave and made in the same way as popcorn.

There is global admiration for a pecan pie, presuming one has an overtly sweet tooth... I don't, however this pecan and macadamia pie made with the earthy sorghum flour, natural sugars and salt, is perfectly balanced. If your health food shop does not sell sorghum syrup or molasses, date or carob syrup and muscovado sugar add the same level of refined sweetness, and are easier to source. Sweet, salty, rich and nutty, this is a real hug in a slice, especially when garnished with some popped kernels for added texture. This is a perfect dessert for a celebratory Thanksgiving meal, a dinner party of any night of the week if so desired...

Salted Pecan, Macadamia & Amaretti Sorghum Pie

ingredients (serves 8-10):
1 cup / 140 g sorghum flour
½ cup / 35 g finely ground hazelnuts
½ teaspoon salt
2 tablespoons / 30 g vanilla sugar
½ cup / 100 g unsalted butter
1 egg yolk + 2 tablespoons cold water

for the nut filling:
1 cup / 115 g pecan halves
1 cup macadamia halves
⅓ cup / 85 g unsalted butter
⅔ cup / 150 g dark molasses /muscovado sugar
1 teaspoon salt
3 eggs, beaten
⅔ cup / 200 ml sorghum syrup
2 teaspoon vanilla extract
4 tablespoons amaretti liqueur

for serving:
vanilla ice cream, crème fraiche & popped sorghum

Method:

- ❖ *preheat the oven to 180 °C / 350 °F / Gas Mark 4*
- ❖ *make the pastry: place the flour, hazelnuts, salt, sugar & butter in an electric mixer until it resembles breadcrumbs, I use vanilla sugar, as I always have a jar of in my cupboard & complements the nutty flavours, but caster sugar will do too, add the beaten egg & enough cold water until a soft pastry forms, remove, flatten into a disc & wrap in cling film, chill for 20 minutes*
- ❖ *toast the pecans & macadamia halves in the oven for 3 to 4 minutes, watching them like a hawk so they aren't too dark and taste bitter, set aside*
- ❖ *roll out the pastry on a floured surface to the thickness of 3mm & line a 22 cm / 9 in tart tin, place baking parchment over the pastry, fill with baking beans & bake blind for 10 minutes, remove the paper & beans & return to the oven for 5 minutes, until golden brown, remove from the oven & reduce the temperature to 150 °C / 300 °F / Gas Mark 2*
- ❖ *make the filling: melt the butter with the dark molasses & salt in a saucepan on a gentle heat, remove from the stove & one at a time whisk in the eggs, until fully incorporated, add the sorghum or date syrup, vanilla extract & amaretti, which gives a warm almond flavour, before adding the toasted nuts, mix well & pour into the tart case, return to the oven for 25 minutes or until the filling is just set but still has a slight wobble in the centre, leave to cool completely before serving with vanilla ice cream or crème fraiche*

**Salted Pecan, Macadamia &
Amaretti Sorghum Pie**

Teff

Teff (*Eragrostis tef*) is an annual cereal grass and a member of the Poaceae plant genus. Originating in Ethiopia and Eritrea, it was domesticated from wild grass over 6000 years ago, and has since become the main staple of African cuisine. Known also as William's Lovegrass, this indigenous seed was so minute it was named *teffa* in the Amharic language, meaning "lost". Tiny in stature and packed full of nutrients, this "tufted" cereal has gained huge, global recognition as a gluten-free alternative grain, and has since found a place as a healthy addition to many Western cuisines.

Teff has always been considered a dependable low risk crop. Unlike many of its ancient relatives, it has a faster growing speed and can thrive in poor soils and almost any climatic conditions. The teff seed, described by Trevor Lacey from Australia's Department of Food and Agriculture as "the smallest-grained cereal in the world", plays a huge role in the farming and culinary cultures of the Horn of Africa, which includes Ethiopia and Somalia. Sustaining a population of over one hundred million, this small, self-pollinating grain provides well over half the region's nutritional source.

In 2008, Dr Catherine D'Andrea, a paleoethnobotanist from the University of Toronto who conducted extensive research on agricultural communities in Ethiopia, claimed that the history of teff and its domestication from a wild grass is poorly understood, possibly due to the lack of remnants of this cereal in archaeological excavations. D'Andrea's research indicates that the domestication of this grass cereal took place in the pre-Aksumite Christian civilisation circa 100 BCE, and originated in the northern highland area of Tigray. Its wild progenitor was presumed to be Eragrostis Pilosa, which archaeobotanists involved in the research assumed to be a "weedy" derivative, mainly valued as fodder grass, rather than a staple grain.

Although mainly confined to the soils of Ethiopia and Eritrea, teff found its way to Yemen and the British colonies of India towards the end of the 1800s, where it was thought to have initially been grown for animal feed and hay. This antiquated grain has remained the principal crop grown in African countries as food for its populace, but due to its nutritional content, the seed is beginning to make a play in the grain market in India, Yemen, America and Australia alongside wheat, barley and rye.

Teff is revered for its nutritional value as a gluten-free grain, its flavour profile and its longevity but also because it is a sustainable crop. Regrettably, there has been little investment or agricultural development in this grass, which provides an income to farmers, maintains excellent soil health, and forms a nutritious diet for the poverty-stricken regions where it is grown. When grown for other uses, such as fodder for livestock or as hay or thatch for shelter, this little seed provides a much-needed profit for African and Indian farmers. However, it still lacks its full potential on the export market, possibly due to its labour-intensive harvesting.

Teff is relatively quick to germinate after planting, which is often later in the season than other wheats and grains. In less developed agricultural regions, the arduous and protracted task of planting these minute seeds is still performed by hand. Within a few months of sowing and before full maturation, the seeds are ready for harvesting, which in Ethiopia and Eritrea, remains another manual task, the teff being threshed using handheld tools, similar to those used for freekeh. In warm and windy conditions, the fully mature seeds can easily fall to the ground whereupon their labour, income and more importantly their annual yield which feeds and nourishes their family, is lost.

Each seed of the *Eragrostis tef* grain is made up of only the bran and germ, and is therefore organically gluten-free. There are three varieties, ranging in colour from dark brown to red to ivory, similar to the pseudocereal quinoa, with each one varying in intensity in its earthy, grassy flavour. Protein rich, full of essential vitamins and minerals, and with a low glycaemic index, this whole grain superfood is attracting attention as a global food for elite athletes, coeliac and diabetes sufferers, as well as health conscious, vegan foodies.

Teff has a culinary versatility and can be used as a thickener in soups, as a breakfast cereal similar to porridge, as a textural element in salads, and as a soft flour for baking. Steamed, boiled or roasted, it produces a nutty flavour that bursts into each dish. In India, *ragi*, known in English as "Finger Millet" is a gluten-free cousin of red teff, with many of the same uses, flavour and hue as the tiny seed, but with a different genetic makeup and genus. It is often found climbing on the superfood bandwagon that teff has recently claimed, particularly in America and Canada.

The Ethiopian unleavened sour flatbread "injera" is made from the gluten-free teff seed. As in so many global cuisines, bread forms an integral part of each meal, and injera has become renowned as a national dish. Injera is prepared from fermented dough, resulting in the distinctly tangy tasting bread, with a soft, spongy texture. Traditionally, there are only two ingredients in this flatbread, tef flour ground from the ancient grain and water. Latterly, however, salt has been added to most recipes. The batter is naturally fermented over a number of days in the same way as a sourdough starter, until the dough is almost rancid and bubbling in the bowl, a stage it must reach before it can be cooked. Injera was baked on a traditional clay *mitad*, a free-standing cooking tool that dates back to the domestication of the teff grain itself and which can still be found in some poorer rural areas, although a griddle pan is more widely used now in African communities. The batter is thinly spread over the pan, and when cooked, results in a flatbread that resembles a thickened, springy crepe. It is baked to accompany the main dish of vegetables or legumes. The bread is used to mop up the rich juices at the bottom of the plate, made even more palatable by the sour tasting flavour of the injera.

Eragrostis tef, thought to be one of our "lost crops", has been making a comeback in the gluten-free global food market. With its nutty flavour and exra nutrients, we will be seeing a lot more of Ethiopia's indigenous seed on our plates and in our cooking, together with sorghum and the ancient grains of barley and rye.

The injera flatbreads are most definitely an acquired taste. Unlike most Middle Eastern flatbreads that are soft and flavoursome from the addition of herbs, spices and olive oil, these Ethiopian fermented flatbreads have a distinct sourness to them, that does works well when mopping up a spicy or sweet stew of vegetables and pulses or in a rich creamy dip of labane or hummous, but not really on their own...

Injera: Ethiopian Fermented Flatbreads

Ingredients (makes 4 flatbreads):
1 cup / 150 g white teff flour
1 cup / 150 g plain flour
1 teaspoon salt
2 ½ cups / 250 ml warm water
vegetable oil, for frying

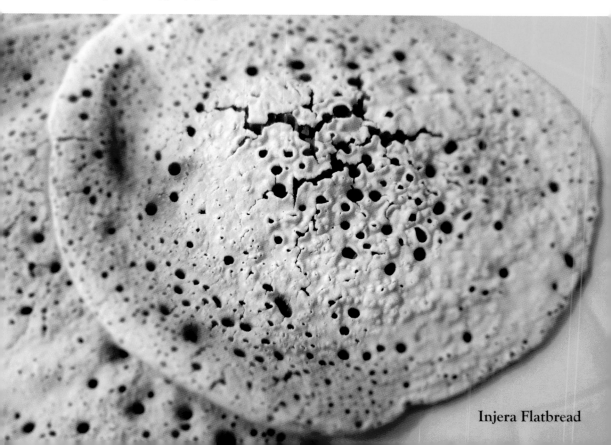

Injera Flatbread

Method:

❖ *place the teff, plain flour & salt in a medium mixing bowl & mix to combine*

❖ *in a steady stream, add the warm water, stirring continuously until a light, smooth batter is formed, cover with kitchen towel & leave overnight in a warm, dry place*

❖ *the following morning, small bubbles should be starting to form, and the batter may smell slightly sour, gently mix, cover & leave overnight, repeat a further 2 times, by which the batter should smell quite tangy and acidic & will be bubbly & spongy, mix to combine*

❖ *heat a lightly oiled frying pan or griddle over a medium heat until hot, before placing a ladle of batter into the pan, moving the batter around until a thin layer is formed, slightly deeper than a crepe, cook for 3 to 4 minutes until bubbles form all over the surface of the flatbread & it is dry, do not be tempted to turn the flatbread over like a crepe, as this is not necessary*

❖ *once cooked, remove from the pan onto a serving plate and repeat until all the batter is cooked, adding a little touch of more vegetable oil, if needed*

❖ *serve warm with lentils or a spicy vegetable stew*

Chapter six

Re-emergence

The re-emergence of wild wheats and ancient grains has seen a resumption of the debate about whether these lost staples should be classified as ancient, heirloom or landrace. The terms differ significantly in meaning between culinary historians, agriculturalists, millers and bakers, however, the definitions relating to the botanical explanation of grains, taken from the *Collins English Dictionary*, are as follows, with each claiming their place in the current revival:

❖ *Ancient: belonging to the distant past, preceding the period in history before the fall of the Roman Empire, circa 1453*

❖ *Heirloom: old cultivars, unchanged over the past 50-100 years, post World War II, 1945, handed down through the generations*

❖ *Landrace: primitive pre-hybrid grains, that have adapted to their environmental conditions over time*

It is of no real consequence to the consumer whether early grains are called ancient, heirloom or landrace. What is important is that they are a part of our cultural and culinary heritage, and that their role is preserved in our existing diet. They connect our culinary and agricultural past to our present diets, through generations of farmers, millers, bakers, botanists and cooks who have held onto the traditional values of each of the lost or forgotten grains. Even through the relentless climatic and environmental revolution, whole grains have stayed authentic in their composition and nutritional value.

The literal meaning of "landrace" stems from the German word *landrasse*, meaning "country breed", suggesting that the wild cultivars of wheat, barley and other grains from early domestication have adapted over time from their indigenous terroir to local environmental conditions, and remained in global food chains. French bakers created a flour from a landrace species of wheat called *blés de population* or "population wheats". These were grown together on the same patch of land during the farming season, allowing the wheats to adapt to the same environmental influences over the same time period. This produced an identical yield, flavour and genetic profile, giving a fixed and secure income from the wheat, on an annual basis.

Annika Michelson, a senior lecturer and researcher in agri-environmental studies, believes that "landraces were developed throughout millennia, and they are living an open-pollinated life in an open ecosystem. Only by using them will it be possible to produce food in a way that allows humans to thrive." She continues with the theory that the forgotten landrace grains of the Fertile Crescent had grown naturally in the region's rugged terrain for thousands of years. They endured the severe and unpredictable climate and survived through self-pollination and agricultural practices and customs that had kept communities and civilisations alive for centuries, mainly through the grain's principal characteristic of adaptability.

Heirloom grains are similar to landrace cereals in their characteristics and adaptation, but passed down from agricultural generations prior to the modern hybridising techniques that were introduced in the twentieth century. Heirlooms are not constrained to a locality, soil or climatic condition. Debate continues among plant geneticists and culinary historians, as to whether the heirloom grains, or heritage grains as they are often referred to, were named following a specific time period pre-1900, known as the "pre-hybrid" era.

The journey of natural rediscovery began at the turn of the twentieth century. Ancient grains were selectively bred to replicate the wild grain, but the growth and yields struggled to compete with modern agricultural practices. By the 1960s farmers throughout America and parts of Europe, benefitting from the arid climate and poor soil, began to grow the wheat and cereal crops that they believed were superior in flavour and nutritional value to the modern varieties. Reviving the growth of einkorn, spelt and khorasan was understood to provide a healthier wholegrain crop, that would start changing global eating habits and diets in the coming decades, and a decision to return to growing and harvesting grains of our ancestors. This took into consideration environmental, agricultural and socio-economic factors, well as health, nutrition and the change in culinary trends.

In order to ensure the authenticity of the crops, archeobotanists and plant geneticists looked at the early domestication of wheat, only to realise that as einkorn formed only one grain per flower and emmer produced two, neither would deliver a sizeable yield in comparison to the modern wheats. Selective domestication was undertaken with seeds from the wild cultivars together with the seeds from old and previously forgotten landraces. This produced a natural mutation of genetic similarity that would harvest a whole "ancient" grain with as much protein and minerals as the original "mother wheat". Nutrient dense, ancient grains contained three parts to the kernel, the bran, the germ and the endosperm, which unrefined or processed, left the whole grain with all its original nutritious properties. This coincided with the hybridisation of the modern wheats and the use of fertilisers and pesticides in the soil, rendering the kernels with less nutritional value and ultimately a distinct lack of flavour, which in turn increased the popularity of the ancient grains with both the food experts and the health conscious. The ancient grain revival had begun...

The early 1990s saw a shift in food trends towards a more wholesome and sustainable diet, with rising demand for "healthier staples". Attitudes were changing towards cooking, baking and breadmaking using the ancestral whole grains, as media and celebrity chefs began the conversation on their versatility, nutritional value and unequivocal superior flavour.

However, the re-emergence of the ancient grain was not without its challenges, particularly for the humble farming communities of rural Palestine, mid-west America, Ethiopia and South America, whose heritage lay firmly in traditional agricultural practises, and especially in the production of freekeh and khorasan. They were soon to find that through a new and increasing demand and mounting costs, the grains of sustenance had become the fuel of their hunger. Controversy from the grain resurgence ensued, as soon it became a socio-economic issue, concerning agriculturalists, nutritionists and public health experts, grasping the enormity of global disparity in diet equality.

The International Institute of Agriculture, founded in the early 1900s by the Polish agriculturalist David Lubin (1849–1919), was set up to advocate the world's concerns about the industry. Lubin recognised that external factors such as conflict, climate, economy and the environment were challenging the farmers on a large scale, so he set up the institute as a body of support and aid to farming communities, primarily through data collection. The Second World War saw the demise of the institute; however, with the backing of Eleanor Roosevelt, the United Nations Food and Agriculture Organisation (FAO) was established in 1945 by British economist Frank L. McDougall (1884–1958). He sought to address the hunger and famine of farmers and their communities, following years of war, starvation and economic ruin.

The organisation adopted the motto "let there be bread" (*fiat panis*) in a global effort to feed the hungry and sustain the malnourished with the principal staple for maintaining life. In the early 1960s, the FAO created the World Food Programme, which took on the task of cultivating strains of wild wheat and other ancient grains that would harvest high density yields. More importantly, the organisation encouraged rural economic stability through employment for the local farming communities to advance the export of crops and promote whole grain in their diets. Through summits and strategic planning, the FAO was committed unreservedly to eradicating world hunger by the beginning of the year 2000, and with it came the global resurgence in the ancient wheats and cereals from the fertile fields of Palestine and the Near East.

The archaic culinary practices and customs of our ancestors faded, as the grains and cereals of ancient cultivars were rekindled in global cuisines, diversifying into our modern diets as the healthy, sustainable alternative to wheat. Freekeh, barley, rye and spelt had come full circle from being one of the first species listed as offerings in the Old Testament to the popular grains of today's foodies. The cultural processes of gathering grains, roasting the kernels on open fires in the fields, hand sieving the chaff from the burnt wheat, fermenting doughs in the hot sun with natural airborne yeasts and the cooking of doughs on clay and stones, had been replaced by complex machinery, dried yeast and electric ovens, yet the natural whole grains were irreplaceable in nutritional value, versatility and flavour profile.

Ancient grains have renewed our culinary attention to the food of our ancestral roots and allowed us to return to the processes, customs and cooking methods of our past with a renewed passion and desire to recreate the food of neglected cuisines and eras. Ancient grains were often used for bland, insipid dishes, yet their revival into modern cooking has paired them with fresher, spicier and more palatable flavourings of notable dishes from history.

Gruel was always the staple of the poor, needy and sick, often made from ground barley or rye, the grains associated with hardship and deprivation. In the Victorian workhouse of Charles Dickens' *Oliver Twist*, the orphaned boys were fed on meagre bowls full of watery gruel, and beaten harshly if dared ask "for more...". Vats of the anaemic gruel were made with a little ground oatmeal mixed into a lot of water, with the occasional addition of salt or allspice. In this workhouse recipe of 1872, treacle is added, more as a thickening agent than for flavour:

16 ounces oatmeal, 8 pints of water, 4 ounces treacle, Allspice to be used occasionally, mix and boil

In his 1895 compendium *Cookery, Its Art and Practice*, the German-born doctor and biochemist J.L.W. Thudichum (1829–1901) described gruel as "thin or liquid porridge" which was "given as nutriment to able-bodied paupers". He goes on to suggest a recipe whereby "gruel may be bound or thickened with a liaison of two yolks of eggs to the pint, and then should not be heated to boiling". This recipe was supposedly put on the menu in the standard third class of the *Titanic*, as a breakfast dish, jazzed up as 'Oatmeal Porridge and Milk'.

Porridge made with nutritious grains has long been considered the national breakfast dish of Scotland. Remains of the indigenous rolled oats from the de-husked groats that prospered in the bleak climatic conditions have been found by archaeologists in cooking pots in the Outer Hebrides, dating back to over 2500 years ago. Traces of "whole barley grains stewed with milk" were stuck to the pots, suggestive that a more sumptuous cereal dish was evolving, using other cereals.

The first recipe for porridge was in the tenth century cookbook *Kitab al-Tabikh* ('Book of Dishes') written by the scribe Ibn Sayyar al-Warraq and later translated by Iraqi food historian and researcher, Nawal Nasrallah.

It was understood that his cookbook was simply compiled from a list of dishes cooked in the caliphs' kitchens, that were the served to the kings and leaders of the realm. The porridge was called Harisa and made with cracked wheat, likely to have been emmer or spelt, and made into a spiced savoury dish. The wheat was boiled in water with meat or chicken and flavoured with meat fat, cumin and cinnamon. The vat of porridge was cooked slowly on an open fire overnight and then beaten until the wheat was smooth and thickened from absorbing the meaty stock.

A. J. Arberry (1905-1969) a scholar of Arabic and Islamic literature, translated this recipe for Harisa from the original manuscript:

The way to make it is to take six pounds of fat meat, cut it up in elongated pieces and throw them in the pot [with water to cover]. Kindle the fire under it until it is nearly done. Then take (the meat) out, remove the meat from the bones, shred it (*yunashshal*) and return it to the pot. Take four pounds of good wheat which has been husked, washed and pounded, and throw it on. Then kindle the fire under it continuously from the beginning of night until the (first) quarter (of the night has passed), stirring it the whole time. Then leave it on a good fire, and throw jointed hens and sticks of cinnamon on it, and leave it until the middle of the night. Then beat it well until it becomes smoothly thickened.

Throw the necessary amount of salt on it. If it needs water, add hot water. Leave it until dawn, then beat it again, then take it up. Melt fresh tail fat and put it on its surface when you ladle it out. Throw finely ground cumin and cinnamon on it separately. Eat with aged soy sauce and fresh lemon juice.

This recipe was undeniably the forerunner of the Arabic traditional dish of freekeh, which has remained one of cuisine's traditional staples. The immature harvested wheat is placed in a basic broth, made from a whole chicken covered in water, with a few simple spices of whole black peppercorns, cinnamon bark and some salt thrown in. The stock is left to simmer gently for hours, to extract as much flavour as possible, which absorbs into each grain, a method that has never left the chefs and home cooks of the Arabic cuisine and is still very much a part of cooking in the Middle East. Aged soy sauce however was not, and a very surprising addition to the recipe, which is a far cry from the hot, spicy "harissa" condiment of the North African cuisine.

Freekeh risotto is a contemporary take on the traditional dish, cooked in Israel by innovative restaurants and private chefs, using local vegetables and herbs with the young, freshly harvested smoked wheat. I cooked up this recipe with Israeli chef and baker Avner Laskin, who delighted in combining the flavours of the Middle East and Mediterranean in one pan of delicious food, reviving the ancient grain for the modern palate.

Freekeh Risotto

Ingredients (serves 4):
1 cup / 150 g freekeh
2 cups / 500 ml boiling water
4 tablespoons / 60 ml extra virgin olive oil
1 large leek
1 parsnip
1 fennel bulb
2 garlic cloves
1 green chilli
½ cup / 125 ml white wine
¼ cup / 60 ml fresh tomato passata
½ cup / 50 g sugar snap peas
salt & pepper

Method:

❖ *slice the leek finely & peel & chop the parsnip into chunks, place half the olive oil into a large saucepan together with leek & parsnip & place on a medium heat, add some salt & stir to coat the vegetables in the olive oil, slice the garlic cloves & chilli, removing the seeds depending how much heat you want, add to the vegetables, stirring for a minute or two, leave to cook on the heat & slice the fennel bulb, stir into the mix & continue to cook for on a medium heat for a further 10 minutes, until the vegetables are sweet and beginning to caramelise, stirring occasionally & adding the remaining olive oil if it looks a little dry or the vegetables are sticking to the pan*

❖ place the freekeh in a bowl, cover with cold water & set aside for 5 to 10 minutes, drain in a fine mesh sieve & rinse well under the cold tap so that all the grit & chaff is removed, add to the vegetables, deglaze the pan with the glug of white wine & add the tomato passata, stir well to combine before pouring in the water to cover all the vegetables, simmer on a gentle heat without a lid for 10 to 15 minutes until the freekeh is beginning to absorb the liquid and starting to soften

❖ preheat the oven to 200 °C / 400 °F / Gas Mark 6

❖ top & tail the sugar snap peas & slice on the diagonal into 2 cm / 1-inch pieces, add to the risotto at the end of the 15 minutes & stir, before placing the pan in the oven for 10 more minutes

❖ the risotto will be ready when the flavours of freekeh and vegetables have amalgamated & softened, serve warm with an extra drizzle of olive oil & a hunk of fresh bread

Avner Laskin's Freekeh Risotto

It was around 1600 that the word porridge replaced "pottage", a Middle English word that defined all manner of thickened dishes that are today known as a stews, soups or broths. All varieties of grains and cereals, meat and vegetables were placed at the heart of the dish, so that the pottage was affordable to peasants as well as the wealthy. In 1723, John Nott, head chef to the Duke of Bolton who resided in St James's Street, London, was so inspired by the luxurious ingredients he used for his recipes, that he compiled a compendium of dishes which was published as *The Cooks and Confectioners Dictionary* and otherwise known as *The Accomplish'd Housewives Companion.* In his publication he describes how to make a barley pottage, possibly one of the first recipes that likened the pottage to a bowl of porridge, that has the expectations of today's breakfast dish and indulges in the use of cream, spice and sweeteners:

To make Barley Pottage.
Lay a Pound of hull'd, or Pearl Barley, to steep in two Quarts of Milk, boil it a little, then put in a Quart of Cream, some Salt, Mace, and a Stick of Cinnamon, broken into small Pieces; when it is thick enough, scrape in fine Sugar, and serve it up

The pottage was ladled into and more often than not, drunk out of a "porringer", a small bowl with one or two handles and made of earthenware or wood. For the richer of society, the porringers were made out of pewter

A 16th century Porringer
© North Carolina Online History resource

or even silver, and often engraved with the family name. The vessel was claimed by the Scots to be most appropriate for eating porridge, who by then had determined that the bowl of creamy grains, be it barley or oats, was native to them.

The weak, watery, oatmeal gruel, became a thicker pottage from the addition of coarser grains, emerging into a rich, velvety porridge made from the nutritiously whole kernels. Full of protein and rich in nutrients, freekeh and barley have revived the bland and insipid bowl of cereal, fit only for the sick and poor of society, to a far superior dish with spice, nut milks, fruits and natural syrups, all allowing porridge the affluence it now so richly deserves.

This overnight spelt porridge is an adaptation of the no-cooking method of oat porridge, quick and easy to make and ready for whenever you want to eat your breakfast, undoubtedly on the hoof... The flavours are up to you, substitute whatever you like or have to hand, but this is the easier, healthier and fresher tasting way of making porridge, to kick start your day. Spelt flakes are easy to find and contain less gluten than wheat flakes, which will still fill you up, but shouldn't leave you feeling bloated. A really modern take on a traditional classic with an ancient grain...

Overnight Spelt Porridge

Ingredients (serves 2-4):
1 cup / 120 g whole spelt flakes
1 teaspoon ground cinnamon
2 teaspoons vanilla sugar, optional
½ cup / 100 ml almond milk
½ cup / 100 ml Greek yoghurt
¼ cup / 60 g tinned apricots in natural fruit juice
2 tablespoons /30 ml natural fruit juice from tin
fresh raspberries, pomegranate kernels & toasted flaked almonds, to serve

Method:

❖ soak the spelt flakes in a bowl of water for about an hour & then drain, before placing in a plastic container with a tight-fitting lid, by soaking the spelt flakes first, this will soften the grain and make the porridge smoother and richer, add the cinnamon & vanilla sugar, if adding & mix to combine, as I may have mentioned, I do not have a particularly sweet tooth, so the sweetness from the milk & the natural fruit juice is enough for me, and I simply add ½ teaspoon of vanilla extract or bean paste for the added flavour

❖ add the almond milk, Greek yoghurt & fruit juice & mix until all the spelt flakes are covered in the liquid, put the lid on the container & place in the refrigerator overnight

❖ when ready to eat the following morning, remove the container from the refrigerator & mix well, adding a little more fruit juice if needed, place the porridge in bowls

❖ chop the apricots into quarters & add to the porridge with fresh raspberries, pomegranate kernels & toasted almonds before serving, use whatever tinned or fresh fruit you have in your larder cupboard and add raisins, dried fruits or seeds if you prefer...

Overnight Spelt Porridge

Bread has been known throughout history as the "staff of life". From the flat, unleavened cake of affliction to the gloriously fashionable sourdough, bread has emerged into our diets with a renewed vigour, using ancient whole grains and understated seeds of times past, ground into flour for the bread that we share on our tables. This has shifted the cultural emphasis from the traditional to the progressive, in all the aspects of producing bread, from crop harvesting, milling of the grain, fermentation for the dough and baking of the loaf.

Bread unites and divides in equal measure, and the grain, colour, texture and flavour of each loaf tells of the social standing of the baker and the consumer. Bread and health have long been closely associated, going back to 1895 when it was evocatively described by the physician J.L.W. Thudichum, who wrote equally on cookery and medicine:

> The tests of a good bread are that is should have a flinty, light-brown crust... it should be spongy on fracture; and the bubbles of the sponge should be uniform in size; it should be white in colour; agreeable in smell and taste, sweet and nutty.

He clearly states the colour of bread "should" be white; the loaf of social standing from 1700 to 1800. White bread was baked for only those who could afford the finely milled flour, refined to purity from the removal of the undigestible husks surrounding the whole grains. Brown bread was discarded to the poor, vulnerable and villains, as a cheap way to feed all lower classes. With the bran, germ and endosperm of the grain intact, the brown bread was considered unhealthy and unpalatable, despite paradoxically sustaining life. Bread was to become the main influencer in culinary trends, dividing nations on the choice of grain and nutritional values, driving a wedge between race and class in what was to become America's "social marker". The debate over the benefits of white over brown raged throughout the decades with inequality at its core. The once white fluffy loaf of the upper classes, became the "trash white" of the poor, with all traces of the ancient, whole and nutritious grain removed from the thin, sliced, crustless bread and churned out by industrial bakeries at a fraction of its original cost. As with so many other commodities, bread became a determination of fashion and worth to all consumers, acknowledging culinary diversity back into our diets and the choice for a healthier grain.

By the end of the 1900s bakers from every corner of the world, whether baking in large commercial bakeries, small handcrafted bread shops or modest domestic kitchens, took the art of bread making to new heights, in a global effort to revive the culinary traditions of previous millennia. Grain scientists, food anthropologists, chefs and food writers were the voice behind ensuring the grains of our heritage became part of our modern diet, which would help to combat the growing concerns of obesity, starvation and malnutrition from the world's largest cash crop. The real challenge came in tempting the lower classes to invest in wholesome, nutritious eating for their future health benefits, but at an affordable price.

Food insecurity and sustainable eating has remained on the political agenda and the reintroduction of ancient grains into global food chains, allows for the affordable, more nutritious cereals that have been part of our diet since the hunter gathering communities, secure nutritious food and stabilise economies, for generations to come.

In 1870, Moshe Rozental, a young Polish immigrant arrived in Palestine, only knowing how to bake bread and bagels, made predominantly from rye flour. He sold his handmade loaves in the markets on the outskirts of Jaffa, until he managed to scrape enough money together to open a bakery in the small town of Petah Tikva. Five generations later, Hagay Ben Yehuda has maintained his traditional roots and set up an artisan bakery adjacent to his house on Kibbutz Einat, not far from where his great, great grandfather first started out. Hagay focuses on producing sourdough breads from ancient whole grains, that have been sieved in his original Breton Stone Mill.

Moshe Rozental's Bakery, Petah Tikva, 1870.

Frenchman Samuel Polan built this style of stone mill, called 'Atelier Pais' to maintain the nutrients and above all flavour from the whole grain, by separating the bran, from the germ and the endosperm. Hagay Ben Yehuda's bakery bakes wholesome, delicious sourdough breads, made from a variety of ancient wheats including emmer, einkorn and the Swiss "yellow" wheat, all handcrafted before being baked in a traditional stone oven. Although these whole grains contain less gluten than modern wheats, the remaining gluten needs to have broken down sufficiently in the fermentation process to create a fluffy, even rise.

As a fifth generation baker reviving the ancient grains, the sourdough of his ancestors is made from Polish wheat, as well as from the ancient emmer and einkorn, handcrafting individual loaves, whilst reviving the family traditions of artisan bakers for Tel Aviv restaurants and modern foodies.

Our culinary history emphasises, that wild and whole grains have been consumed as part of the ancient diets of many lost and forgotten civilisations.

Ancient Wheats, Modern Sourdough

Various methods of crushing or pounding the kernels were used to make the grains more palatable and easier to digest, but not withstanding preserving the health benefits of the grain. As the refining process of the modern wheats stripped the grain of its bran and germ, it left only the endosperm, the part of the grain containing the least amount of nutrients and the highest amounts of carbohydrates. The whole grain scraps that were discarded to the poor, unwittingly contained all the nutrients, despite the refined cereal, commanding the cost. The issue of cost remains a concern for artisan baker Hagay Ben Yehuda, who realises the price of reviving these ancient grains is one that the consumer is not always prepared to pay, despite the quality and nutritional value in the bread. Because of the modest yields of most of the true ancient grains and the cost of importing and milling, an extra 50% is placed on each loaf to ensure a meagre profit to the baker, which despite flavour and trend, is not always sustainable in current economical climates.

When industrial milling began refining the ancient whole grains, the process of modification from the grain's natural structure removed the majority of the healthy components, which after further harsh mechanical pulverisation of the remaining endosperm, a starchy white flour emerged, bereft of all nutrients and capable of damaging the health of the nation. The refinement process was introduced to produce a fine textured flour that became known as the "all-purpose flour" with a longer shelf life for all its baked products. This business advancement emanated nutritional deficiencies through the lack of essential vitamins, minerals and iron and the advancement of serious disease. During the 1940s, governments stepped in and began demanding refined grains be fortified with vitamin B, folic acid and riboflavin, and so it became law for bakeries and bakers to use enriched grains from then on. However, the dietary fibre that was an essential part of the whole grain, remained absent and unable to be replaced through enrichment, continued to be a source of concern to physicians and dieticians, but which is gradually fading, due to the re-introduction of whole grains into our diets.

However, towards the end of the 1990s, a surge in obesity particularly amongst children resulted, together with the rise of type 2 diabetes, prevalent primarily amongst the poorer communities of Western countries, whose diets lacked the dietary fibre required to maintain blood sugar levels, a lower cholesterol and a feeling of fulfilment. A calorie-dense, nutritionally compromised, high carbohydrate diet was set to wreak havoc on both the body and mind. This set off the global campaign for healthy eating and the call for the reinstatement of whole grains into our diet, uncompromising in nutrients, oils and requirements for healthy living.

The revival of ancient grains has been influenced by their health properties, the reduction or absence of the natural protein gluten, versatility in cooking, their flavour profiles and the global trend of returning to our culinary heritage and cooking "grandma's recipes". The grains from our historical, biblical and cultural traditions allow the cook and baker an insight into the ingredients and methods of cooking from our ancestral roots together with the social culture of sharing what food they had, irrelevant of class, background or circumstances. The grain culture has become part of the wider issue of globalisation with the ancient cuisines no longer stuck in past traditions, but modernised for future generations through technology, ingredients and culinary influencers.

Evolution has been significant in the re-emergence of the ancient grains, making the wild genus of the whole kernels and seeds tastier than the modern hybrids, that have had the flavour bashed out of them. However, the rudiments of baking, created a barrier for even the most experienced of bakers using emmer, einkorn and other ancient grains, due to the wheats structure, gluten elasticity and crumb texture. With poor agricultural yields, leading to reduced production, it was the artisan pioneers of baking who promoted the whole grains in speciality breads, which inevitably tasted far superior but came with a hefty price tag attached. Flours, ground from freekeh, spelt and rye were beginning to appear in supermarkets and not just on the shelves of health food shops as chefs, bakers and home cooks returned to their family roots, experimenting with flavours and textures and recreating the recipes of forgotten eras, in a bid to bring the generations of culinary culture to the family table.

The return of the ancient grain coincided with the growing trend in healthy eating and the plant-based diet, a throwback to the hunter gatherers before the dawn of agriculture. Grain scientists advanced their research in the chemistry of the characteristics of the ancient grains and the nutritional components influenced by the poor yielding crops, confirming the health effects from whole grains in the making of bread. The production of ancient grains and flours increased globally and the baking industry took to new heights in the form of natural yeast starters for sourdough bread, which saw whole meal and whole grain loafs piled high on bakery shelves. Freekeh, emmer, einkorn, barley, rye, sorghum, khorasan and teff have been called "supergrains", and become part of the contemporary global diet, taken to new heights by innovative chefs and bakers, whose menus and creations return the eater to their original culinary heritage, with modern twists to delight the palate.

A classic example of an old-fashioned humble dish made from basic ancient grains that has become a modern influencer, is the biblical dish known as Ezekiel bread. A variety of grains and legumes made up the recipe that became known as the prophet's bread, included "wheat, barley, beans, lentils, millet, and spelt" (Ezekiel, 4:9).

This heavy blend of starch was considered by culinary historians to have been more like a stew of wheat, pulses and plants, rather than a dough, but kept to the original ancient Hebrew language, that called it bread. Although packed full of nutrients, proteins and vitamins, this amalgamation of staples cooked in water, provided an unappealing plate of food and considerably lacking in taste, but fulfilling to those that survived on it.

In contrast to this ancient interpretation, Ezekiel bread has become a health food phenomenon in the United States, using the nutritional powerhouse of germinated sprouting grains for its base. Sprouted grains are whole wheat kernels that have germinated from both heat and moisture, budding tiny shoots off the seed and allowing for the nutrients of the whole grain to be

Ezekiel Bread, The Old (left) & The New (right).

readily absorbed, adding flavour and texture to the whole grain loaf.

Ezekiel bread is an illustration of how the grains and cereals from historical diets have transitioned over the centuries into food for healthy eaters, whilst embracing the ancient processes of fermentation, baking and cooking, creating food that is also more appealing to the eye and the palate.

This recipe uses the traditionally harvested freekeh soaked in boiling water to make a healthy salad. It is best made with freshly harvested freekeh, which still has the smokiness from the roasting process. Cooking outside with Hanadi Higress and Amal Badarny from the Arab town of Sacknin in the Galilee, this dish was easy to prepare and even easier to eat. Full of textures and fresh flavours, this salad often accompanies the traditional freekeh soup at the Iftar meal during Ramadan, whilst savouring the memories of this ancient process.

Arabic Freekeh Salad

Ingredients (serves 6):
1 cup / 150 g freekeh
2 cups / 500 ml boiling water
1 bunch of long-stemmed spring onions (4-5)
1 bunch of fresh spinach, rocket or jarjir
1 red onion
1 red, yellow & green pepper
2 mini cucumbers
1 bunch of basil
4 tablespoons / 60 ml extra virgin olive oil
1 lemon
1 tablespoon sumac
salt & pepper
½ cup / 65 g pinenuts or almonds
for the tahina dressing:
½ cup / 120 ml tahini paste

½ lemon
1 teaspoon salt
½ cup / 125 ml cold water

Method:

❖   rinse the freekeh well under running cold water to remove any remnants of ash
    or grit, drain & place the freekeh in a bowl, cover with boiling water & set aside
    for 15 to 20 minutes, similar to how you would soften couscous or burghul

❖   prepare the salad by washing the vegetables and leaves well, and finely slicing
    the spring onions, including the green parts of the onion, the spinach, rocket
    & basil, jarjir is an edible leaf from the wild rocket family, indigenous to the
    Middle East and with a mild peppery flavour, you can substitute watercress
    or lettuce or whatever is available, roughly chop the red onion, peppers and
    cucumbers into cubes & add everything into a large salad bowl, mixing well
    with your hands

❖   put 2 tablespoons of olive oil into a saucepan with the pinenuts or sliced
    almonds, toast on a medium heat for a few minutes until golden brown, keep
    your eye on them and stir regularly as they with burn if you neglect them, I

Arabic Freekeh Salad

love the combination of both nuts with this salad, but if you have only the one or other nuts & seeds available, they work just as well

❖ *make the tahina dressing; place the tahini paste in a bowl, add the juice of half a lemon & the salt, mix well then slowly pour in the cold water, mixing continuously until you have the consistency of double cream, set aside*

❖ *assemble the salad; the freekeh should by this time have absorbed almost all of the water & soft enough to add to the salad, take handfuls of the freekeh out of the bowl, squeezing any excess water if any and scatter liberally across the top of the salad, add the nuts and drizzle the tahina all over the top... simply delicious as an accompaniment to any dish or on its own with bread*

Retired professor of Grain Science, Sir Geoff Palmer, who has extensively researched the processes that turned ancient grains into malt for brewing, opened the *Encyclopaedia of Grain Science* with the words: "Grains are the staff of life. Mindful of this, it is impossible to contemplate a world devoid of grain".

As grain has always been the foundation for sustaining life, it is indeed unimaginable for the tiny seeds and kernels of wheat, barley and indeed all the grains of our ancestry to disappear from our diets. We cannot forget the culinary traditions and cultural processes of the hunter-gatherers, the first farmers from our historical and biblical heritage, who threshed the grains by hand and roasted them over open fires to stave off hunger and bring out the flavour of each grain.

Freekeh was a lost crop from the Fertile Crescent. Within lush areas of the Middle East including Northern Israel, Lebanon and Egypt, the seasonal harvesting of the immature green wheat remains of cultural importance to the Arabic farmers, providing the staple grain for the coming year, as well as financial stability. The seasonal work of winnowing and roasting of the kernels on the open field fires are as traditional now as from when freekeh was first thought to exist as "kali", together with the eternal memory of sharing the grain with those in need.

"When thou cuttest down thine harvest in thy field, and hast forgot a sheaf in the field, thou shalt not go again to fetch it: it shall be for the stranger, for the fatherless, and for the widow: that the LORD thy God may bless thee in all the work of thine hands" (Deuteronomy 24:19).

The re-emergence of ancient grains into our cooking, diets and lifestyle have fostered memories from our historical and biblical ancestors, the forgotten agricultural traditions and practices of ancient civilisations and a desire to commemorate the culinary heritage at our table. The anthropology of food links the vanished crops to the current global issues of food chains and production, with a narrative that evokes a passion for cultivating these forgotten cereals and the ancient cuisines they once belonged to. With healthy and sustainable eating on all food agendas, returning to the grains of our past evaluating our current eating habits, is crucial to preventing disease, hunger and economic collapse.

Recipe developers, chefs and food writers are influencing what we eat and cook, while championing local farmers and businesses selling seasonal, organic produce in every corner of the world. Cereals, grains and seeds of the forgotten past are an increasing part of our culinary future. With their versatility, breads, soups, salads, cakes and pastries made with freekeh, wild wheats and the resurging ancient grains provide a delicious pathway for the healthy and modern diet.

Ancient Wheat Harvesting

Recipes

Breads & pancakes
Soups & salads
Mains & sides
Cakes & biscuits
Desserts

Breads & pancakes

Freekeh flour is a whole wheat flour, that has the distinctive smoky flavour from the roasting of the immature kernels on open fires. It can be used for baking bread, cakes and pastry in the same way as all-purpose wheat flours. As a speciality flour, it is not sold in supermarkets or wholefood shops, but the cracked wheat is readily available, so simply grind the kernels in a spice or coffee grinder and make your own. This is an easy bread to make and full of flavour.

Gruyère & Thyme Freekeh Soda Bread

Ingredients (makes 1 loaf):
1 ½ cups / 200 g freekeh flour
2 ½ cups / 300 ml wholemeal flour
1 teaspoon salt
2 teaspoons bicarbonate of soda
2 cups / 500 ml buttermilk
1 egg, beaten
1 cup / 200 g Gruyère cheese, finely grated
1 teaspoon sweet paprika
2 tablespoons lemon thyme leaves
handful of pumpkin seeds

Method:

❖ *preheat the oven to 180 °C / 350 °F / Gas Mark 4*
❖ *dust a cast iron pan with wholemeal flour & set aside*
❖ *in a large mixing bowl, place the freekeh & wholemeal flours, salt, bicarbonate of soda, Gruyère cheese, sweet paprika & thyme leaves & mix to combine, I like the flavour of lemon thyme, but use any thyme you have in the garden or your refrigerator, or rosemary if you prefer*
❖ *whisk the beaten egg into the buttermilk & pour into the dry ingredients, buttermilk is easy to make, as explained in Emmer Soda Bread with Za'atar & Parmesan (see pp. 106-7)*
❖ *mix the dough until it all comes together, without over mixing, turn the dough out onto a lightly floured surface & give a couple of quick kneads,*

before shaping into a round & placing it in the floured cast iron pot

❖ *with a sharp knife, score a cross about 25 mm / 1 in deep through the top of the loaf & sprinkle with pumpkin seeds, place a tight-fitting lid on top*

❖ *place in the preheated oven for 30 to 35 minutes until golden brown, remove from the oven & check the loaf is done by tapping the base, which should sound hollow, allow the bread to cool for 5 to 10 minutes & serve warm with lashings of butter & a hunk of good cheese*

The round "cob" was a popular bread in Middle England, served at feasts and banquets as an edible bowl to hold soup or stews, and eaten at the end once sodden from the flavoursome broths. It was believed to have preceeded the sourdough in England and was much simpler to make. Wholemeal emmer flour pairs perfectly with the earthiness of the walnuts and enhances the nutty flavour of the wild wheat.

Wholemeal Emmer Wheat & Walnut Cob

Ingredients (makes 1 loaf):
4 cups / 500 g wholemeal emmer flour
1 teaspoon dried yeast
1 teaspoon sugar
1 teaspoon salt
1 ½ cups / 350 ml warm water
2 tablespoons / 30 ml walnut oil
¾ cup / 75 g walnuts + a few extra for garnish

Method:
❖ *place the emmer flour, yeast & sugar in a large bowl & mix to combine*
❖ *pour in the warm water & mix gently with a blunt knife until a lumpy dough begins to form, add the salt & walnut oil & bring everything together with your hands to form the dough, turn out onto a floured surface and*

knead for about 5 minutes until smooth & elastic, place in a floured bowl or proving bowl if you have one, cover with a tea towel & leave for 1 hour in a warm kitchen to rise

❖ *turn the dough out onto a floured surface & knock back the dough a couple of times before adding the walnuts, knead through until evenly mixed throughout*

❖ *place the dough on a lightly oiled or floured baking tray, cover with a tea towel & leave to rise for a further 30 minutes*

❖ *preheat the oven to 200 °C / 400 °F / Gas Mark 6*

❖ *place in the preheated oven for 30 to 35 minutes until the crust is golden brown & the bottom sounds hollow when tapped, remove from oven & leave to cool*

❖ *serve for lunch with some hard cheese, celery & walnuts and a glass of chilled white wine*

Wholemeal Emmer Wheat
& Walnut Cob

S aidel's Jewish artisan baking centre in Israel's West Bank is the leading expert in the baking of traditional biblical breads using the indigenous wild wheats and ancient grains. Their recipe for barley bread is rich in nutrients from the barley and whole wheat flour, and flavoured with warm spices of turmeric, an ancient root used in herbal remedies for centuries. The loaf has a light textured crumb and is fragrantly spiced. Serve alongside soups and stews.

Saidel's Spiced Barley Bread

Ingredients (makes 1 loaf):
1½ cups / 180 g barley flour
1½ cups / 180 g whole wheat flour
1½ cups / 350 ml warm water
1½ teaspoons dried yeast or 5 g fresh yeast
2 teaspoons salt
½ teaspoon turmeric
½ teaspoon ground coriander
½ teaspoon garlic granules
½ teaspoon za'atar spice

Method:

❖ *in a large mixing bowl or electric mixer with dough paddle, place the flours, salt & spices & mix to combine, za'atar spice blend is made from the za'atar plant which is a member of the marjoram and oregano family, so if you don't have any za'atar in your cupboard, you can use dried oregano or finely chopped oregano leaves*

❖ *place the yeast in a jug & pour over the warm water, mix well before pouring into the dry ingredients, mix to form a dough & knead on a floured surface for 10 minutes, or in the electric mixer for 5 minutes until the dough is elastic and smooth, place in a lightly oiled or proving bowl, cover with a clean tea towel & leave to prove for 30 minutes in a warm kitchen*

❖ *knock back the dough & shape into an oval loaf, lightly dust the base of a rectangular 1 kg loaf tin with whole wheat flour, before placing the dough inside, leave for a second prove for 90 minutes*

❖ *preheat the oven to 200 °C / 400 °F / Gas Mark 6*

❖ *place in the preheated oven for 30 to 35 minutes until the crust is golden brown, remove from the oven, checking the loaf is done by tapping the base, if baked it should sound hollow, allow the bread to cool & serve with a bowl of warming soup*

As an ex-student of Leiths cookery school, I have always used their cookery bibles for certain recipes, in particular their pastry. I adapted this recipe from the *Leiths Baking Bible*, which produces a bread that is similar in colour and texture to the traditional Russian Black Bread. Rye bread has a distinct flavour profile with extra richness from the additions of the bittersweet date syrup and cocoa powder. The plump golden raisins add a softness to the texture of the loaf, that are randomly scattered throughout.

Rye & Golden Raisin Sourdough

Ingredients (makes 1 loaf):
for the starter:
1 teaspoon dried yeast
½ cup / 150 ml warm water
2 tablespoons date syrup
1 cup / 120 g strong bread flour
4 tablespoons / 55 g dark rye flour

for the dough:
½ cup / 55 g rye flour
½ cup / 55 g strong bread flour
½ cup / 55 g strong whole wheat flour
2 tablespoons / 30 g cocoa powder
1 heaped teaspoon salt
2 teaspoons dried yeast or 10 g fresh yeast
2 tablespoons / 30 g butter, melted
2 tablespoons / 30 g light brown sugar

⅓ cup / 50 to 75 ml warm water
½ cup / 75 g golden raisins

Method:
For the starter:
❖ mix the teaspoon of yeast into the warm water & add the date syrup, pour into a mixing bowl & add the flours, mix to combine, cover with cling film & leave in a cool place overnight to activate

For the dough:
❖ place the flours, cocoa powder & salt together in a mixer bowl with a dough hook add the starter & 2 teaspoons of yeast & mix briefly, add the melted butter, sugar & enough warm to water to bring the dough together, start with about 50 ml and very slowly pour in a little more as you need it to make the dough smooth and pliable, knead for 5 minutes in the mixer or 10 minutes by hand, place in a lightly oiled or proving bowl, cover with cling film or a tea towel & leave to prove in a warm place until doubled in size
❖ knock back the dough on a floured surface & add the raisins randomly throughout, knead into the dough for a further minute or two until evenly distributed, then shape into an oval loaf & place on a lightly oiled or floured baking tray, leave for a 2nd prove for 30 minutes until the dough is soft & pillowy
❖ preheat the oven to 190 °C / 375 °F / Gas Mark 5, slash the top of the loaf on the diagonal 3 times about 1 cm / ½" deep & place in the preheated oven for 30-35 minutes until the crust is a rich brown and the loaf sounds hollow when the base is tapped, cool before eating with soft creamy cheese & bitter leaves

I long for the beginning of the British Spring and for the pungent aroma of wild garlic wafting through woodland and gardens, to be picked and turned into pesto, butter and salads. A close relative of the onion, the versatile, edible leaves of the *Allium ursinum* are used to wrap around the cheese of Cornish Yarg, as well as to flavour pastry, breads and these delicious scones, which can be eaten straight from the oven with a bowl of soup or lavishly spread with butter or cream cheese and served for afternoon tea.

Wild Garlic & Cheddar Spelt Scones

Ingredients (makes 8-10 scones):
1½ cups / 175 g spelt flour
1 teaspoon baking powder
1 teaspoon salt
1 teaspoon sweet paprika
½ teaspoon caster sugar
¼ cup / 45 g butter
¾ cup / 75 g mature cheddar cheese
2 tablespoons / 30 ml milk
¼ cup / 50 ml natural yoghurt
1 large handful / 10 g wild garlic leaves
1 egg, beaten + 12 small 1 to 2 inch wild garlic leaves

Method:
❖ *preheat the oven to 200 °C / 400 °F / Gas Mark 6*
❖ *line a baking tray with parchment paper or dust with flour*
❖ *place the spelt flour, baking powder, salt, paprika & sugar into a large*

Wild Garlic & Spelt Scones

mixing bowl & stir to combine, add the butter & with your fingertips rub into the dry ingredients until it resembles fine breadcrumbs, grate the cheese & add into the mix, chill for 5 to 10 minutes in the refrigerator

❖ place the milk, yoghurt, wild garlic leaves & a pinch of salt into the bowl of a mini food processor & pulse until the leaves are finely chopped and the liquid is flecked green from the leaves, pour into the chilled dry ingredients & bring together to a soft dough using a palate knife or your hands, be gentle and do not overmix as this will prevent the light fluffy texture of the scone, cover with cling film & set aside to rest for 10 minutes

❖ turn the dough out onto a floured surface & roll the scone dough into a circle 3 cm thick, using a 5 cm cutter, stamp out the scones, reforming the dough until all is used up, place the scones on the tray, brush the tops with the beaten egg & place a small wild garlic leaf on top of each scone for decoration, place in the oven to bake for 12 to 15 minutes or until risen and golden, remove from the oven & serve warm with butter

Flatbreads are unleavened doughs made from flour and water that originated in Ancient Egypt. They date back to pre-agriculture when wild wheats and wild barley were gathered, ground by hand into flour and formed the staple diet of many ancient cultures. Every cuisine has their own interpretation of the flatbread, using native flours, leavening agents and flavourings. The mix of za'atar with extra virgin olive oil is a traditional topping in Arabic cooking, which lends itself well to the nuttiness of khorasan flour, which is now grown in the fields of central Israel.

Khorasan Flatbreads with Za'atar

Ingredients (makes 4 flatbreads)
2 cups / 250 g khorasan flour
1 teaspoon dry yeast or 7g fresh yeast
½ cup / 180 ml warm water
3 tablespoons / 45 ml extra virgin olive oil
1 teaspoon salt

for the za'atar topping
6 tablespoons / 75 ml extra virgin olive oil
4 tablespoons za'atar spice blend

Method:

❖ *place the flour into a large mixing bowl, mix the yeast with the warm water then add to the flour, lightly mix to a lumpy paste, add the oil & salt & mix together with your hands to form the dough*

❖ *knead for about 5 minutes, until soft, smooth and elastic, then transfer the dough into a clean, lightly oiled bowl, cover & leave to prove for 1-2 hours in a warm, dry place, until double in size*

❖ *on a lightly floured surface, knock back the dough lightly to release some air & knead again for a further 5 minutes, cut the dough into 4 equal pieces & roll into balls*

❖ *lightly flour a large baking tray, then roll each dough ball into a flattened circle approximately 10 cm / 4" with either a rolling pin or your hands, depending on how rustic you want them to look, place on the baking tray evenly apart & cover with a clean tea towel, leave to rise for 30 minutes*

❖ *preheat the oven to 200 °C / 400 °F / Gas Mark 6*

To make the za'atar topping:

❖ *put the za'atar spice blend in a small bowl & add the extra virgin olive oil, mix well to make a smooth paste & set aside*

❖ *once the flatbreads have had their final rise, spread the za'atar paste liberally onto each piece of dough, then place in the preheated oven for 8-10 minutes until golden brown, puffed up & slightly crisp at the edges, serve warm with hummus, labane or tahina*

Jowar is the Hindi name for sorghum, used primarily as the staple grain across India. Sorghum is from the flowering plant family, known as Poaceae and therefore naturally gluten-free, used as the alternative to wheat. Packed full of nutrients, sorghum is grown as much for its human grain consumption as for its animal fodder. Jowar flatbreads, also known as *roti* or *dosa* are the staple food across India using the gluten-free jowar flour. They are served at almost every meal to accompany curries and chutneys.

Jowar Flatbreads

Ingredients (makes 8 flatbreads):
2 cups / 250 g jowar (sorghum) flour + extra for dusting
1 ½ cups / 375 ml water
1 teaspoon salt

Method:

❖ *in a medium saucepan, bring the water to a rolling boil with the salt before slowly adding the flour & mixing continuously to incorporate all the flour and to form a dough, similar in consistency to choux pastry, remove from the heat, place a lid on the saucepan & set aside for 15 to 20 minutes to cool*

❖ *once cool enough to handle, turn out onto a lightly floured surface & knead for about 2 to 3 minutes until you have a soft, smooth dough, transfer to a clean bowl, cover & set aside for 10 to 15 minutes*

❖ *on a lightly floured surface, cut the dough into 8 equal pieces & roll each one into a ball, dust a rolling pin with a little extra flour & roll each ball flat into a 3 to 4 mm thick flatbread*

❖ *heat a frying pan or griddle over a medium heat & when hot, cook each flatbread on each side for 3 to 4 minutes or until cooked through & slightly charred, remove from the pan onto a serving plate and repeat until each one is cooked, serve warm with any dipping sauce or chutney of your choice*

I have never been a fan of making muffins since my father took an instant dislike to my first attempt at a blueberry muffin. Breakfast muffins are the healthy alternative to toast or cereals when made with wholewheat emmer flour and a glut of seasonal fruit. Using an abundance of apples, dates and date syrup, these fresh tasting, not overly sweet moist cakes are a great way to start the day with a steaming cup of coffee...

Emmer Breakfast Muffins

Ingredients (makes 12 muffins):
for the apple sauce:
2 firm apples
½ lemon, juiced
½ cup / 125 ml water

for the muffins:
1 cup / 120 g wholemeal emmer flour
1 ⅔ cups / 180 g plain flour
1 ½ teaspoons / 7.5 g baking powder
1 ½ teaspoons / 7.5 g bicarbonate of soda
1 teaspoon / 5 g cinnamon
½ teaspoon salt
2 eggs, beaten
½ cup / 100 g soft light brown sugar
¼ cup / 65 g apple sauce
½ cup / 65 ml light olive oil
½ cup / 125 ml natural yoghurt
2 tablespoons date syrup
1 eating apple
½ cup / 90 g dates

for the topping:
¼ cup / 25 g light brown sugar
2 tablespoons / 30 g emmer flour
2 tablespoons / 30 g rolled oats
½ teaspoon cinnamon
2 tablespoons / 30 ml light olive oil

Method:

❖ *preheat the oven to 180 °C / 350 °F / Gas Mark 4 & line a 12-hole muffin tin with paper cases*

❖ *peel, core & roughly chop the apples for the sauce & place in a saucepan with the lemon juice & water, cook on a low heat for 10 minutes until soft, remove from the heat & mash to a smooth sauce, set aside to cool*

- ❖ mix all the dry ingredients together in a bowl & in a separate bowl whisk together the eggs, sugar, apple sauce, oil, yoghurt & date syrup, pour into the dry ingredients & mix well, peel, core & roughly chop the apple & the dates, then gently fold into the mix
- ❖ spoon a couple of tablespoons of batter into each muffin case to about ⅔ full
- ❖ mix the all the topping ingredients together in a bowl & sprinkle a little over each one for a added crunch when baked
- ❖ bake in the preheat oven for 20 minutes until risen & golden

These light, fluffy pancakes are a delicious treat for a Sunday brunch. Rye flour contains less gluten than wheat flour and will give a slightly denser batter, however the addition of the airy egg whites will lighten the batter, so be very careful when folding them in, not to over mix and knock out too much air. This will soften the mixture and with the addition of the ricotta, create a perfect pancake. For a gluten-free pancake, substitute the rye flour for teff.

Rye & Ricotta Pancakes

Ingredients (makes 8 pancakes):
⅔ cup / 200 g ricotta cheese
2 eggs, separated
⅓ cup / 90 ml milk
1 teaspoon vanilla extract
½ cup / 60 g rye flour
1 teaspoon baking powder
a pinch of salt
¼ cup / 60 g butter
maple syrup & fresh berries, to serve

Method:
- ❖ place the ricotta, egg yolks, milk & vanilla extract in a bowl & mix to

combine, add the flour, baking powder & salt, whisk with a balloon whisk to a thick batter, the mixture will appear to be quite dense at this stage, but this is normal as the addition of the egg whites will lighten it

❖ in a clean bowl, whisk the egg whites to stiff peaks & with a large metal spoon gently fold a spoonful at a time into the batter, until all is incorporated and the batter is smooth & aerated

❖ melt ⅓ of the butter in a frying pan & drop a heaped tablespoon of the mixture into the pan, slightly flattening the top to form a round pancake, add 1 or 2 more spoonfuls depending on the size of the pan, try to be patient & not overcrowd the frying pan with more than 3 to allow the pancakes to cook evenly, cook on a medium heat for 2 to 3 minutes on either side until golden and fluffy, transfer to a plate & continue until all the mixture is used up, re-greasing the pan each time with a little more butter

❖ serve warm with lashings of date syrup or chocolate sauce, stone fruits and fresh berries

Rye & Ricotta Pancakes

These gluten-free crepes can be eaten for breakfast, brunch or as a simple after dinner dessert, creating lots of fun for the family along the way. Sorghum popcorn is as easy to make as regular popcorn, by simply popping the kernels in a lidded pan or microwavable container and wait to hear from the sound of the sorghum popping, which takes a few minutes at best... no need to wait for pancake day to try these...

Sorghum Crepes

Ingredients (makes approximately 8):
1 cup / 235 ml milk
3 eggs, beaten
1 cup / 125 g sorghum flour
a pinch of salt
1 tablespoon butter, melted
butter for greasing the pan

filling:
⅓ cup / 100 g ricotta cheese
2 tablespoons vanilla sugar or 1 teaspoon vanilla paste
date syrup & sorghum popcorn, to serve

Method:
❖ *place the sorghum flour & salt in a bowl & set aside, beat the eggs with the milk & slowly add the flour whisking continuously to a thin batter, add the melted butter & set aside in the refrigerator until required*

To make the ricotta filling:
❖ *place the ricotta in a bowl, add the vanilla sugar or if you would rather omit the sugar, just the vanilla paste & beat until smooth, add any other flavourings of your choice, maybe some citrus zest for freshness*

or even a touch of liqueur for a dinner party dessert, refrigerate until required

❖ *lightly grease a crepe or frying pan with butter & pour a ladle of the batter into the hot pan, swirl to form a thin layer, cook for 2 to 3 minutes or until the edges start to come away from the pan before flipping the crepe and cooking on the other side until golden, transfer to a plate & continue until all the mixture is used up, re-greasing the pan each time with a little more butter, this mixture makes approximately 8 crepes*

❖ *serve with a spoonful of the soft ricotta, a drizzle of date syrup and some sorghum popcorn.*

Sorghum Crepes

Soups & salads

A delicately spiced, hearty soup for those cold, dark winter days. Toasting the pearl barley in a dry pan before simmering in the aromatic stock imparts a nutty flavour, which, when added to the warmly spiced squash, makes for a healthy and satisfying lunch. There are many options for vegetable stock on the market, you may even be tempted to make your own, however I use stock pots which are easy to reconstitute and add some flavour. It is your choice, use what you have available or if not, water with a couple of bayleaves and black peppercorns thrown in does the job.

Spiced Butternut Squash & Toasted Barley Soup

Ingredients (serves 6-8):
½ cup / 100 g pearl barley
2 tablespoons / 30 ml extra virgin olive oil
1 large red onion
2 large carrots
1 butternut squash
1 teaspoon ground cumin
1 teaspoon ground coriander
a handful of fresh thyme sprigs
6 to 8 cups / 1 ½ to 2 litres vegetable stock
salt & pepper
pumpkin seeds & fresh thyme leaves, to serve

Method
❖ *place the pearl barley in a dry saucepan & toast over a medium heat for 3 to 4 minutes, shaking the pan intermittently until the barley smells nutty and begins to take on a golden brown colour, remove from the pan & set aside*
❖ *prepare the vegetables by peeling, deseeding & roughly chopping into dice, place the olive oil in the pan, add the onions & carrots & sweat over a medium heat with a lid on for about 10 minutes until they*

begin to soften, add the butternut squash dice, toasted barley, cumin, coriander, salt & pepper & thyme & stir to combine, keep on the heat for a further 2 to 3 minutes stirring to coat everything with the oil & spices

❖ add the vegetable stock & bring up to the boil, reduce the heat & cover with a lid, simmering gently for 30 to 40 minutes or until the barley and vegetables are soft, and the broth is a beautiful orange hue, check for seasoning & add more salt & pepper if needed

❖ serve in bowls with pumpkin seeds & fresh thyme leaves, toasting the pumpkin seeds in a dry pan, if you wish

**Spiced Butternut Squash
Toasted Barley Soup**

This soup is a hearty, Italian inspired minestrone soup with added nutrients from the sorghum grain, instead of rice or pasta. With a nutty flavour and chewy texture, this small ancient white pearl has the added benefits of being gluten-free. It takes longer to cook than other ancient grains, but this winter warmer is well worth the wait. Use whatever vegetables you have in your vegetable rack and any other legumes you wish to add.

Winter Vegetable, Cannellini Bean & Sorghum Soup

Ingredients (serves 8):
½ cup / 100 g sorghum grain
2 tablespoons / 30 ml olive oil
1 large red onion,
2 large cloves garlic
4 large carrots
3 celery sticks
2 courgettes
½ cup / 225 g butternut squash
1 teaspoon oregano
1 teaspoon za'atar
handful of fresh coriander leaves
1 x 400 g tin of cherry tomatoes in juice
1 x 400 g tin of cannellini beans
5 cm / 2 in piece of parmesan rind, optional
6 cups / 1 ½ litres vegetable stock
salt & pepper
grated parmesan cheese, to serve

Method
❖ *place the sorghum grains in a medium saucepan cover with boiling water & simmer over a low heat for 45 to 60 minutes until most of the water has been absorbed & the sorghum grains are soft, drain & set aside*

❖ *peel, wash and roughly chop all the vegetables & set aside, place the olive oil & onion in a large saucepan & fry over a medium heat for 2 to 3 minutes until beginning to soften, peel & crush the garlic & add to the onion & cook for a further 30 seconds before adding the carrots, celery, courgettes & squash, stir the vegetables to coat in the oniony oil & cook for 10 minutes or until the vegetables begin to soften & brown*

❖ *add the dried herbs, roughly chopped coriander, cherry tomatoes with juice & drained cannellini beans & add the vegetable stock, salt, pepper & parmesan rind if using, mix well & bring to a simmer & leave to cook for 30 to 40 minutes uncovered until the vegetables are soft, add the sorghum & cook for a further 10 minutes, serve with parmesan cheese & extra coriander leaves*

A freekeh salad that is full of the fresh flavours of the Middle East, using plenty of fresh herbs and fragrant spices to flavour the smoky freekeh, and finished off with a dollop of tangy labane, or yoghurt. Baharat is a spice blend that combines the warm spices of cinnamon, cloves and nutmeg with a touch of heat from black peppercorns. Many Arabic women make their own blends from the herbs and spices available to them. To enhance the cultural flavours of this dish, serve at room temperature.

Freekeh Salad with Pistachios & Labane Dressing

Ingredients (serves 4-6):
2 bunches large bulb spring onions
1 tablespoon / 15 g butter
2 tablespoons / 30 ml olive oil
4 cups / 120 g spinach
1 cup / 180 g freekeh
½ teaspoon cinnamon / cinnamon stick
1 teaspoon baharat
2 cups / 500 ml vegetable stock or boiling water
½ cup / 30 g flat leaf parsley
½ cup / 30 g mint

½ cup / 30 g coriander
pistachios
zest of 1 lemon, for garnish

for the labane dressing:
½ cup / 150 ml labane or natural yoghurt
2 teaspoons of za'atar
2 teaspoons olive oil
½ lemon, juiced
salt & pepper

Method:

❖ soak the freekeh in cold water for 10 minutes, then rinse & drain to remove
the chaff & grit, place in a medium saucepan with the cinnamon & baharat,
add the vegetable stock or water, stir to combine & bring to a boil, reduce the
heat & simmer for 20 minutes until the freekeh is tender & the liquid has
absorbed into the grain, remove from the heat, place a tight-fitting lid on the
saucepan & leave to steam for a further 10 minutes, place in a large serving
bowl

Freekeh Salad with Pistachios
& Labane Dressing

To make the labane dressing:

❖ *mix the labane or yoghurt with the za'atar, olive oil & lemon juice, season with salt & pepper & set aside in the refrigerator until ready to use*

❖ *finely slice the spring onions then place the oil & butter in a large frying pan over medium heat & add the spring onions, cook for 5 minutes until soft, then add the spinach & stir for 2 to 3 minutes until wilted but still green & vibrant, season with salt and pepper, remove from the heat & add to the freekeh*

❖ *roughly chop all the fresh herbs & pistachios & mix into the freekeh, combining all together, top with labane, lemon zest, an extra sprinkling of za'atar & pistachios*

❖ *serve at room temperature*

Tahina is roasted, ground, hulled sesame paste, the staple condiment of the Levantine cuisine and primarily used in the making of hummous. It is also a harmonious match with the nutty ancient grains and smoky wild wheats. Roasted cauliflower is on culinary trend, used as a substantial alternative to meat. Doused in the earthy spice mix of za'atar, this is a fulfilling salad, which will satisfy any plant-based foodie

Freekeh with Roasted Cauliflower & Tahini Dressing

Ingredients (serves 4-6):
1 cup / 180 g freekeh, rinsed & drained
2½ cups / 500 ml water
2 small cauliflowers, cut into florets
extra virgin olive oil
3-4 heaped tablespoons of za'atar
a squeeze of lemon juice
salt & pepper
100 g pinenuts, toasted
1 bunch flat leaf parsley, finely chopped

for the tahini dressing:
4 tablespoons tahina
2 tablespoons lemon juice

1 teaspoon salt
ice cold water

Method:

❖ *preheat the oven to 190 °C / 375 °F / Gas Mark 5*
❖ *place the cauliflower florets in a saucepan of boiling salted water & parboil on a medium heat for 5 minutes until al dente, drain & place in a roasting tray, season with salt, liberally pour over olive oil & plenty of za'atar, then place in the oven for 30 to 40 minutes, until the florets are soft & charred at the edges, remove & set aside*
❖ *soak the freekeh in cold water for 10 minutes, then rinse & drain before placing in a saucepan, cover with water & bring to the boil, lower the heat & simmer for 15 to 20 minutes until the freekeh is soft but with a slight bite & the water has been absorbed into the grains, turn off the heat & leave to steam for 10 minutes with a tight-fitting lid*
❖ *place in a salad bowl, season with salt & pepper & drizzle over a little extra*

Freekeh with Roasted Cauliflower & Tahini Dressing

virgin olive oil, a squeeze of lemon juice, some finely chopped parsley & most of the toasted pinenuts, leaving a handful for garnish, mix well to combine

To make the tahina dressing:

❖ *place the tahina in a bowl, add lemon juice & salt & mix with a whisk, very slowly add the cold water, mixing continuously until you have a smooth liquid the consistency of double cream, set aside*

❖ *once the cauliflower florets are roasted, add them to the freekeh with all the delicious za'atar flavoured oil from the roasting pan, pour over the tahini dressing & garnish with the remaining pinenuts & a little extra flat leaf parsley, serve at room temperature*

Bulgur or cracked wheat is the traditional staple used for making tabbouleh throughout the Levant, a vegetarian dish of soaked wheat, flavoured mainly with lots of fresh herbs. The earliest species of wheat used for this dish was a variety called salamouni, which is still grown in the Beqaa Valley in Lebanon. Spelt gives a nutty flavour and texture to this dish, but as spelt grains are whole and not cracked, they need cooking to become soft and palatable. This salad can also be cooked with whole gluten-free sorghum grains and pistachios can replace the pinenuts and sweet pomegranate jewels added for freshness.

Cherry Plum Tomato, Rocket & Pinenut Spelt Tabbouleh

Ingredients (serves 4-6):
1 cup / 180 g spelt grains
2½ cups / 600 ml boiling water
2 cups / 350 g cherry plum tomatoes
oregano sprigs
6 tablespoons / 75 ml extra virgin olive oil
zest & juice of 1 lemon
1 cup / 25 g flat leaf parsley
1 cup / 25 g mint leaves

salt & pepper
1 bunch large bulb spring onions
½ cup / 100 g pinenuts, toasted
2 cups / 50 g rocket
micro leaves or herbs, for garnish

Method:

- ❖ *preheat the oven to 200 °C / 400 °F / Gas Mark 6*
- ❖ *rinse the spelt grains under cold water for 2 to 3 minutes, before placing in a medium saucepan & cover with the boiling water, place on a low heat & simmer for 30 to 40 minutes until the spelt is tender but with a slight bite to the kernel, remove from the heat & drain any residual water, set aside*
- ❖ *place the whole cherry plum tomatoes on a baking tray with the oregano sprigs, season with salt & pepper & drizzle 3 tablespoons of the olive oil over the tomatoes, place in the oven for 25 to 30 minutes until the tomatoes start to blister and soften, remove & cool*
- ❖ *place the spelt grains in a salad bowl whilst still warm, pour over the remaining 3 tablespoons of olive oil, lemon zest & juice, finely chopped parsley & mint & season well with salt & pepper, mix to combine, place the roasted tomatoes, finely sliced spring onions, pinenuts & rocket on top of the spelt & garnish with micro leaves or more herbs, for added protein and a summer supper dish, add slices of fried halloumi*

Crisp apples, crunchy cobnuts, soft pearl barley and sweet, caramelised fennel combines the fresh flavours of autumn in one nourishing bowl. Full of natural goodness from seasonal produce, this salad requires very little cooking. As cobnuts have a short season, you can replace them with hazelnuts, which when toasted adds yet another dimension to this dish. Add some creamy blue cheese or smoked cheddar and enjoy for lunch with a glass of crisp white wine...

Apple, Cobnut & Barley Salad

Ingredients (serves 4-6):
6 tablespoons / 90 ml extra virgin olive oil

2 fennel bulbs
1 cup / 190 g pearled barley
2 cups / 450 ml boiling water
4 large bulbed spring onions
1 tablespoon / 15 g butter
2 eating apples
juice of 1 lemon
3 tablespoons / 45 ml apple cider vinegar
salt & pepper
3 tablespoons fresh dill
⅓ cup / 50 g cobnuts

Method:

❖ preheat the oven to 190 °C / 375 °F / Gas Mark 5
❖ cut the fennel into quarters & place on a roasting tray, drizzle with 2 tablespoons of olive oil & season with salt & pepper & roast in the oven for 20 minutes until soft & charred at the edges, remove & set aside
❖ heat a tablespoon of olive oil in a saucepan & add the pearl barley, cook for 1 to 2 minutes stirring occasionally to toast the grains until beginning to smell nutty and turn golden brown, add the boiling water & a good pinch of salt & simmer for 20 to 25 minutes until the grains are soft but still have a slight bite and most of the water has been absorbed, drain & place in a serving bowl
❖ mix the remaining 4 tablespoons of olive oil with the apple cider vinegar in a small bowl, season well with salt & pepper & pour over the warm barley, stirring to coat all the grains, leave a tablespoon or two to drizzle over at the end
❖ melt the butter in a small frying pan, slice the spring onion on the diagonal & add to the pan, cook on a medium heat for 5 minutes until soft, add to the barley with all the buttery juices, finely chop the dill & mix into the barley with the onions
❖ core the apples, but leave the skin on for added texture, slice the apples thinly & toss in the lemon juice to prevent browning, arrange the apple with the fennel quarters & cobnuts on top of the barley & garnish with a few extra cobnuts, dill or fennel fronds & the extra dressing

Mains & sides

Pearled spelt is a robust alternative to rice for a risotto, as coined by the word *speltotto* from the celebrity chef and food writer, Hugh Fearnley-Whittingstall. This comforting dish is full of nutrients from kale, a curly-leaved variety of cabbage that originated in 2000 BCE and was referred to as Sabellian kale by writers such as Pliny and enjoyed at Roman banquets. It has since become a superfood, grown in allotments and gardens throughout the UK.

Spelt Risotto with Spring Onion, Kale & Thyme

Ingredients (serves 4):
2 tablespoons / 30 g butter
4 large bulb spring onions
2 tablespoon / 30 g fresh thyme leaves
¾ cup / 150 g pearled spelt, rinsed well under cold water
2 cups / 600 ml hot vegetable stock
½ cup / 75 g fresh peas
4 cups / 120 g kale
2 tablespoons / 30 g mint
¼ cup / 30 g parmesan cheese
salt & pepper

Method

❖ *finely slice the spring onion, then melt the butter in a large pan, add the spring onions & thyme leaves & fry gently for 6 to 8 minutes until soft*

❖ *rinse the pearled spelt under cold running water for a few minutes, drain & add the the onions, mix well until all the spelt is coated in the buttery mixture, add the hot stock, of which I have used a stock pot, salt & pepper & stir well, place a tight-fitting lid on the pan & simmer on a gentle heat for 30 to 40 minutes, stirring occasionally until the spelt is tender & most of the liquid has been absorbed*

❖ *while the risotto is simmering, blanch the kale in boiling salted water for 2 minutes, drain & refresh under cold water, if using large kale leaves, roughly chop*

❖ *once the spelt is tender & most of the liquid has been absorbed, stir in the fresh peas, blanched kale & half of the mint, which should be finely chopped, cook for a further 5 minutes on a gentle heat, check seasoning adding more salt & pepper if needed*

❖ *serve in warm bowls with plenty of freshly grated parmesan cheese, the remaining mint and a fresh green salad*

Stuffed vegetables of all shapes and sizes are authentic to Levantine cuisine, usually made with rice and spice. Stuffing vegetables and leaves were synonymous with battle and hunger, when any morsel of food found could be stuffed inside a rotting vegetable and eaten for sustenance. This recipe for stuffed peppers is with freekeh, a change from the usual rice stuffing and packed with sunny Mediterranean flavours. A delicious, easy, vegetarian supper with a crisp, green salad.

Stuffed Red Peppers with Freekeh, Olives & Feta

Ingredients (serves 4):
4 red peppers, halved & deseeded
6 tablespoons / 90 ml extra virgin olive oil
½ cup / 100 g freekeh, soaked, rinsed & drained
1 cup / 250 ml boiling water
2 bay leaves
2 banana shallots, roughly chopped
2 garlic cloves, crushed
a large handful of oregano, flat leaf parsley & mint leaves, finely chopped
10-12 black olives, pitted & chopped
6-8 sundried tomatoes, chopped
2 tablespoons of capers
1 lemon, zest & juice
1 teaspoon dried mint
100 g feta
½ cup / 50 g pinenuts, toasted (optional)
salt & pepper

Method:

- ❖ preheat the oven to 190 °C / 375 °F / Gas Mark 5
- ❖ place the pepper halves on a roasting tray cut side down, season with salt & pepper & drizzle with 4 tablespoons of olive oil, place on a baking tray & roast for 15 to 20 minutes until the flesh is tender & the edges starting to char, remove from the oven & set aside
- ❖ place the rinsed freekeh in a saucepan & cover with the boiling water, throw in the bay leaves & simmer for 15 to 20 minutes until all the water has all been absorbed, place a tight-fitting lid on the pan & set aside to steam for 10 minutes

To make the stuffing:

- ❖ heat the remaining 2 tablespoons of olive oil into a pan, add shallots & garlic & cook on a low heat for 5 minutes until soft, mix in all the chopped fresh herbs, dried mint, lemon zest, juice, olives, tomatoes, capers, salt & pepper & cook for a further 5 minutes, remove from the heat & add in the crumbled feta & pinenuts before adding the mixture to the freekeh, mix well to combine
- ❖ turn over the pepper halves & stuff each half with the stuffing, sprinkle some extra pinenuts, feta or mint over the top & return to the oven for 15 minutes until warmed through

Red Peppers Stuffed with Freekeh, Olives & Feta

Fritters are small pieces of meat, fish, vegetable or fruit, coated in a light batter and fried until golden brown. A latke is the Yiddish term for a fritter, that was traditionally made with the affordable potato, but becoming more popular using other vegetables with or without the potato. The versatile cauliflower, when paired with delicate Middle Eastern spices, makes a delicious latke, particularly when bound with the nuttiness of spelt flour. Inspired from an Ottolenghi recipe, this battered little vegetable is a perfect accompaniment to any main course or even as a starter with a dip.

Cauliflower Spelt Latkes

Ingredients (serves 4):
1 small cauliflower
½ cup / 65 g spelt flour
2 tablespoons / 30 g flat leaf parsley
2 tablespoons / 30 g fresh coriander
1 shallot
2 garlic cloves
2 eggs, beaten
1 teaspoon ground cumin
½ teaspoon ground coriander
½ teaspoon ground cinnamon
½ teaspoon ground turmeric
1 teaspoon salt
1 teaspoon black pepper
1 cup / 250 ml sunflower oil, for frying

Method
❖ *cut the cauliflower into florets & place in a saucepan of salted boiling water, cook on a low heat until soft, drain well*
❖ *finely chop the herbs, shallot & crush the garlic & place in a bowl, add the spelt flour, spices, beaten egg & a good seasoning of salt & pepper, mix well to combine until you have a smooth batter*

Cauliflower & Coriander Latkes

❖ mash the cauliflower florets with a fork & mix well into the batter

❖ pour the sunflower oil into a large pan & heat until hot, then place 2 tablespoons of the batter mixture into the pan & press with the back of the spoon to form the latke, work in batches of 3 or 4, cook for 2 to 3 minutes per side until golden brown, repeat until all the mixture has been used up, drain on kitchen towel & serve with a yoghurt dressing and plenty of chopped fresh coriander.

Bourekas originated in Spain and Portugal as a signature pastry of the Sephardic Jewish cuisine. They have become one of the most popular street foods in Israel today. Made with many types of pastry, including

filo, brik or yeasted, these savoury parcels are made from an Arabic pastry, called *f'tir* & packed with nutrients for the healthy snack.

Kale, Feta & Mint Einkorn Bourekas

Ingredients (makes 8):
1 cup / 125 g einkorn flour
1 cup / 125 g wholewheat flour
1 teaspoon dried yeast
1 teaspoon salt
½ teaspoon sugar
¼ cup / 60 ml extra virgin olive oil
¼ cup / 60 ml warm water
½ cup / 110 g butter, melted

for the yoghurt dip:
½ cup / 100 ml natural yoghurt
1 teaspoon sumac
a squeeze of lemon juice
fresh mint

for the filling:
2 tablespoons / 30 ml extra virgin olive oil
2 cloves of garlic, crushed
1 ½ cups / 250 g kale
1 teaspoon dried mint
½ teaspoon sweet paprika
⅔ cup / 100 g feta
salt & pepper
1 egg, beaten
sesame seeds

Method
❖ mix the flours, yeast & sugar in a mixer with a dough hook, before adding the salt & olive oil, mix to combine then on a slow setting, add the warm water until a soft dough is formed, knead for 5 minutes in the mixer until smooth & firm, cover & leave to prove in a warm place for 30 minutes

To make the filling:

❖ put the 2 tablespoons of olive oil into a pan, crush the garlic into it & cook on a low heat to soften, add the kale & cook for 2 to 3 minutes until soft & wilted, add the dried mint, paprika, salt & pepper & mix to combine, remove from the heat, crumble in the feta, mix & set aside

To make the dressing:

❖ chop the mint finely & mix all the ingredients together for the yoghurt dip, refrigerate until needed

❖ preheat the oven to 200 °C / 400 °F / Gas Mark 6, turn out the pastry onto a floured surface & divide into 8 balls, roll out each one to a rectangle, making it as thin as possible stretching it out gently with your hands to about 15 x 10 cm / 6 x 4 in, brush the dough all over with melted butter, then place a line of filling horizontally at one of the long edges, roll the dough over into a log, seam side down, before rolling the log into a spiral from one end into the middle, tucking the edges underneath, place on a clean parchment lined baking tray & repeat with all the dough balls, brush them with the beaten egg & sprinkle over the sesame seeds, place in the oven for 25 to 30 minutes until crisp and golden, serve warm with the yoghurt dip & extra mint

Barley flour has a mild, earthy taste to it which pairs really well with walnuts. It is a healthy substitute to all-purpose flour. This pastry has a crumbly texture and may need a little more than the 2 to 3 tablespoons of cold water to bind together. It can be added to whole wheat flours to become a little less short, with a ratio of 100 g barley flour to 75 g whole wheat or half & half if you prefer.

Leek & Taleggio Tart with Barley & Walnut Pastry

Ingredients (serves 6-8):
1 ½ cups / 175 g barley flour
1 teaspoon salt
½ cup / 100 g butter
½ cup / 50 g walnuts, ground
2 to 3 tablespoons iced cold water

for the filling
2 tablespoons / 30 ml extra virgin olive oil
2 tablespoons / 30 g butter
5 cups / 450 g leeks
3 large bulb purple spring onions
5 cups / 150 g baby spinach leaves
1 tablespoon of thyme leaves
1 teaspoon dried mint
grating fresh nutmeg
2 egg, beaten
½ cup / 50 g parmesan cheese
1 ½ cups / 125 g taleggio cheese
salt & pepper

Method:

❖ lightly flour a 25 cm / 10 in round tart tin

❖ place the flour, salt & butter into a mixing bowl, using your fingertips rub the butter into the flour until it resembles fine breadcrumbs, or place in a mixer & bring together with a beater, add the ground walnuts & 2 to 3 tablespoons of iced water, or a little more if you think it still looks a bit dry & bring the pastry together to a smooth dough, wrap in clingfilm & chill in the refrigerator for 15 to 20 minutes

❖ preheat the oven to 190 °C / 375 °F / Gas Mark 5, roll out the pastry to ½ cm thickness & line the tart case with the pastry, prick the base all over with a fork & cover with baking parchment & baking beans & place in the preheated oven for 10 minutes, remove the baking parchment & beans & cook for a further 5 minutes, remove from the oven & set aside, turn the oven down to 180 °C / 350 °F / Gas Mark 4

To make the filling:

❖ slice the leeks & spring onions, melt the butter in a frying pan with the oil, add the leeks & spring onions, put a lid on the pan & cook on a gentle heat for 5 to 8 minutes until the alliums are beginning to soften, add the spinach to the pan & mix until wilted, followed by the thyme leaves, dried mint & nutmeg, beaten eggs, grated parmesan, salt & pepper, stir just to combine then remove from the heat

❖ place the mixture into the pastry case & top with cubes of taleggio, place in the oven for 25 to 30 minutes, until the cheese is melted and golden on the top, remove from the tin & serve warm with a green salad

This tart packs a real punch of autumnal flavours. I love the sweet flavour of the chestnut mushrooms, but use any type that you like or have foraged for all which work with the smokiness from the garlic. The rye flour pastry has a richness to it, from using the combination of wholemeal and white flour, enhanced by the smokiness of the garlic and the earthiness of the chestnuts, a real winning combination to impress at a lunch or supper party.

Mushroom, Chestnut & Smoked Garlic Rye Tart

Ingredients (serves 6-8):
1 cup / 110 g whole rye flour
⅔ cup / 75 g white rye flour
½ teaspoon salt
½ cup / 100 g unsalted butter
1 egg yolk
2 to 3 tablespoons iced cold water

for the filling:
2 tablespoons / 30 ml olive oil
2 tablespoons / 30 g unsalted butter
2 banana shallots
3 ½ cups / 350 g mushrooms
2 cloves smoked garlic
2 tablespoons fresh thyme leaves
⅔ cup / 100 g chestnuts
1 egg
½ cup / 120 ml crème fraiche
a grating of fresh nutmeg
½ cup / 50 g Gruyère cheese
salt & pepper
flat leaf parsley

Method:

❖ *preheat the oven to 190 °C / 375 °F / Gas Mark 5, lightly flour a 36 x 12 cm / 14 x 5 in rectangular tart tin, place the flours, salt & butter* into a mixing bowl, using your fingertips rub the butter into the flour until it resembles fine breadcrumbs, or place in a mixer with a beater, add the egg yolk & 2 to 3 tablespoons of iced cold water & bring the pastry together into a smooth dough, wrap in clingfilm & chill for 30 minutes

❖ roll out the pastry to ½ cm thick & line the tart case, prick the base all over with a fork, line with baking parchment & fill with baking beans, place in the preheated oven for 10 minutes, remove the baking parchment & beans and cook for a further 5 minutes, remove from the oven & set aside, turn down to 180 °C / 350 °F / Gas Mark 4

❖ melt the butter with the oil in a frying pan, roughly chop the shallots & add to the pan, cook on a medium heat for 2 to 3 minutes until starting to soften, add the mushrooms, which I like to slice, crushed garlic & thyme leaves. cook for a further 7 to 8 minutes until the mushrooms are cooked & dry, remove from the heat & add the chestnuts, halved or quartered & place the mixture in the tart shell, beat the egg with the crème fraiche & nutmeg & season well with salt & pepper, mix into the mushroom mixture & grate the Gruyère over the top with a sprinkling of chopped flat leaf parsley, place in the oven for 15 minutes, until the custard has set & the cheese is golden & melted on the top, remove from the tin & serve a slice warm with a salad of your choice

Mushroom, Chestnut & Smoked Garlic Rye Tart

Cakes & biscuits

Freekeh flour is made by simply grinding cracked freekeh kernels to a fine powder in a spice or coffee grinder. For this cake, I put the flour through the grinder a couple of times, to give it a fine texture. This is a celebration cake, full of warm wintery flavours of roasted maple pumpkin, smoky freekeh and fragrant spices... true harmony in every mouthful.

Freekeh, Pumpkin & Maple Syrup Cake

Ingredients (Serves 8-10):
2 ½ cups / 300 g pumpkin
2 tablespoons / 30 ml walnut oil
1 ½ cups / 200 g freekeh flour
1 teaspoon baking powder
1 teaspoon bicarbonate of soda
1 cup / 200 g light brown sugar
2 teaspoons expresso powder
1 teaspoon cinnamon
1 teaspoon mixed spice
½ teaspoon cloves
a good grating of fresh nutmeg
3 eggs, beaten
1 cup / 250 ml buttermilk
⅓ cup / 80 ml sunflower oil
1 teaspoon vanilla paste
4 tablespoons / 60 ml maple syrup
¼ cup / 50 g golden raisins
¼ cup / 50 g walnuts

for the cream cheese frosting:
½ cup / 115 g unsalted butter, softened
1 cup / 225 g cream cheese
1 teaspoon vanilla essence
1 tablespoon maple syrup
⅓ cup / 75 g icing sugar
walnut halves & edible flowers, for decorating

Method:

- ❖ preheat the oven to 180 °C / 350 °F / Gas Mark 4
- ❖ peel, deseed & cube the pumpkin & place in a roasting tin, drizzle with the walnut oil & 2 tablespoons of the maple syrup, roast for 20 minutes until soft, if you don't have walnut oil, light olive oil will do, remove from the oven & mash, set aside
- ❖ grease & line the base 23 cm /9" springform baking tin with baking parchment
- ❖ in a large mixing bowl, mix together all the dry ingredients, in a separate bowl whisk together all wet ingredients until smooth & add the mashed pumpkin, fold into the dry ingredients & mix well with a large spoon, add in the walnuts, which need only be roughly chopped & raisins & pour into the prepared tin, bake for 45 to 50 minutes until a skewer inserted into the middle of the cakes comes out clean, remove from the oven & set aside to cool

To make the frosting:

- ❖ place the butter, cream cheese, vanilla essence & maple syrup into a mixer & whisk until smooth, slowly add the icing sugar until the soft & fluffy, I find if the ingredients are all at room temperature, then they beat into a smoother frosting, spread the frosting evenly over the top & sides of the cake & decorate with extra walnuts & edible flowers

This is a dark, moist, spiced ginger cake that smells just as good as it tastes. The rye flour lends itself well to the flavours of both fresh and dried ginger, so play around with the quantities of each to suit your own taste. I know there seems to be a lot of ingredients in this recipe, however it is simply a "throw together" traybake & in about hour you will have a delicious afternoon tea cake.

Rye & Ginger Cake

Ingredients (serves 12):
½ cup / 150 ml date syrup

2 tablespoons / 30 ml treacle
1 cup / 250 ml milk
1 teaspoon bicarbonate soda
1 ½ cups / 185 g white rye flour
½ cup / 65 g plain flour
2 teaspoons / 10 g baking powder
1 teaspoon of ground ginger, cinnamon & mixed spice
a good grating of fresh nutmeg
a twist of black pepper & ½ teaspoon salt
1 cup / 200 g golden caster sugar
¾ cup / 150 g dark brown sugar
3 large eggs, beaten
2 teaspoons fresh ginger, peeled & grated
1 teaspoon vanilla paste
½ cup / 120 ml almond oil
¼ cup / 60 ml sunflower oil
⅔ cup / 100 g golden raisins

for the icing:
¾ cup / 85 g icing sugar
3 tablespoon lemon juice
stem or crystalised ginger, finely diced for decoration

Method:

❖ *preheat the oven to 180 °C / 350 °F / Gas Mark 4*
❖ *grease & line the base 21 cm / 8 in square baking tin with baking parchment*
❖ *place the date syrup, treacle & milk in a small saucepan & warm through mixing well to combine, stir in the bicarbonate of soda & set aside to cool*
❖ *place the flours, baking powder & spices in a bowl, mix & set aside, in an electric mixer, whisk the eggs, grated ginger, vanilla paste & oils, before adding the date syrup mixture, which should have expanded from the addition of the bicarbonate of soda, then add in the dry ingredients & mix well to combine*
❖ *pour the batter into the prepared baking tin, bake for 45 to 55 minutes- or until a skewer inserted into the middle of the cake comes out clean, remove from the oven & set aside to cool completely*

To make the icing

❖ *sift the icing sugar into a bowl & add the lemon juice, mixing to a smooth consistency, drizzle over the cake & sprinkle the ginger dice over the icing*

Modern wheat flours are hybrid species which have a very different gluten structure to the ancient wheat flours of einkorn and spelt. With a lower gluten content, einkorn flour does not tend to rise quite as much as the modern flours, so requires a little more raising agent in the mix and less handling to preserve the structure. Packed with flavour, this is a delicious carrot cake that looks more complicated than it really is.

Einkorn Carrot Cake with Cream Cheese Frosting

Ingredients:
1 cup / 140 g einkorn flour
1 cup / 140 g spelt flour
2 teaspoons baking powder
½ teaspoon bicarbonate of soda
½ teaspoon salt
1 teaspoon of cinnamon & mixed spice
a good grating of fresh nutmeg
¾ cup / 35 g desiccated coconut
½ cup / 110 g vanilla sugar
½ cup / 110 g light brown sugar
¾ cup / 150 g golden raisins
¾ cup / 150 g walnuts
3 cups / 150 g carrots
¾ cup / 175 ml sunflower oil
1 ½ cup / 350 ml Greek yoghurt
2 teaspoon vanilla essence

for the cream cheese frosting:
½ cup / 115 g unsalted butter, softened
1 cup / 225 g cream cheese
2 teaspoons vanilla essence
zest of 1 orange
2 cups / 250 g icing sugar
walnuts & edible flowers, for decorating

Method:

- ❖ preheat the oven to 180 °C / 350 °F / Gas Mark 4
- ❖ grease & line the base of two 20 cm / 7 in round baking tins with baking parchment
- ❖ in a large mixing bowl mix together all the dry ingredients, make a well in the centre, add the grated carrots, sunflower oil, yoghurt & vanilla extract & fold everything together gently until mixed, add the raisins and chopped walnuts & spoon the mixture equally into the prepared baking tins, bake for 20 to 25 minutes until a skewer inserted into the middle of the cakes comes out clean, remove from the oven & cool

To make the cream cheese frostings:

- ❖ place the butter, cream cheese, zest of the orange & vanilla essence into a mixer & whisk on a low speed until smooth, I find that if the butter & cream cheese are both at room temperature, they become smoother than if beaten from cold, slowly add the icing sugar until the mixture is soft & fluffy, refrigerate until the cakes are cool & you are ready to assemble the cake
- ❖ place one of the cakes on a serving plate & spread ½ of the frosting over the top, place the second one on the top & spread the remaining frosting over it, decorate with whole & chopped walnuts & edible flowers, if you make double the quantity of frosting, you can cover the sides too which makes for a real celebration cake

Einkorn Carrot Cake

Light and buttery, these little biscuits have a hit of citrus zing and a nuttiness from the khorasan flour and pistachios. Like so many Middle Eastern sweetmeats, a syrup is lavished on each biscuit immediately they come out of the oven, to enhance the delicious flavours. Rose water or orange blossom water can be added to the sugar syrup to give a floral note to the biscuits.

Pistachio & Lime Khorasan Shortbread

Ingredients (makes 20 biscuits):
5 tablespoons / 75 g unsalted butter
¾ cup / 150 g golden caster sugar
2 cups / 250 g khorasan flour
¼ teaspoon salt
1 large egg, beaten
2 -3 drops of almond essence
zest of 1 lime
¼ cup / 30 g pistachios

for the syrup:
¼ cup / 50 g golden caster sugar
⅓ cup 75 ml boiling water
2 teaspoons / 10 ml lime juice

Method:

❖ *preheat the oven to 180 °C / 350 °F / Gas Mark 4, line a large baking tray with baking parchment*

❖ *beat the butter & sugar in an electric mixer until combined, add the beaten egg, almond essence & lime zest, followed by the khorasan flour & salt until it all comes together similar to pastry, remove & flatten into a disc, wrap in cling film & chill for 20 minutes*

❖ *roll out the shortbread on a floured surface to the thickness of 3mm & stamp out rounds with a 7.5 cm / 3 in fluted cutter & place on the baking tray,*

*continue until all the dough is cut into rounds & chill in the refrigerator for
a further 30 minutes*

To make the sugar syrup:

❖ *place the golden caster sugar & water in a small pan, put on a low
heat until the sugar has dissolved, then leave to simmer for a further 5
minutes until syrupy, add the lime juice & stir, remove from the heat &
set aside*

❖ *remove the shortbread from the refrigerator, sprinkle with the pistachios,
which should be finely chopped or leave more rustic if you prefer & place in
the preheated oven for 10 to 12 minutes until golden brown, remove from the
oven & immediately brush each shortbread with the lime syrup, then leave to
cool and harden, before serving*

Pistachio & Lime Khorasan Shortbread

Flapjacks are a healthy snack and simple to make, combining wholesome nutritious grains with dried fruits and nuts, to suit your taste and store cupboard. I love the Middle Eastern flavours of date and tahini, which when combined with chocolate is a match made in heaven. I came across the chocolate tahini in my local continental shop, but regular tahini paste is very easy to find and adds a deeper sesame flavour to these flapjacks, rather than a richer chocolatey taste, up to you...

Date, Chocolate & Tahini Ancient Grain Flapjacks

Ingredients (makes 16):
½ cup / 115 g butter
¼ cup / 50 g dark brown sugar
¼ cup / 90 ml date syrup
½ cup / 120 g chocolate tahini or tahini paste
1 teaspoon vanilla essence
1 cup / 150 g wheat flakes
1 cup / 150 g oats
1 teaspoon cinnamon
1 cup / 100 g Medjool dates
1 cup / 100 g chocolate chunks

Method:

❖ *preheat the oven to 150 °C / 300 °F / Gas Mark 2, grease & line a 20 x 20 cm / 12 x 12 in square baking tray*

❖ *melt the butter, sugar, date syrup, tahini & vanilla essence together in a small saucepan over a gentle heat*

❖ *stone & roughly chop the dates & place them with the wheat & oat flakes, cinnamon, & chocolate chunks into a large bowl & mix to combine*

❖ *once the syrupy butter mixture is bubbling, pour over the dry ingredients & gently mix until all the flakes are coated with the sticky syrup, pour into the greased tin & flatten the top with a palette knife*

❖ *place in the preheated oven & bake for 20 to 25 minutes until golden on top, remove from the oven & while the flapjacks are still warm and* soft, mark out the 16 squares with a sharp knife, place in the refrigerator allow to cool completely in the tin, before cutting into 16 squares & serving

❖ once up to room temperature chocolate will soften and the flapjack with be rich and gooey in the centre

These summer berry crumble bars are a delicious treat when there is a glut of summer fruits and you are not sure what to make with them. Most fruits work well with this recipe, especially tart blackcurrants, blackberries or raspberries, which should be frozen first to stay whole, keep their shape and so be easier to use. A bag of frozen fruits of your choice from the supermarket work too. These bars have the added benefit of being completely gluten-free from the millet flakes and sorghum flour.

Summer Berry Sorghum & Millet Crumble Bars

Ingredients (serves 12):
1 ½ cups / 150 g millet flakes
1 ½ cups / 180 g sorghum flour
¼ teaspoon salt
¾ cup / 130 g dark brown sugar
½ teaspoon baking powder
1 teaspoon cinnamon
⅔ cup / 175 g unsalted butter, softened

for the filling:
2 teaspoons / 10 g cornflour
2 tablespoons lemon juice
½ cup / 150 g raspberry or strawberry jam
4 cups / 400 g frozen summer berries

Method:

❖ *preheat the oven to 190 °C / 375 °F / Gas Mark 5, grease & line a 20 cm / 8 in square baking tin with greaseproof paper*

❖ *mix the millet flakes, sorghum flour, salt, sugar, baking powder & cinnamon together in a large mixing bowl, add the butter & rub it into the dry ingredients until it resembles breadcrumbs*

❖ *place ⅔ of the crumble mix into the prepared tin, spread it all over the bottom & press down firmly to cover the tin about 5 cm / ½ in thick like pastry, place in the preheated oven & bake for 15 minutes until golden, set aside the rest of the crumble mix*

❖ *while the base is cooking, mix the cornflour & lemon juice together in a separate bowl to form a thin paste, stir in the jam & frozen berries & mix well to combine, set aside*

❖ *remove the base from the oven and cool slightly, spread the fruit filling over the base evenly, then sprinkle the remaining crumble mixture over the top, return to the oven for 20 to 25 minutes, until the filling is bubbling around the edges & the top golden & crunchy, remove from the oven & set aside to cool*

❖ *cut into squares & serve with a cup of tea or a scoop of vanilla ice cream*

Desserts

Crumbly whole wheat pastry, soft filling, slightly charred apple slices and a sweet, sticky glaze makes this tart a real crowd pleaser during the cold winter months and provokes an interesting conversation with dinner guests about the healthy attributes of the pastry. The freekeh and einkorn flours together make very short whole wheat pastry with a slight smokiness from the freekeh. Substitute wholemeal flour for the einkorn if you don't have any, but do grind your own freekeh kernels in a spice or coffee grinder if you can, to get the authentic taste of this smoky unripe wheat in your pastry.

Apple & Lemon Thyme Tart with Freekeh Crust

Ingredients (serves 8):
1 cup / 150 g freekeh flour
½ cup / 75 g einkorn flour
2 tablespoons / 30 g vanilla sugar
¾ cup / 125 g unsalted butter
1 egg yolk + 2 tablespoons iced cold water

for the apple filling:
6 eating apples
¼ cup / 50 g vanilla sugar
1 teaspoons ground cinnamon
3 tablespoons / 45 ml apple juice
⅔ cup / 100 g golden raisins
2 tablespoons calvados or brandy
½ cup / 100 g ground hazelnuts
2 teaspoons lemon thyme
2 tablespoons honey
2 tablespoons demerara sugar

3 tablespoons of apricot jam, to glaze

Method:

❖ *grind the freekeh into a fine flour & place with the einkorn, sugar & butter in an electric mixer until it resembles breadcrumbs, add 2 tablespoons of iced* cold water to the beaten egg & add to the flour mixture until it all comes together as a soft pastry, remove, flatten into a disc, wrap in cling film & chill for 20 minutes

❖ peel, core & quarter 4 of the apples & place in a saucepan with the vanilla sugar, cinnamon & apple juice, cover with a tight-fitting lid & place on a low heat to cook for 10 to 15 minutes until the apples are just beginning to soften but still holding their shape, remove from the heat & set aside

❖ place the golden raisins in a small saucepan with the calvados, heat gently for 2 to 3 minutes, turn off the heat & leave to cool

❖ preheat the oven to 190 °C / 375 °F / Gas Mark 5, roll out the pastry on a floured surface to the thickness of 3mm & line the bottom & sides of a 23 cm / 9 in pie dish, place baking parchment over the pastry & fill with baking beans, bake blind in the preheated oven for 10 minutes before removing the paper & beans & returning pie dish to the oven for a further 5 minutes, until golden brown, remove from the oven

❖ spread the ground hazelnuts over the base of the crust, mix the raisins in with the stewed apple quarters & fill the pie case with the mixture, leaving the skin on the remaining 2 apples, core & slice very thinly, cover the filling with

Apple & Thyme Tart with Freekeh Crust

overlapping slices of apples, drizzle over the honey & thyme leaves, sprinkle with demerara sugar & bake in the oven for 40 to 45 minutes until the crust is crisp & the apples soft & slightly charred at the edges, remove from the oven & set aside to cool,

❖ *warm the apricot jam in a saucepan with 2 tablespoons of hot water & pass through a sieve, glaze the tart with the jam & serve with crème fraiche or double cream*

The glut of ripe plums falling from the trees heralds the warm, autumnal puddings of crumbles, crisps and cobblers. Whatever the name, the concept is the same, soft fruit stewed lightly with complementary flavourings and a crunchy topping, made from butter and wheat. This recipe pairs the sweetness from the fruit with a piney aroma from the fresh rosemary and a nuttiness from the einkorn and hazelnut topping. No crumble, crisp or cobbler should be served without a dollop of cream, custard or ice cream...

Plum & Rosemary Einkorn Crisp

Ingredients (serves 6-8):
10 cups / 1 kg plums
½ cup / 100 g light brown sugar
zest & juice of 1 orange
2 sprigs of rosemary
2 teaspoons einkorn flour

for the crisp:
½ cup / 125 g unsalted butter
1 cup / 125 g einkorn flour
½ cup / 75 g rolled oats
½ cup / 60 g hazelnuts
¼ cup / 50 g light brown sugar

¼ cup / 50 g dark brown sugar
1 teaspoon cinnamon
a grating of fresh nutmeg
custard, cream or vanilla ice cream, to serve

Method:

❖ preheat the oven to 180 °C / 350 °F / Gas Mark 4
❖ wash, halve and stone the plums & finely chop the rosemary leaves, place in a large bowl with the brown sugar, 2 teaspoons of einkorn flour, zest & juice of an orange & mix to combine, place in a roasting dish, cover with tin foil & place in the oven for 15 to 20 minutes or until the plums are beginning to soften, but still holding their shape, remove from the oven & set aside

To make the crisp topping:

❖ roughly chop the hazelnuts & place in a bowl with the einkorn flour, oats, brown sugars & spices, mix to combine, melt the butter in a saucepan or microwave & pour onto the dry ingredients, mix into clumps with a wooden spoon to form the crisp
❖ sprinkle evenly on top of the plums & return to the oven for 25 minutes until the plum juices are bubbling & the crumble topping has turned a rich golden brown
❖ serve with custard, cream or vanilla ice cream

This Middle Eastern version of a sticky toffee pudding was adapted from a recipe by the 2005 Masterchef Winner, Thomasina Miers, using spelt flour and warm spices. Her love of strong flavours sing out in all her dishes and this moreish dessert is no exception. This pudding is a sheer delight, but you might just want to make plenty of the sticky date sauce which is pure heaven...

Date, Pecan & Tahini Cake with Sticky Date Sauce

Ingredients (serves 8):
½ cup / 100 g fresh Medjool dates, pitted

1 cup / 250ml date syrup
½ cup / 100ml tahini paste
¾ cup / 180 g unsalted butter
⅔ cup / 120 g light muscovado sugar
4 large egg, beaten
1 cup / 100 g pecans
1 cup / 100 g spelt flour
2 teaspoons / 10 g baking powder
½ teaspoon ground cardamom, mixed spice & freshly grated nutmeg
pinch of salt

for the sticky date sauce:
½ cup / 120 g butter
1 cup / 250 ml date syrup
1 cup / 400 ml double cream

Date, Pecan & Tahini Pudding with Sticky Date Sauce

Method:

- ❖ preheat the oven to 160 °C / 325 °F / Gas Mark 3, grease & line the base 24 cm / 9 in square baking tray with baking parchment
- ❖ place the dates, date syrup & tahini in a mini blender & blitz to a smooth purée, adding 2 to 4 tablespoons of hot water to loosen the mixture
- ❖ cream the butter & sugar in an electric mixer, until light & fluffy add the date purée followed slowly by the beaten eggs & mix to combine, roughly chop the pecans & add to the mixture
- ❖ mix all the dry ingredients together in a bowl before adding to the wet mixture & gently mix together until all is combined, pour in the prepared baking tray & bake for 50 to 55 minutes or until a skewer inserted into the middle of the cake comes out clean, remove from the oven & set aside

To make the sticky date sauce:

- ❖ place the butter & date syrup into a small saucepan over a low heat, stir until the butter has melted into the date syrup, then add in the double cream, mixing continuously until you have a light coffee coloured sauce, keep the heat low, so the sauce does not split
- ❖ serve squares of warm cake with the hot sticky sauce & a dollop of any 'creamy addition' of your choice...

This fruit cake makes the perfect afternoon tea cake, but is equally deserving of a dessert when served with soft roasted peaches on the side and cream, crème fraiche or vanilla ice cream. A moist almond sponge with a hint of thyme, complements the peaches or any seasonal stone fruits, that are in abundance. This cake freezes very well.

Peach, Almond & Thyme Cake with Roasted Peaches

Ingredients (serves 8):
¾ cup / 185 g unsalted butter
¾ cup / 165 g vanilla sugar

3 eggs, beaten
1 cup / 100 g khorasan flour
½ cup / 50 g ground almonds
2 teaspoon / 10 g baking powder
1 ½ cups / 250 g peaches
1 tablespoon / 15 g thyme leaves
½ teaspoon almond essence
½ cup / 50 g flaked almonds

for the roasted peaches:
3 cups / 500 g peaches, halved & stoned
3 tablespoons / 45 ml honey
2 tablespoons / 30 ml Amaretto liqueur, optional
thyme leaves

Method:

❖ preheat the oven to 180 °C / 350 °F / Gas Mark 4, grease & line the base 20 cm / 7 in round baking tin with baking parchment

❖ place the butter & vanilla sugar in an electric mixer & beat until light & fluffy, add the eggs slowly followed by flour, ground almonds & baking powder, beat until combined then fold in the thyme leaves & almond essence

❖ wash, halve, stone & roughly chop the peaches & set aside, pour ½ of the cake mixture into the prepared baking tin, followed by half of the chopped peaches, repeat until all the mixture covers the fruit, then scatter the remaining peaches on the top, pressing them lightly into the batter so that they are only just showing through, sprinkle over the flaked almonds & bake for 40 to 45 minutes- or until a skewer inserted into the middle of the cake comes out clean, remove from the oven & set aside to cool

To make the roasted peaches:

❖ wash, halve and stone the peaches & place in a shallow roasting dish, drizzle over the honey, thyme leaves & Amaretto, if using & roast in the oven for 20 minutes until the peach halves are soft but still holding their shape and any juice is a little syrupy, before removing from the oven, you could replace the Amaretto with orange juice or sweet white wine, if preferred

❖ place the cooled cake on a serving plate and cut into 8 slices, serve with roasted peaches and some thickened cream or crème fraiche

This is a gooey, fudgy gluten-free chocolate cake made with teff flour, which lends itself well to unleavened baking. This chocolate cake is definitely more suited to becoming a rich, decadent dessert, than an afternoon tea cake. I like to add some Amaretto liqueur into the cream, for a boozy, almond hit that adds a touch of warmth to the bitter chocolate, but a few drops of almond essence will also do the trick.

Boozy Chocolate Fudge Teff Cake

Ingredients (serves 8):
⅔ cup / 150 g unsalted butter
1 cup / 175 g 70% dark chocolate
2 tablespoons brandy
¾ cup / 95 g teff flour

Boozy Chocolate Fudge Teff Cake

1 cup / 200 g golden caster sugar
¼ teaspoon salt
1 teaspoon expresso coffee powder
3 large eggs, beaten
1 teaspoon / 5 ml vanilla essence

for the Amaretto cream:
1 cup / 250 ml double cream
2 tablespoons Amaretto liqueur
dusting of cocoa powder & fresh berries, to serve

Method:

- ❖ preheat the oven to 170 °C / 350 °F / Gas Mark 4, grease & line a 23 cm / 9 in cake tin with baking parchment
- ❖ break up the dark chocolate & place with the butter cubes in a heatproof bowl over a pan of simmering water, melt until smooth & combined, remove from the heat & cool, add the brandy into the chocolate or whatever booze you have & mix to combine
- ❖ place the teff flour, sugar, salt & expresso powder in the bowl of an electric mixer & mix to combine, pour in the melted chocolate mixture & beat for a few seconds to combine, add the eggs & vanilla essence & beat on a medium speed for 2 to 3 minutes until the batter looks light & fluffy
- ❖ pour into the prepared tin & bake for 30 minutes, a crust should have formed on the top & a skewer inserted into the middle will come out clean, if there is still the odd crumb on the skewer, do not worry as it just makes the cake even more gooey on the inside, remove from the oven & cool
- ❖ in a separate bowl, whip the double cream with a couple of 2 tablespoons of Amaretto liqueur to luscious soft peaks & serve with a slice of cake, dusted with cocoa powder & plenty of fresh berries or orange segments for freshness

The sorghum pastry for this fruity tart is a short, crumbly gluten-free crust. Sorghum and almond really complement each other and add delightful herbaceous notes to the summer fruits. I used black and red currants from the summer pickings on our allotment, and this offsets

the cream filling with tart notes. Frozen summer fruits work just as well or
any berries that you have your own supply of.

Blackcurrant & Redcurrant Cream Tart

Ingredients (serves 8):
2 cups / 200 g sorghum flour
½ cup / 50 g ground almonds
¼ cup / 50 g vanilla sugar
½ cup / 125 g unsalted butter
1 egg yolk + 2 tablespoons iced cold water

for the filling:
3 egg yolks
½ cup / 90 g golden caster sugar
1 tablespoon / 15 g cornflour
2 teaspoons almond extract

Blackcurrant & Redcurrant Cream Tart

1½ cups / 360 ml double cream
1 cup / 200 g black & red currants, fresh or frozen
crème fraiche or vanilla ice cream, for serving

Method:
❖ place the flour, ground almonds & vanilla sugar in a bowl, rub in the butter until it resembles breadcrumbs, add the egg yolk & 2 tablespoons of iced cold water until it all comes together as a soft pastry, remove & flatten into a disc, wrap in cling film & chill for 30 minutes

❖ roll out the pastry on a floured surface to the thickness of 3mm & line the bottom & sides of 36 x 12 cm / 14 x 5 in rectangular tart tin, prick the pastry base with a fork & freeze for 15 minutes

❖ preheat the oven to 190 °C / 375 °F / Gas Mark 5, line the case with baking parchment & fill with baking beans, bake blind in the preheated oven for 10 minutes before removing the paper & beans & returning the tart case to the oven for a further 5 minutes until the pastry is golden brown, remove from the oven & brush the inside of the case with a little of the left-over egg white, which will seal the pastry case

To make the filling:
❖ whisk the egg yolks, sugar, cornflour & almond extract together, add the double cream & whisk until combined, pour into the tart case, add three quarters of the currants into the filling, letting them sink into the tart, then bake for 15 minutes, before adding the remaining currants on the top, return to the oven & bake for a further 15 minutes until the filling has set & golden in colour, remove from the oven & serve with any extra currants and some crème fraiche or vanilla ice cream

Cranachan is a traditional Scottish pudding, much like the English trifle. It is usually made with Scottish porridge oats, but rye flakes make a crunchier alternative, which when added with nuts, more like a granola topping. This is a delightful fruit dessert, made all the more enjoyable to make when the apples and blackberries are home grown or picked from the hedgerows.

Blackberry & Apple Rye Cranachan

Ingredients (serves 4):
1 cup /100 g whole rye flakes
½ cup /50 g blanched hazelnuts
½ cup / 100 g vanilla sugar
1 teaspoon ground cardamom
¼ cup / 50 g unsalted butter
2 eating apples, peeled, cored & cubed
2 tablespoons / 30 ml elderflower cordial
2 cups / 200 g blackberries
1 to 2 tablespoons cassis
1 cup / 250 ml double cream
½ cup/120 ml Greek yogurt
2 tablespoons honey
1 teaspoon vanilla extract

Blackberry & Apple Rye Cranachan

Method:
For the apples:
- ❖ place the apple cubes, 2 to 3 tablespoons of the vanilla sugar depending how tart your apples are & the elderflower cordial into a small saucepan, cover & heat on a low light for 10 to 15 minutes until the apples are soft but still holding their shape, set aside to cool

For the cranachan:
- ❖ place the rye flakes, hazelnuts, 2 tablespoons of vanilla sugar & cardamom into a food processor & pulse together 2 to 3 times, melt the butter in a pan & pour the pulsed mixture into the melted butter, cook on a gentle heat for 4 to 5 minutes, stirring regularly, until the flakes and nuts are slightly caramelised and a rich golden brown, set aside
- ❖ in the same processor, add the blackberries, reserving a few for decoration & blitz for a few seconds with the remaining vanilla sugar & cassis to form a rough purée
- ❖ whip the cream to soft peaks, add the Greek yoghurt & honey & ¾ of the rye flake mixture and mix gently to combine

To assemble:
- ❖ place some apple cubes at the bottom of the glass or bowl, add some blackberry purée followed by a dollop of the cranachan cream & a sprinkling of the reserved rye flake mix, decorate with some whole blackberries & mint leaves

Bibliography

Aaronsohn, Aaron. *Agricultural and Botanical Explorations in Palestine*, Washington: Government Printing Office, 1910.

Abendi Massaad, Barbara. 'My Culinary Journey Through Lebanon', blog [http://myculinaryjourneythroughlebanon.blogspot.com].

Albala, Ken. 'Shakespeare's Culinary Aesthetic', *Actes des congrès de la Société française Shakespeare*, 29, 2012: 1-11.

Arranz-Otaegui, Amaia, et al. 'Archaeobotanical evidence reveals the origins of bread 14,400 years ago in north eastern Jordan', *PNAS*, 115 (31), 2018: 7925-7930.

Balinska, Maria. *The Bagel: The Surprising History of a Modest Bread*, Yale University Press, 2008.

Baye, Kaleab. *Teff: Nutrient Composition and Health Benefits*, International Food Policy Research Institute, 2014.

Behre, Karl-Ernst. 'The history of rye cultivation in Europe', *Vegetation History and Archaebotany*, 1, 1992: 141–156.

Bloom, Cecil. 'Aaron Aaronsohn: forgotten man of history?', *Jewish Historical Society of England*, Vol. 5, 2005: 177-196.

Bonjean, A.P., & Angus, W.I. *The World Wheat Book: A History of Wheat Breeding*, Laroisier Publishing, Paris and Intercept, 2001.

Bos, Gerrit. *Maimonides, On the Elucidation of Some Symptoms and the Response to Them*, Hotei Publishing. 2019.

Bostock, John. *The Natural History. Pliny the Elder*, London: Taylor & Francis, 1855.

Brown, Lisa, et al. 'Cholesterol-lowering effects of dietary fiber: a meta-analysis', *American Journal of Clinical Nutrition*, Vol. 69, 1, 1999: 30-42.

Brown, T.A. et al. 'The complex origins of domesticated crops in the Fertile Crescent', *Trends in Ecology & Evolution*, Vol. 24, 2, 2009: 103-109.

Brush, S.B. *Farmers' Bounty: Locating Crop Diversity in the Contemporary World*, Yale University Press, 2004.

Burton Brown, Elizabeth. *GRAINS: An Illustrated History with Recipes*, Prentice-Hall International, 1977.

Cook, Orator Fuller. *Wild Wheat in Palestine*, Washington Printing Office 1913.

Cooper, Raymond. 'Re-Discovering ancient wheat varieties as functional foods', *Journal of Traditional & Complementary Medicine*, 5, 2015: 138-143

Curna, V., & Lacko-Bartosova, M. 'Chemical Composition and Nutritional Value of Emmer Wheat (*Triticum dicoccon Schrank*): A Review', *Journal of Central European Agriculture*, 18 (1), 2017: 117-134

Dalby, Andrew (ed.). *Cato: On Farming (De agri cultura)*, Prospect Books, 1998.

Dalby, Andrew. *Food in the Ancient World from A–Z*, Routledge, 2003.

Dalby, Andrew, & Dalby, Rachel. *Gifts of the Gods: A History of Food in Greece*, Reaktion, 2017.

D'Andrea, A.C. 'T'ef (Eragrostis tef) in Ancient Agricultural Systems of Highland Ethiopia', *Economic Botany*, Springer University Press, Vol. 62, 4, 2008: 547-566.

Davidson, Alan. *The Oxford Companion to Food*, Oxford University Press, 1999.

De Wet, J. M., & Huckabay, J.P. 'The Origin of Sorghum Bicolor. Distribution & Domestication', *Evolution*, 21 (4), 1967:787-802.

Dickstein, Tova. 'A new look at Hametz, Matza and everything in between', Neot Kedumim Park [https://www.neot-kedumim.org.il/index-articles-about-biblical-food/hametz-matza/].

Dommers Vehling, Joseph. *Cookery and Dining in Imperial Rome, A Bibliography, Critical Review and Translation of the Ancient Book known as Apicius de re Coquinaria*, University of Chicago, 1926

Ensminger, Audrey H. & M. E. *Foods & Nutrition Encyclopedia*, CRC Press, 1994.

Evans, L.T & Peacock, J.W. (eds.). *Wheat Science: Today and Tomorrow*, Cambridge University Press, 1981.

Field, Henry. 'Ancient Wheat and Barley from Kish, Mesopotamia', *American Anthropologist*, Vol. 34, 2, 1932: 303-309.

Friedman, David D. & Cook Elisabeth. *A Miscellany* [http://www.daviddfriedman.com/Medieval/Misc10/Misc10.pdf].

Galen: On the Properties of Foodstuffs (De alimentorum facultatibus), trans. Owen Powell, Cmabridge Ujoiversity Press, 2003.

Gonen, Rivka. *Grain: Dagon Collection: Archaeological Museum of grain handling in Israel*, Shikmona Publishing Company, 1979.

Goodman Kaufman, Carol. 'Counting on Barley' [https://forward.com/food/218470/counting-on-barley/].

Grant, Mark. *Galen on Food and Diet*, Routledge, 2000.

Grant, M.D. 'Food and diet in late antiquity: a translation of books 1 & 4 of Oribasius' *Medical Compilations* with an introduction and commentary', Phd thesis, University of Saint Andrews, 1987.

Grocock, Christopher & Grainger, Sally (eds.). *Apicius: A Critical Edition with an Introduction and English Translation*, Prospect Books, 2006.

Harlan, J. R. 'A Wild Wheat Harvest in Turkey', *Archaeological Institute of America*, Vol. 20, 3. 1967.

Hazlitt, Henry. *The Conquest of Poverty*, New York: Arlington House, 1973.

Heun, Manfred et al. 'Site of Einkorn Wheat Domestication Identified by DNA Fingerprinting', *Science*, Vol. 278, Issue 5341, 1997:1312-1314.

Horace, 'Sermones 2.6: The Country Mouse and the City Mouse', edited and translated by Daniel Fleming, 2018 [http://www.usu.edu/markdamen/Latin1000/Readings/38Horace1.pdf].

Ibn Al-H Al-Baghdadi, M. *A Baghdad Cookery Book: The Book of Dishes (Kitab Al-Tabikh)*, trans. Charles Perry, Prospect Books, 2005.

Jackman, Nicole D. 'Tef and Finger Millet: Archaeobotanical Studies of Two Indigenous East African Cereals', MA thesis, Simon Fraser University, Canada, 1999.

Jacomet, S, et al. 'Identification of cereal remains from archaeological sites' *IPAS*, Basel University, 2006. [https://ipna.duw.unibas.ch/fileadmin/user_upload/ipna_duw/PDF_s/AB_PDF/Cereal_Id_Manual_engl.pdf]

Khlestkina, Elena, et al. 'A DNA fingerprinting-based taxonomic allocation of Kamut wheat', *Plant Genetic Resources*, 4 (3), 2006: 172-180.

King, Philip J., & Stager, Lawrence E. *Life in Biblical Israel*, Westminster John Knox Press, 2002.

Kislev, M. E. 'Emergence of Wheat Agriculture', *Paléorient*, 10-2, 1984: 61-70.

Kitto, John. *A Cyclopaedia of Biblical Literature*, A & C Black, 1849.

Kissing Kucek, Lisa et al. 'A Grounded Guide to Gluten: How Modern Genotypes and Processing Impact Wheat Sensitivity', *Comprehensive Reviews*, Vol. 14, 3, 2015: 285-302.

Larsson, Mikael. 'Barley grain at Uppåkra, Sweden: evidence for selection in the Iron Age', *Vegetation History and Archaeobotany*, Vol. 27, 2018: 419-435.

Lieber, Elinor. 'Galen on Contaminated Cereals as a Cause of Epidemics', *Bulletin of the History of Medicine*, Vol. 44, 4, 1970: 332-345.

Liu, Li et al. 'Fermented beverage and food storage in 13,000 y-old stone mortars at Raqefet Cave, Israel: Investigating Natufian ritual feasting', *Journal of Archaeological Science*, Vol. 21, 2018: 783-793.

MacDonald, Nathan. *What did the Ancient Israelites Eat?*, Eerdmans, 2008.

Magnus, Hugo. *Ophthalmology of the Ancients*, J.P. Wayenborgh, 1998.

McClatchie, Meriel. 'A long tradition of cereal production', *Seanda* 6, 2011:

8-10.

Morgounov, A. et al. 'Effect of climate change on spring wheat yields in North America and Eurasia in 1981-2015 and implications for breeding', *PloS One*, 13 (10), 2018.

Mortlock, Stephen. 'The Ten Plagues of Egypt', *The Biomedical Scientist*, 2019.

Nadel, D. et al. 'New evidence for the processing of wild cereal grains at Ohalo II, a 23 000-year-old campsite on the shore of the Sea of Galilee, Israel', *Antiquity*, 86 (334), 2012: 990-1003.

Nathan, Joan. *The Foods of Israel Today*, Knopf, 2001.

Naum. Jasny. 'The Daily Bread of the Ancient Greeks and Romans', *Osiris*, Vol. 9, 1950:.227-253.

Nesbitt, M., & Samuel, D. 'From staple crop to extinction? The Archaeology and History of Hulled Wheats' *Proceedings of the first international workshop on hulled wheats*, 1996: 41-100.

Newman, C.W., & Newman, R.K. 'A Brief History of Barley Foods', *Cereal Foods World*, 51 (1), 2006: 4-7.

Nott, John. *The Cooks and Confectioners Dictionary*, London: Rivington, 1723.

Ohnishi, Ohmi. 'Discovery of the Wild Ancestor of Common Buckwheat', *Fagopyrum*, 11, 1990: 5-10.

Ohnishi, Ohmi. 'Search for the Wild Ancestor of Buckwheat III. The Wild Ancestor of Cultivated Common Buckwheat, and of Tatary Buckwheat', *Economic Botany*, Vol. 52, 2, 1998: 123-133.

Oliveira, Hugo R. et al.. 'Multiregional origins of the domesticated tetraploid wheats', *PLoS ONE*, 15 (1), 2020.

Oren, Sarah. 'Wild Wheat: the 'mother' of all wheat' Neot Kedumim Park, [https://www.neot-kedumim.org.il/index-plant-of-the-month/wild-wheat/].

Ozkan, Hakan et al. 'Geographic distribution and domestication of wild emmer wheat (*Triticum dicoccoides*)', *Genetic Resources and Crop Evolution*, 58 (1), 2011: 11-53.

Pavlik, Jeff. 'Reproducing the 18th Century English Sea Biscuit', *Journal of Early Americas*, Vol. 1, 11, 2001.

Percival, John. *The Wheat Plant, A Monograph*, Duckworth & Co, 1921.

Pray Bober, Phyllis. *Art, Culture, and Cuisine: Ancient and Medieval Gastronomy*, University of Chicago Press, 1999.

Preece, Catherine, et al. 'How did the domestication of Fertile Crescent grain crops increase their yields?' *Funtional Ecology*, Vol. 31, 2, 2017: 387-397.

Rodinson, M., Arberry, A J., & Perry, C. *Medieval Arab Cookery*, Prospect Books, 2006.

Rogosa, Eli. *Restoring Heritage Grains, The Culture, Biodiversity, Resilience, and Cuisine of Ancient Wheats*, Chelsea Green Publishing, 2016.

Rosner, Abbie. 'The Pilgrimage to El Babour – A Functioning Mill in the Nazareth Market', *Food and Markets: Proceedings of the Oxford Symposium on Food and Cookery 2014*, Prospect Books, 2015.

Rubin, Shira. 'Israel's millennia-old 'biblical diet'', BBC Travel, 2018 [http://www.bbc.com/travel/story/20180508-israels-millennia-old-biblical-diet].

Sharpe, Pamela. 'The female labour market in English agriculture during the Industrial Revolution: expansion or contraction', *Agricultural History Review*, Vol. 47, 2, 1999: 161-181.

Shizhen, Li. *Compendium of Materia Medica (Bencao Gangmu)*, Foreign Languages Press, 2003.

Stollar, Carol. A. 'Seated at the Sabbath table with Rashi and Rambam', *Nutrition Reviews*, Vol. 67, 3, 2009: 147-154.

'The Natural History of Wheat', Encyclopaedia.com [https://www.encyclopedia.com/food/encyclopedias-almanacs-transcripts-and-maps/natural-history-wheat].

The Story of Food: An Illustrated History of Everything We Eat, DK Publishing, 2018.

Thudichum, J.L.W. *Cookery its Art and Practice: The History, Science and Practical Import of the Art of Cookery*, Warne, 1895.

Treasure Trove of Benefits and Variety at the Table: A Fourteenth-Century Egyptian Cookbook, Brill, 2017.

Uval, Batya. 'The Book of Ruth: Reaping Redemption' Neot Kedumim Park [https://www.neot-kedumim.org.il/index-general-articles/the-book-of-ruth/].

Van Der Crabben, Jan.' Agriculture in the Fertile Crescent' [https://janvdcrabben.medium.com/agriculture-in-the-fertile-crescent-2e1b6f028d9e].

Vergauwen, David. 'From early farmers to Norman Borlaug: the making of modern wheat', *Current Biology*, Vol. 27, 17, 2017: 858-862.

Weiss, E, et al.. 'Small Grained Wild Grasses as Staple Food at the 23,000-year-old Site of Ohalo II, Israel'. *Economic Botany*, Vol. 58. 2004.

'Wheat & Wheat Products in the Bible', Old Dominion University, Virginia USA, 2006.

[https://ww2.odu.edu/~lmusselm/plant/bible/wheatandproducts.php].

Whittaker, A et al. 'A khorasan wheat-based replacement diet improves risk profile of patients with type 2 diabetes mellitus (T2DM): a randomized crossover trial', *European Journal of Nutrition*, Vol. 56, 2017: 1191–1200.

Wrigley, Colin, Corke, Harold, & Walker, Charles E. *Encyclopaedia of Grain Science*, Elsevier Science, 2004.

Yen, C, & Yang, J. *Biosystematics of Triticeae: Volume I. Triticum-Aegilops Complex*, Springer, 2020.

Zurayk, Rami, & Rahman, Sami Abdul. *From 'Akkar to Amel', Lebanon's Slow Food Trail*, American University of Beirut, 2008.

Acknowledgements

It has been a real delight, researching, writing, recipe testing and eating all things related to freekeh, wild wheats and ancient grains, which I would not have nearly enjoyed as much, had it not been for the help, support and tastebuds of family, friends and food writing colleagues.

I want to firstly thank Catheryn Kilgariff, Prospect Books for bringing this tempting title to me and believing that I would do it justice with my knowledge of the lush, green freekeh fields and traditional fare of Northern Israel. I hope I have done you proud.

Without doubt, the unreserved support from Drew Smith, the *Guardian* restaurant columnist and editor of the *Good Food Guide* for a number of years has boosted my confidence in this genre of culinary writing, whilst mentoring me to publication. Thank you Drew for your time, wisdom and most of all your continual encouragement, and for steering me in the right direction when I veered a little off piste...

To my photographers and friends Neil Mercer and Adam Bloom, whose treks across the lush landscape of the Golan Heights captured such beauty, from the wild wheats and grasses natural habitat.

I have to acknowledge and thank the Guild of Food Writers, who have embraced the challenges of the past year and created a welcoming, supportive network of talented food writers, who are only too willing to share their experience and knowledge. The interesting zoom workshops have been an inspiration and the much needed, friendly banter on the various social media forums, has provided endless support and plenty of discussion, on recipe conversions and indexing...

As most of the manuscript was written in lockdown, I had very little opportunity to travel to Israel to witness the freekeh harvest, discover of the home of the 'Mother of Wheat' and view archaeobotanical evidence of wild wheat. Cooking traditional staple dishes with local Arabic women and baking with artisan bakers was put on hold, whilst I relied on the networks of my colleagues and contacts to meet over Zoom, and for that I am truly grateful. When I finally managed to travel to Israel, I was humbled by the openness and friendliness of chefs, bakers, millers, farmers, archaeologists, professors and museum directors, all who imparted their knowledge and expertise with enthusiasm and kindness, thank you one and all. This was helped financially by the very generous research bursary that I was lucky enough to have been awarded by The Guild of Food Writers for the travel expenses, which was gratefully received in these challenging times.

Lastly, my thanks go to my wonderful boys Sam and Ben, who put up with my innovative recipe ideas and concoctions, with humour and gusto. With regards to your palates and tastes, you are the polar opposite, one refuses to try anything new, and the other will eat anything put in front of him... I thank you both for being who you are and for your love and support to me whilst putting pen to paper on this cookbook.

About the Author

Winner of the Gourmand Special Category Cookbook Awards for Peace and for Culinary Tourism in 2018, with her debut cookbook *The Galilean Kitchen*, Ruth Nieman has established her position as a Middle Eastern food writer, having grown up with traditional cuisines handed down from generations of Jewish and Arabic matriarchs. Her recipes showcase traditional Arabic dishes using local ingredients from rural Galilee, and are inspired by women from the Druze, Muslim, Christian and Bedouin communities, so cultural flavours ooze from every page.

Through her love and extensive knowledge of Middle Eastern food, Ruth Nieman has become an authority on historical, biblical and cultural customs, and on the culinary uses of the ancient supergrains that sustained our hunter gathering ancestors in the Fertile Crescent.

Picture credits
(unless otherwise stated)

Adam Bloom: page 94

Meriel McClatchie: page 114

Neil Mercer: pages 8, 12, 16, 18, 36, 66, 70, 71, 76, 80, 82, 83, 99, 102, 103, 143, 209

Ruth Nieman: pages 23, 34, 35, 38, 41, 48, 49, 52, 86, 97, 137, 140, 149, 201, 202, 205, 210 & all photographs of recipes

Anomarel Ogen: pages 46, 132, 136, 188

Index of Recipes

Index